CRITICAL ANTHROPOLOGY

CRITICAL ANTHROPOLOGY
Foundational Works

Stephen Nugent, Editor

Walnut Creek, California

LEFT COAST PRESS, INC.
1630 North Main Street, #400
Walnut Creek, CA 94596
http://www.LCoastPress.com

ISBN: 978-1-61132-178-4 paperback

Library of Congress Cataloging-in-Publication Data:

Critical anthropology: foundational works / Stephen Nugent, editor.
   p. cm.
Includes bibliographical references.
   ISBN 978-1-61132-178-4 (pbk.)
1. Anthropology—Research. 2. Anthropology—Fieldwork. 3. Anthropology—Methodology. I. Nugent, Stephen (Stephen L.)
 GN33.C73 2012
 301—dc23
                         2011048672

Printed in the United States of America

♾™ The paper used in this publication meets the minimum requirements of American National Standard for Information Sciences—Permanence of Paper for Printed Library Materials, ANSI/NISO Z39.48-1992.

Cover design by Piper Wallis

The chapters in this book were originally published as articles in *Critique of Anthropology*, copyright © SAGE Publications, and are reprinted with permission of SAGE Publications:

Ch. 1: vol. 2, nos. 4–5 (1975):110–126; Ch. 2: vol. 5, no. 2 (1985):5–19; Ch. 3: vol. 2, no. 8 (1977):3–32; Ch. 4: vol. 11, no. 2 (1991):171–188; Ch. 5: vol. 11, no. 2 (1991):189–194; Ch. 6: vol. 5, no. 1 (1985):69–96; Ch. 7: vol. 5, no. 3 (1985):69–76; Ch. 8: vol. 7, no. 1 (1987):33–77; Ch. 9: vol. 7, no. 1 (1987):49–51; Ch. 10: vol. 8, no. 3 (1988):7–39; Ch. 11: vol. 8, no. 3 (1988):41–51; Ch. 12: vol. 9, no. 1 (1989):7–23; Ch. 13: vol. 9, no. 1 (1989):25–31.

CONTENTS

INTRODUCTION

This volume is a collection of articles published in the journal *Critique of Anthropology* between 1975 and 1991. Its purpose is to illustrate key trends in what is sometimes referred to as 'critical anthropology', a non-dogmatic Marxist turn within anthropology that has strongly shaped the field. The cohesion among these articles is provided not by fealty to a particular line of argument, but by the lasting influences that the arguments contained within have had on anthropology. Because many of the articles have long been out of print and inaccessible in original form, this book is a teaching resource and, for future generations of scholars, a compendium of original arguments that are of continued relevance to the evolution of the discipline.

In a strong sense, modern (sociocultural, which is to say, UK and US) anthropology has always been 'critical'. Anthropology has been at the forefront of efforts to de-naturalize mainstream assumptions about Euro-American society being 'normal' while other societies, peoples and cultures were portrayed as not only different, but lesser. Traditionally it has done this by challenging received wisdom, raciological and social evolutionist[1] views about the intrinsic superiority of 'the advanced, civilized West'. In that important sense, one of modern anthropology's durable, critical contributions has been simply to disregard the idea that, in any meaningful way, one culture is intrinsically superior or inferior to any other. The idea of a crude, linear, primitive-to-civilized model of human history – and hence culture-as-civilization – was not only expunged from what anthropology as a field represented, but also has been replaced in the wider public sphere.

There is another, less mainstream meaning of critical anthropology, and this one is the main subject of this book. In this tradition of critical anthropology, scholars have argued that the study of social systems as free-standing objects of analysis should be extended to include analysis of the underlying causes of social change. In other words, the premise upon which modern anthropology had advanced understanding of cultural difference should be extended to include analysis of the underlying causes of social change.[2] This broader analysis should be done not on the basis of a collection of case studies of different examples of bounded cultures nor on the basis of a presumed evolutionary idiom – a mono-linear, natural, stagelike progression from simple to complex – but on the basis of compelling arguments concerning the historical formation of economic, political, social and cultural structures and processes that connect peoples as well as provide the basis for differentiation at the level of cultural expression. Modern anthropology emerged in an era in which imperial and colonial power made access to 'anthropological societies' possible, and because of this fact, anthropology was confronted in its basic field research not only with culture/social systems, but also with the circumstances of their containment, the context in which they were available to anthropological scrutiny (see p. 7).

There is another main sense in which critical anthropology departs from the mainstream meaning of 'critical'. Critical anthropology has a materialist orientation rather than the culturalist idealism which has flourished across the field, perhaps especially in the last three decades. Instead of taking the culture concept as defining unambiguous boundaries between and amongst groups, the critical perspective has seen all cultures as, in the words of Roseberry (1989:13): 'Intertwined with a larger set of economic, political, social and cultural processes to such an extent that analytical separation of "our" history and "their" history is impossible'.

While this critical anthropology may contest some of the assumptions of the mainstream, it is also located very much within that mainstream. Critical anthropology is just as much a product of academic culture as are other tendencies within anthropology, but it is more forward in proposing that anthropological practice does not take place in a vacuum or some kind of specially insulated space. The peoples studied by anthropologists might meet the needs and interests of scholarly investigators, but they also live in a world of unequal access to resources and political and economic power, and the political economy that expresses that historical and global complexity is not something *in addition* to anthropology, but the actual setting in which anthropology finds itself.

There is yet another reading of 'critical' anthropology, one that will be returned to at length toward the end of this introduction, that concerns a distinctively reflexive turn (often depicted as postmodernist and literary) according to which, the discipline of modern anthropology itself is seen to be so wrapped up in a representational hall of mirrors, that it no longer provides a unitary, critical stance (which is also to say it lacks a decisively *disciplinary* perspective) from which to authenticate its observations and analyses. In this turn, the object of analysis is neither the remote 'other', nor an historical metanarrative according to which 'the West and the rest' are structurally and processually linked. Instead, it is the discourse of anthropological inquiry itself, a multisited, globalized network of multidisciplinary inquiry which retains crucial links to its disciplinary past (ethnography is still proclaimed distinctive methodologically), but which, by and large, rejects the political economic disposition of the articles represented here as characteristic of the prior version of critical anthropology.

CRITICAL ANTHROPOLOGY (MK I)

Critical anthropology is not a 'school' in the sense of having a privileged, formulaic analysis that is applied to any and all empirical material,[3] and that is both a strength and a weakness. It is a strength in that it promotes a highly developed and critical self-consciousness about the criteria being invoked in analysis, which typically is focused around questions such as: What is the social basis of knowledge claims? Are the universalistic ambitions of a social science appropriate for the accurate representation of cultural diversity? How do identities of 'the other' and 'the non-other' mutually reinforce one another? How are economic development and underdevelopment mutually implicated? Hence, there is a preoccupation with theoretical speculation directly tied to empirical investigation and evidence. On the other hand, this displays weakness in the sense that critical self-awareness is not good for institution-building and creating power bases; 'critique' implies an intrinsic suspicion of the official, the orthodox and the canonical.

If there is an institutional expression of this trend in critical anthropology, it is most evident in journal publications, of which *Critique of Anthropology (CofA)* is a prime example. Commencing as a 'radical student', irregularly self-published journal in the early to mid-1970s, *CofA* became a regular publication under the auspices of the Dutch publisher Luna in the early 1980s, and eventually became a 'proper' peer-reviewed journal of the international publisher SAGE Publications, where it has remained for more than two decades.

This collection of articles published in *CofA* traces a history of critical anthropology. It is not the only history, but is one that documents particularly well the shifting nature of an academic anthropology that once had a somewhat privileged position on the global landscape as specialist in societies that are remote, so-called 'non-Western', preliterate, preindustrial and so forth (in the case of North America, Australia and Brazil, these societies may be internal). That specialist role has been challenged if not superseded by many other interests – international and national NGOs, tourism, consultancies of vast and varied sorts, filmmaking – and it is unclear whether a unified anthropological perspective will ever again command even the limited level of authority it once had as central interlocutor between societies for which anthropological investigation had some cultural capital and those societies that have provided anthropological subjects.

Critical anthropology has also been transformed in an era commonly subsumed under the heading 'globalization'. Once closely associated with a political-economic orientation, critical anthropology has been affected by the turn of the anthropological gaze away from 'outside the West' to 'anywhere and everywhere', as well as by the incorporation into the mainstream of perspectives once viewed as radical or innovative. The anthropology of women and feminist anthropology are key examples of such mainstreaming (see, for example, Segal and Yanagisako eds. 2005), as are many other sub- and cognate fields.

Recognition of the political underpinnings of social science research has been marked in a number of settings over the years. At one extreme there are cases of covert activities, such as those exposed by Boas in the early twentieth century with respect to spying under the pretext of field research; later in the context of the Korean War and the war in Indochina (see Price 2000, 2008) and more recently the Human Terrain Systems (Griffin 2010; Price 2011), activities pursued through embedding anthropologists in the field in Afghanistan and Iraq. Social science in the service of foreign policy aims presents, as in the case of the post– World War II emergence of 'area studies', Project Camelot and various forms of targeted research-funding, complex mixtures of scholarly and political objectives, areas in which the equivocations of professional bodies have divided the anthropological community.[4]

Critical anthropology has been in the forefront in addressing issues raised in these settings, but activist engagement has hardly been its prerogative alone. More pertinent to characterizing critical anthropology has been the conviction that anthropology is not just a way of looking at the world (the so-called 'anthropological gaze'), but is itself the product of particular historical relations between those who look and those who are looked upon. This fundamental political asymmetry informs the stance of a critical anthropology that acknowledges the fact that anthropology didn't 'just happen', but reflects a legacy of expansionary European systems that, from the sixteenth century onward have transformed, in Wallerstein's phrasing, the world from one of many world systems (political/culture domains) to a single world economic system (capitalist world economy) with a global division of labour (in part represented by the diversity of the semi-periphery and periphery). The major theoretical contribution to this perspective from anthropology has come from Eric Wolf, who departs from (and somewhat antedates)

Wallerstein's view by taking more seriously the effects on the total system generated from below, as it were, by sociocultural systems whose cardinal features, far being obliterated, as is often said of Wallerstein's model, maintain their own dynamics.

If there was a polarizing moment when it became more clear what the divisions between a critical anthropology and anthropology were it occurred within the furore surrounding the publication of two edited volumes that continue to this day to feed discussion about the political implications of a science built, in substantial part, around the long-term political, economic and social asymmetries springing from imperial and colonial expansion of the sixteenth century – globalization *avant la lettre*.

The publication of Talal Asad's (ed.) *Anthropology and the Colonial Encounter* (1973) and the near contemporaneous publication of Dell Hymes' (ed.) *Reinventing Anthropology* (1972) represented consolidations of several critical trends that had long been present in anthropology and which continue to be broadly consistent with the general thrust of critical anthropology. While the essays in Asad (1973) are most directly addressed to the UK social anthropology, and those in Hymes (1972) offered a distinctly (but not exclusively) the US perspective, there are significant areas of overlap, particularly with respect to anthropology's role, by and large unbidden, as an expression of imperial interest.

The most mechanical expression of the relationship between anthropology and the extension and maintenance of imperial and colonial political power has been repeatedly traced to the title (but not so much the essay itself) of Kathleen Gough's 1968 essay in *The Monthly Review*, 'Anthropology and Imperialism'.[5] Two inferences drawn from that association persist and continue to be confused. One inference has anthropology in the service of imperialism; the other sees anthropology as arising from, as the Asad title puts it, the colonial encounter. In other words, anthropology would not exist except for the conditions afforded by imperial/colonial conquest, but it is not directly part of the imperial/colonial project.

That ambiguity neatly fits the critical anthropology brief, for critical anthropology is not outside the inequalities that prevail in imperial and postimperial relations between core and periphery, but it is not sponsoring those inequalities. It exists in substantial part because of those particular conditions. It seems unlikely that a Sanumá tribesman would conduct fieldwork in Buckingham Palace or the World Bank, not only because it would not be permitted, but also because it is unlikely to be of much interest in Sanumá terms.[6]

The link between Marxism and critical anthropology is obvious, but also complicated. For a brief period during the 1970s[7] 'Marxist anthropology' was a credible label for work in economic anthropology, historical anthropology, peasant studies, political economy and other subfields. In the *Annual Review of Anthropology*, in 1975, Marxist anthropology was acknowledged in a major article (O'Laughlin 1975), though by 1988 'political economy' was the preferred label (Roseberry 1988). Also in 1975, *Marxist Analyses and Social Anthropology* (Bloch [ed.] 1975) showed the impact of French and structuralist influences of both anthropological (e.g., Terray 1972) and non-anthropological sources (Althusser 1969) and the titles of several edited volumes conjoined Marxism and anthropology with unprecedented visibility, as did Diamond's (ed. 1979) *Toward a Marxist Anthropology*, and the journal he founded, in 1975, *Dialectical Anthropology*.

Critical anthropology of the period was part of a resurgent Western Marxism (generally more academic than activist[8]) and associated with a number of New Left tendencies, but it also drew on traditions within academic anthropology that had long referenced Marx and the historical materialist tradition. Wolf (1982) and Mintz (1974) are among the most prominent, but the influence of materialist traditions in pre– and post–World War II anthropology is evident in networks linking a number of major departments in the United States. Critical anthropology, however much it overlapped with such figures and influences, drew from a wider set, especially from an emergent mix of structuralism and Marxism[9] in France (the primary of the 'Continental' influences) and from figures and areas of inquiry such as dependency theory, which employed models that subsumed the more archaic anthropological objects of analysis (e.g., 'the tribe'). As a result, during the brief, 'golden age' of critical anthropology, there was an attempted integration of a structure-functional approach, the articulation of a modes-of-production approach and dependency theory that suggested a new kind of historical anthropology, one that derived methodological strength from traditional forms of ethnographic, empirically minded field research that derived explanatory strength from maintaining a dual focus on system structure as well as system transformation (production and social reproduction); and that directly engaged with the forms of uneven development that linked the dynamism of the core (figured around capital accumulation) and the variety of social forms to which it was linked on the periphery and semi-periphery.

The ideas that inspired that brief period of fluorescence have hardly disappeared and there is evidence of active and productive research linked to that set of once-integrated concerns; however, the centrality of the political-economic approach has disappeared. Instead, there are many thematic restatements that claim to set the pace in critical anthropology, whether from an expanded remit of indigenism, new social movements, queer theory, consumption studies, cultural studies, social study of technology or media anthropology. Obviously, the critical edge is blunted if everything is 'critical', but rather than a circumstance in which a new overarching model prevails, the situation is one of coexistence and convergence with the general disavowal of the idea that there is single, generic argument that provides a reference for any general anthropological theory.

Critical anthropology had already been nascent or incipient in the development of anthropology as a whole in the first half of the twentieth century through the influence of historical materialism – albeit at times in eccentric form – in archaeology and evolutionist approaches. The rapid expansion of the field (and academia in general) post–World War II was affected by the Cold War's impact on the global social landscape on which featured diverse wars of national liberation – particularly those in Indochina; the emergence of so-called New States from old colonies; the Civil Rights and Free Speech movements and new forms of what would subsequently be grouped under the heading 'globalization'. All of these provided a backdrop for social science staff and students less willing to accept the arbitrary separation of scholarly practice and political awareness. The expansion in student numbers (and, briefly, academic posts) meant that there was a larger, immediate public available to react to what then, and in retrospect, seemed a new sense of academic engagement with the world outside the campus.[10] Furthermore, the involvement of established anthropologists in the antiwar movement, through teachings, for example, and the fact that various wars of national liberation and other forms of bottom-up or grass-roots resistance occurred in many of the fieldwork regions in which anthropology had at least partially established itself, meant that the discipline of anthropology was seen as directly germane to the understanding not just of 'funny people in funny places doing funny things', at its most brutally caricatured, but of the complex relationships amongst societies that produced anthropologists and societies that produced anthropological subjects.

The articles that follow represent particular moments in which a new kind of critical anthropology emerged, staked a claim for attention, and then transformed into or laid the groundwork for a yet another and different kind of critical anthropology (henceforth, New Critical Anthropology or Critical Anthropology Mk II). The connections between the political economic critical anthropology and what followed are still a matter of dispute. In terms of the explanatory power of, say, arguments invoking the notions of articulation of modes of production to help explain how social systems reproduce themselves under the impact of gradual (and uneven) incorporation in the capitalist world system, these arguments have not been refuted. They have been modified, criticized and found wanting, as are all heuristics, but they have not been effectively challenged as fundamentally errant, much less arrant. Mainly, they have become unfashionable as anthropology as a whole has shifted its gaze, becoming increasingly concerned with developing itself as an all-purpose cultural-symbolic explanans machine (hence the 'culture of the water cooler' or 'the anthropology of cell phones'). This is particularly within societies that themselves value anthropology, not the traditional societies of anthropological scrutiny for whom, by and large, the interests of anthropologists are odd and irrelevant.[11]

The political economic approach has also suffered the general decline in confidence in the scientific orientation of modern anthropology.[12] It has always been an issue in anthropology how to calibrate different sets of epistemological and ontological demands (How real is witchcraft for those who believe and on what basis can I trust and/or evaluate their claims?). But increasingly – and largely under the influence of followers of Geertz – the science part of the anthropological equation has been, by and large, and certainly in terms of dominant models, quietly sequestered.[13] It is ironic, to say the very least, that a critical anthropology that arose in part to contest the idea of value-free science should now be susceptible to being portrayed as vulgarly positivistic (Erickson and Murphy 2008:189; and Tyler, this volume).

Critical Anthropology Mk I was clearly political economic in character, but not exclusively so. It was also tied to a variety of political and theoretical departures of the 1960s and 1970s and as such reflected a general ferment associated with the slip from the modern to the postmodern. Its successor form shares much of that theoretical legacy, but also expresses an eclecticism in which a grounding in the political economic is regarded as passé if not retrograde. Its successor version also differs in its mainstream prominence. Where the Mk I version could, with some confidence, be located in an anthropological subfield (economic anthropology), the new version addresses a generalized anthropological discourse whose hybrid character aims to exceed by far the grasp of the old.[14]

THE NEW CRITICAL ANTHROPOLOGY (MK II)

By its very positioning as interlocutor between 'the West and the rest', modern anthropology implied a political character if not necessarily a political theory. As noted earlier, Boas famously sought to chastise anthropological colleagues who had used their fieldwork presence as opportunities to spy on behalf of the US government, though he was himself censured by his professional colleagues for trying to 'bring politics into the profession'. During the war in Indochina, attempts to mobilize professional anthropology to condemn those who betrayed scholarship through duplicitous acts resulted in rejection of those who sought to bring the weight of 'the field' to bear.[15] The fact that the greatest expansion of the academic field took place within the Cold War landscape no doubt highlighted the political implications of much anthropological research.

More prominent than a theory of politics, the politics of theory – cyclically muted and overt – has driven anthropological discourse. The theoretical aspirations of an anthropological science – albeit with 'science' always expressed in rather muted tones – disallowed much in the way of theory as an isolated and special sphere of inquiry. Theory was attached to an explanatory instrumentality as in, for example, the formalist versus substantivist dispute over the rationality of non-market production; to the degree that either 'theory' had explanatory value, it was derived from a capacity to account for results from the field. While in general the discourse of anthropology was stylistically and ideologically marked by adherence to one or another theoretical positions (as often used as terms of abuse as much as terms of affiliation – those 'bloody transactionalists/structuralists/functionalists', etc.), those were markers of competitive scholarship; 'theory' itself, as a free-standing thing or domain of activity did not actually provide much purchase.

Three developments, however, gradually removed such constraints from the modest ambitions of 'theory'[16] and are closely linked to the ushering in of a New Critical Anthropology (Mk II). The first was the ascendancy of a (largely) Geertz-derived[17] theory of anthropological culture; that is, the formal apparatus within which anthropological activity itself was organized, a so-called interpretive approach. Second was the ascendancy of a poststructuralist tendency in which an overdeveloped self-consciousness about epistemological assumptions made it possible to create objects of analysis located in anthropological discourse itself (anthropology becomes the anthropology-of-anthropology). What had previously been a kind of translation problem (what kind of sociologic is to be used to explain the other's sociologic) was put aside by acquiescing to the inscrutability of extreme cultural relativism.[18]

The third development enveloped anthropology rather than springing from its internal shifts, and this was the emergence of a generic idiom of 'globalization'. Within the idiom of globalization, attempts to specify hierarchies of causality (e.g., 'it is the economic in the last instance') are silenced by appeals to a rule-changing, one-world-market of neoliberal fantasy. We will look at these three developments in turn.

1. Geertz's asserted the impossibility (and undesirability, as though it could merely be wished away) of a scientific anthropology[19] because it was impossible to calibrate the interests of observer in relation to those of the observed. This was in part an expression of a widespread tendency

toward viewing the material of observation and analysis as the product of 'social construction',[20] a 'way of seeing', a recognition of a cultural relativism that now allows of little nuance.

The New Critical Anthropology, although spurred in part by challenges to conventional wisdom that were prompted by the political economic moment of its predecessor, much more enthusiastically embraced anthropology-as-humanities or, as depicted by Marcus and Fischer (1986), espoused a more wide ranging 'anthropology as cultural critique' in which the determinative role of the economic was subsumed under the complex of 'culture'. As the successor version of critical anthropology, it is very closely associated with a generic shift in the social sciences that has seen anthropology – often elided with cultural studies – committed to interpretive commentary in a wide range of specialist areas previously beyond its ken.[21]

2. In the elevation and promotion of 'theory' per se as an activity separated from mundane explanatory purpose based on field research observation and evidence, anthropology has achieved a degree of multidisciplinary cachet, not least in the appeal that ethnography or the ethnographic method has gained across cognate fields. The super valorization of ethnographic method, however, is based on the fragile premise, as Stocking (1992) was at pains to show, that there was a relatively high degree of coherence to the method when in fact eclecticism prevailed. One consequence of the appeal of the ethnographic beyond the field is that ethnography now often appears as a kind of voluntary theoretical stance.[22] What began as a set of techniques to accommodate the ignorance and naiveté of a researcher with weak command of local languages, poor grasp of etiquette, mores and manners and so forth, is now a kind of guarantee of qualitative research results.

The contemporary super valorization of ethnography rests in no small part on the programmatic claims made for multisited ethnography, although it is unclear how much of a departure this is from conventional historical anthropology, beyond its theoretical self-consciousness.[23] (The work of, say, Wolf and Mintz, though lacking the multisited claims announced in Marcus [1986, 1989, 1995], could hardly be described as adhering to the allegedly modal, holistic, case study approach.[24])

3. The term globalization is sufficiently ubiquitous in scholarly and journalistic work to have generated a small industry devoted just to defining and redefining the term itself, and despite the prominence of the term in the theoretical framing of contemporary anthropological discussion, it is not evident that a distinctive anthropological take prevails. Within the (narrow?) anthropological tradition, however, there are two (noncompeting) versions that present themselves relatively uncontroversially. One of these refers to the emergence of a single, global market

system in which the dynamic of capital accumulation trumps the political world systems (e.g., Oceania) of the premodern period.[25] In this sense, anthropology itself is a product of globalization – a scholarly practice that reflects both a global division of labour and a division of labour within complex metropolitan systems, as developed, of course, within the particular cultural ambit of centres of accumulation (and hence the different styles of sociocultural anthropology practiced in the UK and the United States).

The second meaning of globalization in this context refers to the emergence of a global financial system less constrained by the state than was the case prior to World War II. Previously depicted in shorthand as a maturing multi/transnational/corporate capital, in this version of financial globalization, differences (cultural, social, political) among global polities are to some degree mitigated and reduced in significance by virtue of membership in markets. This is often spoken of as homogenization or the flattening of cultural difference such that, for example, mere association within a cultural sphere indicates something (trivial, serious, irrelevant, revealing – these are all investigable possibilities in principle) about the interpenetration of cultural worlds. A hunter-gather with a cell phone and GPS; a Nairobi street child in a Pearl Jam t-shirt; genetically modified seed types overtaking local native species and so on.

It is within this latter, globalized landscape that the New Critical Anthropology has staked its claim as an anthropology fit for purpose in a postmodern age. There are both acknowledged and unacknowledged precursors to this change. George Marcus, one of the most enthusiastic proponents of this tendency, notes in his introduction to *Critical Anthropology Now* (1999) the change of outlook documented in his influential, coedited *Writing Culture* (1986), observing in particular what he refers to as the repatriation and refocusing (1999:4) of anthropological interest not just on new (and homebound) geographical locales, but on new objects of anthropological analysis.

One paradoxical manifestation of the new sensitivity toward a globalized anthropology that is central to the New Critical project is the emergence of an 'anthropology of the South', paradoxical because it seems that a 'globalized' anthropology would dissolve or disallow the traditional space-and-culture link which is such a hallmark of both conventional (the study of Others abroad) and critical anthropological (the study of uneven development) premises. The anthropology of the South (which has been extensively discussed in *CofA*) most closely resembles the New Critical Anthropology because, in a word, it cannot resemble any other – both modern anthropology and its first critical complement represented a metropolitan gaze; an anthropology of the South, by definition, is a postmetropolitan configuration of anthropology, or a view from what used to be the margin, but is now reconstituted in light of the effects of development/underdevelopment. The model accessible to it is the tending-toward-post-discipline New Critical Anthropology, less concerned with how the past has shaped the present than it is concerned with, in Foucault's phrase, the history of the present. The layered nature of what is perhaps too casually presumed to be a unity (anthropology) is starkly revealed by an anthropology of the South that takes as its object of analysis not the world system or its constituent sub-systems, but anthropological discourse itself.

The emergence of an anthropology of the South indicates well both continuities and discontinuities between early and later forms of critical anthropology. On one hand, anthropology of the South marks a rising profile of critical social sciences in periphery/semi-periphery where such endeavours were long suppressed politically or where social conditions were inadequate.[26] On the other hand, anthropology of South obscures the historical roots of an anthropology that, crucially, preyed upon the South. The phenomenon to which the anthropology of the South refers coexists with independent national traditions, yet is driven largely by the postmodernist agenda so forcefully articulated (in the main) within the US anthropological establishment, one in which a generalized (some might say multidisciplinary) critical practice challenges the discipline's modernist configuration. In this regard, the kind of critical anthropology revealed in this collection is both a precursor of what was to follow under the banner of an emboldened, postmodernist flag, and a critical legacy in which resides an explicit challenge to some of the tendencies now evident in the New Critical Anthropology. As a precursor, Critical Anthropology Mk I positioned anthropological explanation within an expanded framework, one that included historical analysis, aspects of development studies, the politics of gender and ethnicity, dependency theory and world systems theory, but it did so largely within a fieldwork- (and archive-) based model in a direct lineage of tent-and-notebook anthropology. It was theoretically precocious, but selective in terms of what was relevant on the ground. Its successor reversed the relationship between empirical investigation and theoretical result, insisting that it was the need for sustaining anthropological discourse itself – a dialect that could facilitate anthropological integration into the humanities (perhaps at the cost of forsaking the social sciences) – that determined what the anthropological object might be.

From the perspective of the critical anthropology reflected in this volume, it may well be that 'critical anthropology' was too successful in the sense that it now occupies, as the New Critical Anthropology, not a marginal and hence structurally critical position, but a good portion of the mainstream. This is not an unusual outcome in the unfolding of theoretical dispute within a discipline – that the ostensibly critical loses a necessary edge by succeeding in displacing (or at least shaking) the old guard.[27] The price of such success is often the need then to defend institutional and power gains, not harry powers-that-be.

The articles in this collection set out an agenda for critical anthropology that is still evident in a revised critical anthropology initiative, albeit one that has shifted to a markedly interpretive mode. The postmodernist footing of the New Critical Anthropology has, to a considerable degree, relocated the focus of anthropology away from a differentiated world – us and them in various guises – and back onto the social milieux which themselves gave rise to anthropological speculation. The crucial links, however, between those who recognize an anthropological imperative and those who are recognized by an anthropological imperative have not been effaced, and as the articles in this collection show, that differentiation is part of an extended story told with reference to the past, present and future.

While there has been a gradual shift of the anthropological gaze away from what happens on the periphery and back onto the societies of anthropologists themselves, simultaneously, the idea of world-class-economic-crisis has shifted from the periphery (e.g., the Latin American debt crisis of the 1980s) to the core. Whatever tools are available to a critical anthropology today, whose attention is ever more inward-looking and homeward bound, had their origins in a different sphere, that in which the regulation of societies on the periphery was still defined by Cold War prerogatives and spheres of influence, decline of empire (and rise of new states), wars of national liberation and the emergence of corporate capital increasingly unfettered by national state control. What were then often mis-identified (or over identified) as precapitalist holdovers – as though the capitalist world system began in 1500 for some, 1980 for others – were studied not only as cogent systems in their own right, but also because of what the intersection of capitalist incursion and 'another kind of system' showed us about the dynamics of capitalism and its multilayered unfolding. That the core of capitalism/capitalist culture still embraces other kinds of systems (unvalorized domestic labour continues to be an outstanding example as does the disjunction between received notions of family and kinship and actual systems as well as the ascendency of culturalist idioms over class-based ones) was never a mystery, but what was gained by seeing a de-normalized world through profoundly different societies and cultures is lost through over-valuing the effects of globalization on the periphery. This is not to deny the effects of 'globalization', but the broad inference that the characteristic unevenness of the effects of capitalist domination on the periphery is somehow subdued seems remarkable, not least in light of the decline of material standards on a periphery so long disciplined by the demands of modernization policies administered from the core.

Some of the continuities between critical anthropology and the New Critical Anthropology are purely nominal, while some are substantive. It is no small irony that the turning of the gaze back on to the metropolitan core was accompanied by a downgrading of the importance of political economy as a major preoccupation in the framing of anthropological research. Given the prominence of economic crisis as it now unfolds in such different ways at local, regional, national and international levels, the discarded political economic focus of the recent past may come to command more attention.

NOTES

1. There are strong (residual) evolutionist currents in critical anthropology, but the distinction here is between social evolutionism of the Spencerian, reductionist sort and more metaphorical usages engaged in expressing systematic, multilinear change over time.
2. 'Underlying' in two senses: First, that among causal factors/structures, some might be more important that others, e.g., the economic in the last instance; second, that there is the need to construct/hypothesize a model to explain what appears to be happening empirically.
3. As a discipline, anthropology has been highly susceptible to a tendency – common in other fields of 'the ideological sciences' – according to which the struggle to promote a central, field-wide theoretical centre – what some unsympathetic observers would refer to as an obsession with master narratives – has resulted in much theoretical type-casting and demonizing.
4. In both the USA and the UK, professional bodies have shown enormous reticence when it comes to criticizing the behaviour of members whose scholarly activities and research have, in the view of many, been clearly transgressive. See Price 2000 for introduction to this discussion.
5. The cover of that issue of the *Monthly Review* flags the article as 'Anthropology: Child of Imperialism', but the actual article is entitled 'Anthropology and Imperialism'.
6. In the UK, much of the professional reaction to the film *Meet the Tribe* (Searle 2007) had a very patronizing tone reflecting deep uncertainties about what it meant for the other to pretend to 'do anthropology' in the wrong home.
7. This is not to say that both prior to and following the 1970s there were not serious engagements between anthropology and Marxism (of various types), but for that brief period the boundaries of a 'marxist anthropology' were well defined enough that one could almost talk of a sub-field.
8. That is not to slight those for whom the relationship between theory and practice was more than a seminar topic, but anthropology is largely confined to the campus. Furthermore, research practice – in the field – tends to be highly atomised/individualistic, and not generally a focus of collective action.
9. In many respects the expression 'structural Marxist' was a label of general convenience that acknowledged an overlap between two influential social theoretical trends of the time. There was an actual synthetic claim made by Althusser/Althusserians, but the diversity of both 'structuralist' and 'Marxist' positions represented throughout the humanities and social sciences (and elsewhere) reduced

the luminosity of that particular synthetic claim. More narrowly, in anthropology, structural Marxism had a different kind of coherence given that there was a focus on a particular problem: How was pre-capitalist production articulated with capitalism (not that all of those interested in the problem explicitly adopted a structural Marxist posture)? While the exploration of that problem certainly intersected with structural Marxism more broadly, the theoretical elaboration of the 'modes of production/social formation', as in the work of (non-anthropologists) Hindess and Hirst 1975, exceeded carrying capacity.

10. This was also the case in the UK, albeit on a much smaller scale. The UK professional associations currently have a few hundred members; the American Anthropological Association has eleven thousand.

11. This is not to say that there are not many more national anthropologies (often collectively grouped as 'anthropology of the South'), but these reflect, as in the original countries with anthropology, particular class and interest configurations. A generalized, popular anthropology remains unrealized.

   China represents an interesting variant on the anthropology of the South in as much as China's economic ascendency places it in a unique position vis-à-vis a globalization that seems to close a chapter on the West while opening a new one for China. The new Chinese anthropology has been represented in *Critique of Anthropology* through the work of Wang Mingming (2002).

12. It is a measure of the degree to which economic anthropology, once a vigorous expression of the political economic moment, is less central to anthropology overall that one of the largest studies in recent years (Henrich et al. [eds.] 2004) has stronger associations with evolutionary psychology than it does with mainstream sociocultural anthropology.

13. While many on all sides are exercised, and have long been so, about how to characterize anthropology's relationship with science (a method, an ideology, a heuristic, an institution?) the emergence of evolutionary psychology as a non-denominational (i.e., no need to swear allegiance to sociobiology), explicitly science-defined branch of anthropology has resolved some of the ambiguities.

14. *Cultural Anthropology*, the vanguard journal of Critical Anthropology Mk II, in its very title indicates the mainstreaming of 'critical anthropology'.

15. Professional scrutiny of the furore surrounding the publication of *Darkness in El Dorado* (Tierney 2000) reveals a similar divisiveness (cf. Borofsky 2005).

16. While many remember the period 1975–85 (somewhat nominal dates) as one of excessive theoretical point-scoring (cf. discussions surrounding Hindess and Hirst's *Pre-Capitalist Modes of Production* 1975), there was a conceptual consistency and extension that is no longer so apparent. Currently, for example, it is not unusual to see 'labour', 'work', 'labour power' used interchangeably, just as the term 'ethnographic' applies to even the most fleeting research encounter that does not rely on a survey. For indicative contemporaneous commentaries on PCMP, see Corrigan and Sayer (1978), Taylor (1975, 1976) and Hindess and Hirst (1977).

17. Geertz attracted much support rather than actively pursuing it, but his influence is unmistakable in the highly polarized and prescriptive discussions about where anthropology should be headed (see Segal and Yanagisako [eds.] 2005). His diffident leadership role in this regard is well put by Marcus (1997:90):

   In Geertz's writings on his fieldwork of the 1960s and 1970s, we see first a virtual outline and summary of the major moves of later critique – built on the reflexive study of the conditions of anthropological knowledge not only in terms of its traditional mise-en-scène of fieldwork but also in terms of the broader historic contexts that Geertz tended to elide – and then a hesitation and a pulling back for the sake of sustaining a distanced practice of interpretation.

18. The two volume 'rationality debate' represented in Wilson (1971) and Hollis and Lukes (1982) was resolved in favour of a normative cultural relativism that was consolidated in the mainstreaming of postmodernism. It is salutary – and disorienting – to see in the current vogue for perspectivism/ontological pluralism, echoes of that, much earlier (and widely unacknowledged), discussion.

19. Even if it is rather hard, at mid-century, to locate the core of a rigidly scientific or scientist sociocultural anthropology to which the symbolist/interpretive is such a necessary, palliative reaction. As a social science, long set between the two-culture demands of the natural science/humanities dialectic, reductionist-scientism was, according to many, reflected in the vulgar materialism of Harris, but as Friedman (1974) noted, Harris's relationship to science was highly questionable. In Geertz (1967) Lévi-Strauss bore the brunt of an attack on formalistic and scientific pretention.

20. Ian Hacking offers a particularly cogent critique (1999).

21. The Open Anthropology Cooperative – a web-based association, includes 195 anthropological interest groups including those devoted to the anthropology of roads, humour and laughter and entrepreneurship.

22. The statement of one ethnographic journal, for example, describes its purpose as providing:

> relevant material that examines a broad spectrum of social interactions and practices – in subcultures, cultures, organizations, and societies – from a variety of academic disciplines including, but not limited to, Anthropology, Communications, Criminal Justice, Education, Health Studies, Management, Marketing, and Sociology.

23. In drawing the connection between theory and fieldwork in the era of the New Critical Anthropology, Marcus writes (1995:102):

> There are several inspirations for multi-sited ethnography within the high theoretical capital associated with postmodernism: One might think, for example, of Foucault's power/knowledge and heterotopia (18), Deleuze & Guattari's rhizome (13), Derrida's dissemination (15), and Lyotard's juxtaposition by 'blocking together' (78). These concepts anticipate many of the contemporary social and cultural conditions with which ethnographers and other scholars are trying to come to terms in shaping their objects of study in the absence (p. 103) of reliable holistic models of macroprocess for contextualizing referents of research, such as 'the world system,' 'capitalism,' 'the state,' 'the nation,' etc.

24. And curiously, Marcus acknowledges that Malinowski's work in the Trobriands is 'the archetypal account' of a multisited ethnography (1995:106).

25. Wallerstein's model of the modern world system has been preeminent. Within anthropology, Friedman has been the most consistent world-systems theorist.

26. The designation 'anthropology of the South' does not explicitly refer to, but certainly includes, the many national anthropologies that have existed outside the

Euro-American axis. Both Brazilian and Mexican anthropology, to note but two, represent expressions of anthropological interest, which, while in part shaped by and in scholarly terms respondent to Euro-American institutional weight, pursue independent strategies and contain unique elements not represented in the Euro-American tradition(s). The 'anthropology of the South' more narrowly defined, takes as its defining characteristic an autonomy from the hegemony (it is often put as such) of the traditional metropolitan centres of anthropological authority.
27. See, for example, the noisy response to the appointment of the new editors of the *American Anthropologist* in 1996 [unauthorised.org/anthropology/anthro-l/february-1996/0617.html].

REFERENCES

Althusser, L. (1969). *For Marx*. London: Allen Lane.
Asad, T. (ed.) (1973). *Anthropology and the Colonial Encounter*. London: Ithaca Press.
Bloch, M. (ed.) (1975). *Marxist Analyses in Social Anthropology*. London: Malaby Press.
Borofsky, R. (ed.) (2005). *Yanomami: The Fierce Controversy and What We Can Learn from It*. Berkeley: University of California Press.
Clifford, J. and Marcus, G. (eds.) (1986). *Writing Culture: The Poetics and Politics of Ethnography*. Los Angeles, CA: University of California Press.
Corrigan, P. and Sayer, D. (1978). 'Hindess and Hirst: A Critical Review', *Socialist Register*, Vol. 15, pp. 194–214.
Diamond, S. (ed.) (1979). *Toward a Marxist Anthropology: Problems and Perspectives*. Berlin: de Gruyter Mouton.
Erickson, P. and Murphy, L. (2008). *Readings for a History of Anthropological Theory*. Toronto: University of Toronto Press.
Friedman, J. (1974). 'Marxism, Structuralism and Vulgar Materialism', *Man* (NS), Vol. 9(3), pp. 444–69.
Geertz, C. (1967). 'The Cerebral Savage: The Structural Anthropology of Claude Lévi-Strauss', *Encounter*, Vol. 28(4), pp. 25–32.
Gough, K. (1968). 'Anthropology and Imperialism', *Monthly Review*, Vol. 19(11), pp. 12–27.
Griffin, M. (2010). McFate and Co. www.nthposition.com/mcfateandco.php [accessed May 20, 2011]
Hacking, I. (1999). *The Social Construction of What?* Cambridge, MA: Harvard University Press.
Henrich, J. et al. (eds.) (2004). *Foundations of Human Sociality: Ethnography and Experiments in Fifteen Small-scale Societies*. Oxford: Oxford University Press.
Hindess, B. and Hirst, P. (1975). *Pre-Capitalist Modes of Production*. London: Taylor and Francis.
———. (1977). 'Mode of Production and Social Formation in *PCMP*: A Reply to John Taylor', *Critique of Anthropology*, Vol. 2(8), pp. 49–58.
Hollis, M. and Lukes, S. (eds.) (1982). *Rationality and Relativism*. Cambridge, MA: MIT Press.
Hymes, D. (ed.) (1972). *Reinventing Anthropology*. New York: Pantheon.
Kahn, L. and Llobera, J. (1981). *The Anthropology of Pre-capitalist Societies*. London: Macmillan.

Malinowski, B. (1967). *A Diary in the Strict Sense of the Term*. London: Routledge and Kegan Paul.

Marcus, G. (1986). 'Contemporary Problems of Ethnography in the Modern World System', in J. Clifford and G. Marcus (eds.) *Writing Culture: The Poetics and Politics of Ethnography*, pp. 165–93. Berkeley: University of California Press.

———. (1989). 'Imagining the Whole: Ethnography's Contemporary Efforts to Situate Itself', *Critique of Anthropology*, Vol. 9(3), pp. 7–30.

———. (1995). 'Ethnography in/of the World System: The Emergence of Multi-sited Ethnography', *Annual Review of Anthropology*, Vol. 24(1), pp. 95–117.

———. (1997). 'The Uses of Complicity in the Changing Mise-en-Scène of Anthropological Field Work', *Representations*, Vol. 0(59), pp. 85–108.

———. (ed.) (1999). *Critical Anthropology Now*. Santa Fe: School of American Research Press.

Marcus, G. and Fischer, M. (1986). *Anthropology as Cultural Critique*. Chicago: University of Chicago Press.

Mingming, W. (2002). 'The Third Eye: Towards a Critique of "Nativist Anthropology"', *Critique of Anthropology*, Vol. 22(2), pp. 149–74.

Mintz, S.W. (1974). *Caribbean Transformations*. Chicago: Aldine.

———. (1985). *Sweetness and Power: The Place of Sugar in Modern History*. New York: Viking.

Obeyesekere, G. (1992). *The Apotheosis of Captain Cook*. Princeton: Princeton University Press.

O'Laughlin, B. (1975). 'Marxist Approaches in Anthropology', *Annual Review of Anthropology*, Vol. 4, pp. 341–70.

Price, D. (2000). 'Anthropologists as Spies', *The Nation*, 20 Nov.

———. (2008). *Anthropological Intelligence*. Durham and London: Duke University Press.

———. (2011). *Weaponizing Anthropology: Social Science in Service of the Militarized State*. Petrolia: AK Press/CounterPunch Books.

Roseberry, W. (1988). 'Political Economy', *Annual Review of Anthropology*, Vol. 17, pp. 161–85.

———. (1989). *Anthropologies and Histories: Essays in Culture, History, and Political Economy*. New Brunswick and London: Rutgers University Press.

Sahlins, M. (1985). *Islands of History*. Chicago: University of Chicago Press.

Searle, G. (2007). *Meet the Natives* (Three Part Film, Channel 4). London: Keo Productions.

Segal, D. and Yanagisako, S. (eds.) (2005). *Unwrapping the Sacred Bundle: Reflections on the Disciplining of Anthropology*. Durham, North Carolina: Duke University Press.

Stocking, G. (1992). *The Ethnographer's Magic and Other Essays in the History of Anthropology*. Madison: University of Wisconsin Press.

Taylor, J. (1975). 'Review Article: Pre-Capitalist Modes of Production (Part I), *Critique of Anthropology*, Vol. 2(4–5) (Autumn), pp. 127–55.

———. (1976). 'Pre-Capitalist Modes of Production (Part II)', *Critique of Anthropology*, Vol. 2(6), pp. 56–71.

Terray, E. (1972). *Marxism and Primitive Society*. New York: Monthly Review Press.

Tierney, P. (2000). *Darkness in El Dorado*. New York: Norton.

Wilcken, P. (2010). *Claude Lévi-Strauss: The Poet in the Laboratory*. London: Bloomsbury.

Wilson, B. (ed.) (1971). *Rationality.* New York: Harper and Row.

Wolf, E. (1982). *Europe and the People Without History.* Berkeley, CA: University of California Press.

Wolpe, H. (ed.) (1980). *The Articulation of Modes of Production: Essays from Economy and Society.* London: Routledge and Kegan Paul.

http://unauthorised.org/anthropology/anthro-l/february-1996/0617.html

http://www.census.gov/prod/2004pubs/p20-550.pdf

PART I
Marxism in the American Anthropological Tradition

This article is a response to a review of *Reinventing Anthropology* (Hymes ed. 1972) by David Kaplan.[1] Diamond, Scholte and Wolf particularly address issues raised in and about Diamond's contribution to the volume, and in doing so they outline the general aims of Marx-informed anthropology of the time.

In his book review, Kaplan had presented a clichéd demonization of Marxism common in anthropology in both the United States and the UK. At about the same time that *Reinventing* was published, Asad (ed.) published *Anthropology and the Colonial Encounter* in the UK in 1973. This collection provided an intervention parallel to that of *Reinventing Anthropology*, and both volumes were received in a spirit of 'the-establishment-under-siege'.

Diamond, Scholte and Wolf – all now deceased – were major figures in the post–World War II attempt to reconfigure anthropology as a discipline sensitive to the political conditions (of both academia and the broader world) in which, especially in the 1960s, anthropology was expanding and consolidating its place within the social sciences.

Wolf is one of the most celebrated anthropologists of the 20th century and his work has had the most lasting influence. His early work on peasantries and economic anthropology (based on fieldwork in Puerto Rico and Mexico) set the tone for historical anthropology for many decades and his *Europe and the People without History* (1982) stands to this day as a monument of historical anthropology. Diamond was a key figure in the establishment of the anthropology department at the New School for Social Research and founded the journal *Dialectical Anthropology*. Scholte, after training and teaching in the United States, returned to the Netherlands, where he was a leading anthropological polemicist and celebrated teacher. He was actively involved in editing *Critique of Anthropology*.

27

The second piece in this section, an encounter between Wolf and Godelier (which took place in Amsterdam), is more of a discussion than a heated debate and offers excellent overviews of US and European anthropology of the time as articulated by influential figures. While critical anthropology then was very much in the idiom of the New Left, many Marxist influences in the field dated from an earlier period. Neither Wolf nor Godelier, who has been a prominent figure in French and international anthropology for decades, is speaking 'on behalf' of the field as a whole, but both are clearly allied with an historical approach soon to be challenged by the 'literary turn' allied with an aggressively postmodernist turn in anthropology.

Both anthropologists, though hailed for their singular, specialist contributions, display the features of accomplished generalists as well, comfortable with an anthropology whose explanatory remit is open to history and prehistory. In terms of the development of critical anthropology it is noteworthy that neither Wolf nor Godelier insists on defending a particular, canonical theoretical position, nor is either given to sweeping pronunciamentos, in striking contrast to the heated, prescriptive declarations of much hyper-theoretical anthropology that followed.

Note

1. As the response is addressed to the journal rather than the reviewer it might be fair to infer that the authors take the views expressed in the review to represent more than the opinions of the individual reviewer.

Chapter 1

ON DEFINING THE MARXIST TRADITION IN ANTHROPOLOGY*: A RESPONSE TO THE *AMERICAN ANTHROPOLOGIST*

STANLEY DIAMOND, BOB SCHOLTE AND ERIC R. WOLF

One does not anticipate a knowledgeable response from any establishment that is under attack. Academicians who are reluctant to inquire into their own motives, are ill-equipped to assess radical and dialectical alternatives to analytic scientism in cultural anthropology. They distort or simply talk past an intellectual tradition that commences with Vico and Rousseau, passes through Herder and Kant, becomes explicitly dialectical in Hegel, politically concrete in Marx, and is rendered extemporary with Lukacs, Sartre and many others. Like all exclusively analytic thinkers, Kaplan deals in discrete and reified entities: self *and* other, subject *and* object, committed *or* value-free method, scientific *or* metaphysical beliefs.

In his review of *Reinventing Anthropology*, Kaplan charges that we are voluntaristic, narcissistic, even solipsistic (and therefore irrational, idealistic, metaphysical). Such a psychologistic reduction of what is in fact an epistemological argument is impermissible. The analytic separation between subjectivity and objectivity does not exist in the dialectical tradition; such a categorical separation reflects a mechanistic imagination, which, in turn betrays an essential idealism. As Sartre puts it:

> There are two ways to fall into idealism: The one consists in dissolving the real into subjectivity; the other in denying all real subjectivity in the interests of objectivity. The truth is that subjectivity is neither everything nor nothing; it represents a moment in the objective process (that in which externality is internalized), and this moment is perpetually eliminated only to be perpetually reborn. (Sartre 1963:33)

Kaplan's remarks about Diamond's essay and the interpretation of Marx are symptomatic of his *modus operandi*. First of all, Marx is nowhere treated as an "inspirational Guru" in Diamond's essay (or anywhere else in the book); he is conceived, rather, as the paradigmatic figure of the revolutionary, non-academic, intellectual tradition in the

19th Century – a transformation of the enlightenment – and he is approached critically. Although Diamond's essay is substantially addressed to the question of an ethnology in the mode of Rousseau and Marx, his definition of Marxism, far from avoiding the "contradictions of capitalism," as Kaplan maintains, is as follows:

> If (Marxism) can be epitomized at all it is as a theory of social, hence political constraints on material possibilities. It is, therefore, dialectic in method and must be distinguished from all types of reductive materialism or technological determinism . . . that is, Marxism is based on the social process of exploitation in terms of class conflict; the question of class consciousness becomes the critical political question . . . It is only when men act politically, not only through aesthetic or religious symbols, to change the economic basis of their lives in accord with their "truly human" interests that they may begin to make history. (Hymes 1972:416–17)

For a discussion of surplus value, which Kaplan claims is not part of our Marxist lexicon, we refer him to Diamond's recent book (1974: especially pp. 9–12) which concludes that Marxism, indeed all revolutionary theory must base itself on the fact of "surplus" expropriation. This does not mean that the conventional Marxist analytical categories are inevitably applicable to the understanding of primitive societies since such categories have developed within the revolutionary critique of capitalism. However, the ethnological project remains Marxist precisely because it approaches primitive societies through categories pertinent to *their* operation, and on the basis of the critical Marxist analysis of our own society (Diamond 1972:414, 423–4).

More generally Kaplan is confused about the relationship between the "early" and "late" Marx, a confusion which reflects the limitations and the spirit of his review. He connects the early Marx to Rousseau, whose name as usual seems to be invoked as an epithet. But in *Anti-Duhring* Engels (1939:153–4) disagrees both with Kaplan's chronology *and* interpretation, stating that:

> "*Already in Rousseau, therefore, we find not only a sequence of ideas which corresponds exactly with the sequence developed in Marx's Capital*, but that the correspondence extends also in details, Rousseau using a whole series of the same dialectical developments as Marx used . . ." (Italics added)

Kaplan does not realize that Marx thought of himself as the heir of the French tradition of revolutionary and socialist thought. As the subtlety of his revolutionary insight developed, and his analysis of capitalism sharpened, Marx's antipathy toward imperialism increased; he became *less* Europecentric in his thinking (not more so as Kaplan seems to think). Hobsbawm, for example, has indicated that Marx – after the publication of *Capital* (about 1869) returned to a reconsideration of the primitive commune and its potential because of his increasing revulsion for the capitalist system, thus repudiating his earlier acceptance of imperialism on the basis of its unfortunate but supposedly progressive impact on pre-capitalist societies (1962:49ff). And Krader in his introduction to *The Ethnological Notebooks of Karl Marx*, shows how Marx used the comparison to man's past as the basis for both the critique of the present civilized condition, . . . and the perspective upon the future of society (1972:3, 35). In this connection we note that Marx's comments on the Paris commune reveal that in 1871 (certainly not the early or "Rousseauian Marx") he was anticipating both the dissolution of the state apparatus which had finally achieved the status of a thing in itself during the Second Empire, *and* the defeat of the dominant bourgeoisie. As David Fernbach makes clear in *The First International and After*, Marx "uses the terms Commune and State as opposites . . . [Marx describes] the Commune as a revolution against the State itself the hypertrophy of the bourgeois state was the result of class conflict, but the Commune was to be resumption by the people for the people of its own social life" (1974:38).

Obviously, Marx's attitude to the Commune is of a piece with his dialectical understanding of primitive communism, that "primitive condition" which, as Krader documents, "[he did not regard] as an end, but as a critical weapon to be applied against the antagonisms built into and arising out of civilised society" (1972:61). This we should note is the point of Diamond's recent book (1974) – and of his critical work in general – which bears no resemblance to Kaplan's misrepresentation of it as a romantic primitivism. Thus "the position of the notebooks makes it possible to oppose the condition of primitive men in particular societies to the life of man in the divided, industrial, urban societies" (Krader 1972:21).

It is in the understanding of the historical opposition between primitive societies and civilization which Marx reflected on so well, that the possibility of socialism originates. And it is this primitive communalism which Diamond treats as the "archetype of socialism," the antithesis of civilization, and most particularly of capitalism, in order to shed light on the revolutionary imperatives of our own time. Need it be said that contrary to the impression that Kaplan tries to convey, this does not imply a return to the actual forms of primitive society (see Diamond 1974:48, 174–5); it implies, rather, a dialectical return on a higher level, and in *different* form to certain defining *functions* of primitive society – classlessness, communal command of the basic means of production; integration of labor and related phenomena. This would not include a return to infanticide (Kaplan's implication), but rather a development of the means and relations of production that would render that usage – which has never been ascribed to cruelty – unnecessary. Still, Kaplan might well reflect – as did Marx, Engels and Rousseau, on the depth and extent of civilized crimes against children – crimes noted for their cruelty and senselessness, although one must, of course, contextualize, and make the effort to understand them socially.

Correlatively, it would certainly be a mistake to equate the "dismantling of the industrial apparatus" (Kaplan's phrase) with the socialist transformation of capitalism to which we ascribe, but it is not our mistake. Neither Diamond nor anyone else represented in *Reinventing Anthropology* has ever suggested that industrialism *as such* is the enemy. That is a conclusion in the style of our adversaries; *we* do not reify social institutions or technology, and we are certainly not Luddites. The process of dialectical return that we have outlined constitutes the basis of the Marxist historical method. It is nowhere more evident in Marx's work than at the end of his life (the *Ethnological Notebooks* were written in 1880–82; Marx died in 1883).

Curiously enough, Kaplan himself, in quoting Morgan's famous passage at the end of *Ancient Society* in order to establish the latter's supposed opposition to Social Darwinism seems momentarily to approve of this historical dialectic.

It is clear that Marx was not a scientist in the abstract academic, logico-deductive, hypothetical-propositional, ultimately positivistic sense. As Krader properly observes, he "opposed . . . the (positivist) conception of science as classification and definition, and consequently . . . (the) separation of science and politics" (1972:42–3). Correlatively, Marx was no empiricist in any formal definition of the term; he did not believe that facts speak for themselves. He was a dialectician, and a historian who practiced no particular discipline but focused on the whole range of socio-cultural phenomena in order to discover the key to the exploitation of man by man. His scientific (or realistic) – as opposed to Utopian – socialism included the necessity of political action based on class consciousness and conflict, in society at large. But Marx did not subscribe to universal, positivistic laws. In 1870, he stated,

> Comte is known to the Parisian workmen as the prophet in politics of Imperialism (of personal dictatorship), of Capitalist rule in political economy, of hierarchy in all spheres of human action, even in the sphere of science, and as the author of a new catechism with a new Pope and new saints in place of the old ones. (Harrison 1971:14)

In 1877, Marx denied that he had worked out "a historical-philosophical theory of the general path that every people is fated to tread." In response to the Russian populist N. K. Mikhailovsky, he had argued that

> he has to transform my sketch of the origins of capitalism in Western Europe into a historical-philosophical theory of a universal movement necessarily imposed upon all peoples, no matter what the historical circumstance in which they are placed, and will lead in the last resort, to an economic system in which the greatly increased productivity of social labor will make possible the harmonious development of man. I must protest. He . . . discredits me. (Bottomore and Rubel 1963:37)

Or as Maurice Godelier states: "Marxism is not evolutionism, and history is not the unfolding of a seed" (1975:81). Thus when Diamond supposes that abstract, non-historical, reifying social science will disappear in a classless, communitarian society, he is arguing in a dialectical, rather than an academic mode. For the cognitive categories and related organization of academic social science are symptoms of alienation, of particular social circumstances. But the identification of the structure of the academy with that of civilization itself, and thus the effort to eternalize both, is an old illusion; it goes back to Plato. Any serious attack on the academy is thus perceived as an attack on civilization, and we find Kaplan in the typical stance if the apologist, charging us with opposition to all institutions as such. Unfortunately for our critic, we are not "anarchists," but critical socialists in the Marxist tradition, engaged in the task of analyzing the salient structures of exploitation.

We do, however, certainly envisage the eventual demise of the alienated "expert," and the consequent freeing of social intelligence from disciplinary constraints and monopoly control. This is what Lenin meant in stating that any cook should be able to run the State. Demystification of the historical structure and position of the academy remains a radical, and critical task.

Accordingly, we find it understandable that Kaplan fails to mention Levi-Strauss, whom Diamond characterizes at length as the academic anthropologist – a formalist, reductionist, and "scientific" relativist who denies the connection between theory and practice, and insists on the privileged position of the Western observer. For it is such a definition of science that is rejected in the Marxist tradition. This rejection is no retreat into subjective idealism, but quite the contrary. For the turning of man into an object is both an idealist and a mechanical materialist fallacy ("inverted Platonism," as Lukacs [1971] affirms), a fallacy nowhere more evident than in the sector of anthropology for which Kaplan speaks. Correlatively, we note that the reviewer has overlooked Diamond's appreciation of Boas and his achievement, and of aspects of the work of Lowie, Kroeber, and Radin, both in this book (Hymes 1972:422) and elsewhere, not to mention similar statements by Hymes and other contributors, since they do not square with his contention, that such people have been "harshly maligned and dismissed."

Kaplan thus demonstrates his lack of anthropological understanding of anthropological traditions. He separates logic from sociologic. He reifies the texts of the ethnological theory at the expense of understanding the contexts of ethnological praxis. Logically, this distinction is entirely arbitrary; "criteria of logic are not a direct gift of God, but arise out of, and are only intelligible in the context of, ways of living or modes of social life" (Winch 1958:100). Sociologically, it exhibits that Western scientific ideology which has always pretended to an ultimate objectivity, autonomy, and superiority. Ethnologically, it is inexcusable. What, after all, is more anthropological than the recognition that ". . . histories are multiple and . . . [that] all sciencings occur in the course of histories and are themselves histories" (Nelson 1974:17).

The limitations of Kaplan's sense of history are further evident in his treatment of Wolf's suggestion that the construction of American industry evoked Social Darwinism as "its dominant mode of intellectual response" (1972:252) and that American anthropology "responded to the intellectual mood of Social Darwinism with the elaboration of evolutionist." Kaplan (1974:831) calls this a "somewhat mechanical sociology of knowledge approach that tends to reduce all ideas to 'rationalizations,'" and, moreover, is highly selective in its treatment." He stresses that the roots of cultural evolutionary theory lie most directly in the writings of certain French and Scottish Enlightenment social philosophers; that Darwin's thought was not isomorphic with Social Darwinism; and that neither Morgan, nor Tylor, nor Maine were Social Darwinists. All true, though selectively misplaced. To say that Social Darwinism was a "dominant mode of intellectual response" does not assert that it was the only mode. Elaboration *means* a "process of working out carefully, developing in great detail," rather than "originate." Modern evolutionary theory quite probably has its roots in the Enlightenment, though it is misleading to say this without reference to capitalism which stimulated that notable movement (see inter alia Gay 1966; Hobsbawm 1962; Horkheimer and Adorno 1947; Macpherson 1962). It is also true that Darwin was no Social Darwinist and that Marx and Engels praised him. It is equally certain, however, that in their praise they also warned against a biologizing materialism which saw the driving force of human life in the "struggle for survival," without reference to the changing characteristics of the historical process (*Kapital*, Vol. 1:89, 319). This famous statement in a letter from Marx to Engels, June 18th 1862 is pertinent:

> It is remarkable how Darwin recognizes among beasts and plants his
> English society with its division of labour, competition, opening up of

new market, 'inventions,' and the Malthusian 'struggle for existence.' It is Hobbes's *'bellum omnium contra omnes,'* and one is reminded of Hegel's *Phenomenology,* where civil society is described as a 'spiritual animal kingdom,' while in Darwin the animal kingdom figures as civil society. . . . (Schmidt 1971:46)

Yet this is precisely what Social Darwinism did, and why it became the dominant mode of Capitalism in the United States. The interested reader is referred to the quote from Hofstadter in Wolf's article (p. 251), to Hofstadter's book on *Social Darwinism in American Thought* (1955), and to Gruber's authoritative article, "Racism and Progress in the 19th Century" (Diamond 1974). The main exponents of the Social Darwinist mood in American anthropology were Powell and Briton.

Wolf moreover speaks of "intellectual moods" and "intellectual responses;" it is Kaplan (1974:833) who suggests that Wolf deals with intellectual traditions, as "though the cognitive component in those traditions didn't exist". Surely Kaplan is not suggesting that ideas lead a life of their own. One may readily concede the existence of a cognitive logic. What is in question, however, is not the logical working out of a set of ideas, but the successive replacement of one set of dominant ideas by another when many of the displaced ideas were, and still are, useful and fruitful. What is argued, moreover, in Wolf's paper and constitutes its main burden of argument – is that each of the successive sets of dominant ideas in American anthropology *avoided* contact with certain problems, notably the combined problem of political power and economic exploitation. They are interesting not only for what they said, but for what they did *not* say. The explanation of this notable *absence* invites explanations in terms of factors external to the ideas themselves.

This then brings us back explicitly to the question of objectivity. We can only agree that reality exists, or better, what exists is real. Yet if it is important to distinguish between men, as agents who transform reality, and reality itself, it is equally important to recognize that the opposition entails a relation which pre-supposes that the experimenter is part of the experiment. There are, indeed, various meanings of the term "objectivity." One kind of objectivity, consists in the examination of modes of cognition which men bring to bear upon reality and strives to understand the social, cultural, and psychological determinants of these modes. A second type of objectivity grants the integrity of reality, of the object, and respects that integrity. This aesthetic mode of cognition puts "naïve" observation, perceptual cognition before abstract analysis.

Yet there is a third meaning of objectivity – and this is the mode of objectivity favored by Kaplan. It is, however, also the most grossly subjective. It does away with an interest in the mode of cognition practiced by a socially and culturally determinate group in relation to socially and culturally determinate objects, and substitutes for this a set of historically disembodied scientists, thinking "thoughts without thinkers." These non-personal philosopher kings, moreover, proceed to dismember the objects of their study into abstract components, which are then assigned the status of the "true reality" as against that which is held to be merely "subjective" or superficial.

"Objectivity," Kaplan writes, "refers to the process of applying non-personal critical procedures and canons to the assessment of knowledge claims" (1974:827). What are we to say of an anthropology that takes no account of its modes of cognition? How do we assess the knowledge claims of a discipline which writes accounts of "cultures" abstracted from the contexts of capitalism and imperialism, racism and domination, war and revolution? What are we to say of a discipline which goes to great length to construct uneven samples of geographically and historically isolated cases in the name of science and for the purposes of mathematical comparison, without once asking questions about the possible distortion of the sample because of the existence of a common political economy, the incommensurability of the units of analysis, and so on? These are hardly questions which can be answered by reference to anthropology as a disengaged community of scholars.

In sum, Kaplan's arguments against the dialectical tradition all presuppose the 'innate' virtue of an essentially ethnocentric, technocentric, and merely pragmatic rationality.

As Horkheimer (1947:82), echoing Marx, states: "By its identification of cognition with science, positivism restricts intelligence to functions necessary to the organization of material already patterned according to the very commercial culture which intelligence is called upon to criticize."

Positivism proceeds by insisting on such so-called transcultural "objective" criteria as economy, efficiency, elegance, "value-free" explanation. Kaplan seems to glory, as Mannheim wrote (1936:101), "in his refusal to go beyond the specialized observation dictated by the tradition of his discipline, be it ever so inclusive; (he) is making a virtue out of a defense mechanism which assures him against questioning his presupposition."

To invoke Popper does not help one iota. His rationalism is no more critical or substantive than Kaplan's, it is a simple article of faith. Being scientific, it severs facts from values. Being liberal, it extends scientific methodology to the political domain (e.g., social engineering in the "open" society). Being undialectical, it separates the problem of validity from the question of socio-cultural genesis. It is not, by definition, critical: "questions of fact are prejudged in the form of methodological decisions and the practical consequences flowing from application of such criteria are excluded from reflexion" (Habermas 1968:280).

Finally, Kaplan fails to acknowledge that, most often anthropologists have been self-selected, rather marginal persons who have gone in search of that "common-humanity" (Kaplan's phrase) which contemporary Western Civilization, contrary to his sentimental conclusion, has systematically deformed and failed to define except on its own terms. It is a measure of the bureaucratization of the vocation that Kaplan should deny the relation between the alienation of persons in our society and the growth of the anthropological consciousness. And Kaplan's cognate effort to universalize exploitation, to imply that it is a human constant is also a sign of the times – for it enables him to ignore the *specific* structures of exploitation, which, as Marx pointed out, have reached their peak in the world that capitalism created. Examining, assessing, and seeking to replace such structures is not the result of "guilt," but of historical understanding, and a consequent, freely assumed historical responsibility. Professionals of Kaplan's type may try to discredit such an intent by reducing it to neurotic guilt, but they will find that in the world which we all share, that sort of thing no longer works. The ultimate purpose of anthropology is, we conclude with Rousseau, the revolutionary scrutiny of our own society.

---

*   "On Defining the Marxist Tradition in Anthropology: A Response to the *American Anthropologist*," sent to *Critique of Anthropology* by the authors, is a reply to D. Kaplan's review article of *Reinventing Anthropology* (D. Hymes, ed., New York: Pantheon Books, 1972) published in *American Anthropology*, 1974, 76:824–39.

REFERENCES

Bottomore, T.B. and Rubel, M. (eds.) 1963. *Karl Marx: Selected Writings in Sociology and Social Philosophy*. Harmondsworth: Penguin.

Diamond, S. 1964. "What History Is." In R.A. Manners (ed.), *Process and Patterns in Culture (Essays in honor of Julian H. Steward)*. Chicago: Aldine.

Diamond, S. 1972. "The Root is Man: Critical Traditions." In D. Hymes (ed.), *Reinventing Anthropology*. New York: Random House (Pantheon).

Diamond, S. 1974. *In Search of the Primitive: A Critique of Civilization*. New Brunswick: Transaction Books, E.P. Dutton.

Engels, F. 1939. *Anti-Duhring*. New York: International Publishers.

Fernbach, D. 1974. *The First International and After*. Harmondsworth: Penguin.

Gay, P. 1966. *The Enlightenment*, Vol. 1. New York: Alfred A. Knopf.

Gay, P. 1969. *The Enlightenment*, Vol. 2. New York: Alfred A. Knopf.

Godelier, M. in press. "Towards a Marxist Anthropology of Religion," *Dialectical Anthropology*, Vol. 1(1):81–85. Amsterdam: Elsevier Scientific Pub. Co.

Gruber, J. in press. "Racism and Progress in the 19th Century." In S. Diamond (ed.), *Anthropology: Ancestors and Heirs*. The Hague: Mouton.

Habermas, J. 1968. *Knowledge and Human Interest*. Boston: Beacon Books.

Harrison, R. 1971. *The English Defence of the Commune*. London: Merlin Press.

Hobsbawm, E.J. 1962. *The Age of Revolution*. London: Weidenfeld & Nicolson.

Hofstadter, R. 1955. *Social Darwinism in American Thought*. Boston: Beacon Books.

Horkheimer, M. 1947. *Eclipse of Reason*. New York: Seabury Press.

Horkheimer, M. and Adorno, T.W. 1947. *Dialectik Der Aufklarung*. Amsterdam: Querido.

Hymes, D. (ed.) 1972. *Reinventing Anthropology*. New York: Random House (Pantheon).

Kaplan, D. 1974. "The Anthropology of Authenticity: Everyman His Own Anthropologist." *American Anthropologist* 76:824–39.

Krader, L. 1972. *The Ethnological Notebooks of Karl Marx*. Amsterdam: Van Gorcum.

Lukacs, G. 1971. *History and Class Consciousness*. London: Merlin Press.

Macpherson, C.B. 1962. *The Theory of Possessive Individualism*. Oxford: Oxford University Press.

Mannheim, K. 1936. *Ideology and Utopia*. New York: Harvest Books.

Marx, K. 1923. *Das Kapital*, Vol. 1, 7th ed., K. Kautsky (ed.). Berlin: Dietz.

Nelson, B. 1974. "On the Shoulders of the Giants of the Comparative Historical Sociology of 'Science'." In R. Whitley (ed.), *Social Process or Scientific Development*. London: Routledge & Kegan Paul.

Sartre, J-P. 1963. *Search for a Method*. New York: Vintage Books.

Schmidt, A. 1971. *The Concept of Nature in Marx*. London: New Left Books.

Winch, P. 1958. *The Idea of a Social Science and its Relation to Philosophy*. London: Routledge & Kegan Paul.

Wolf, E. 1972. "American Anthropologists and American Society." In D. Hymes (ed.), *Reinventing Anthropology*. New York: Random House (Pantheon).

Chapter 2

THE WORST OF ARCHITECTS IS BETTER THAN THE BEST OF BEES: A DEBATE BETWEEN ERIC WOLF AND MAURICE GODELIER*

JOJADA VERRIPS

A debate without clashes tends to disappoint the audience. People complain that the discussion was tedious or dull.

Such were the qualifications I overheard after Eric Wolf and Maurice Godelier had discussed a number of important issues in anthropology. The debate was held in Amsterdam on January 26, 1985, and was led by Frans Hüsken (lecturer at the University of Amsterdam). Eric Wolf and Maurice Godelier were said to have been too much in agreement, their discussion lacked vitality. True, the two anthropologists did not attack one another violently. They listened carefully to each other, did not interrupt each other, did not become emotional, never raised their voices and frequently indicated that in general they agreed with what the other had said. Their discussion was anything but an exciting duel, at no point was there any reason for the chairman to intervene. But the fact that the debate – perhaps public conversation is a better term – failed to produce major clashes certainly does not mean to say that it was insignificant. On the contrary, in the course of a few hours Godelier and Wolf put forward a great many interesting and intriguing ideas and views. It was, however, not always easy to understand the drift of their argument. This was partly due to the fact that they assumed that everybody was thoroughly familiar with their work and partly to language problems. English is a second language for both Godelier and the audience. As a result, his arguments, digressions and sudden jumps in the train of thought were sometimes hard to follow.

INTRODUCTORY STATEMENTS

Wolf opened the discussion by giving some comments on the outline of the debate which had been sent to both Wolf and Godelier beforehand. The first question in the outline concerned the relevance of Marx to the study of anthropology. Wolf gave the following introduction.

Before World War II there were no measurable Marxist influences in American anthropology. There were some people who did see the relationship between the Indian population and the American government in terms of domination but that was all. It was not until after World War II that more and more anthropologists developed 'a material interest, not necessarily a Marxist interest, but an interest in understanding societies and cultures in material terms.'[1] Eric Wolf himself recognized the significance of a Marxist approach in anthropology when he started thinking about how societies and cultures that anthropologists normally study became incorporated into the larger world.

> The moment you look at North American Indian groups in relationship to the fur trade or at Central African societies in relationship to the expanding slave trade or to populations in South East Asia in relation to processes of colonization, it becomes evident that all of these cultures have been involved, caught up in, transformed by processes that had their origin in the larger world and that many of the cultures are in fact products of these processes. (. . .)

> So that the kind of units we used to think of as entirely separate, distinct entities suddenly begin to interpenetrate while the boundaries between them become questionable. You then discover that they very often are in fact groups that have divided, fissioned off from each other, joined each other and whose structure and organization, the kind of social and economic relations that hold them together are continuously changing.

This means that you have to find some scheme by which to explain these kinds of processes. You have to make a choice, either to be an empiricist who is not looking for explanations, or to adopt some kind of modernization theory, or you can turn to the Marxist tradition. Wolf choose for the latter because Marx paid attention to the fundamental dynamics of change and phenomena like exploitation, domination and colonialism. Wolf emphasized the continuing process of recreating and restructuring the world. Group transformation is the result of this expansion process. If you take this notion seriously, it is difficult to continue to view societies and cultures as units. Instead of referring to *a* society, *a* culture, one should think in terms of a continuing process of structuring, change and refashioning. According to Wolf this process of the involvement of peoples in the expanding world is governed by the capitalist mode of production and is therefore primarily an economic and political process. However, this process takes place without people's intentions; or, the intentions of people are carried along by the forces that move them. This insight forced him to change his view on cultures and values. It forced him to adapt his worldview and ideology – phenomena which are also a subject to constant change. If the relations between people change, their outlook on how the world is organized also changes. Consequently Wolf does not view ideology as some fixed, structural essence, but as something in a state of flux, something that changes.

Godelier gave a different kind of introduction. Rather than giving an overview of his scientific credo he talked about his wanderings through the academic world. As a young man, having become a member of the communist party, he wanted to fight exploitation and change society. He studied philosophy and later economy. After he came in contact with Braudel and Lévi-Strauss ('he encouraged and shielded the development of Marxist anthropology') Godelier became interested in anthropology. He developed a Marxist anthropological perspective '(. . .) in order to understand contradictions, social development and exploitative processes'. Two notions formed a crucial part of this perspective: that people are the only species which produce societies and that the development of these societies takes place through the exploitation of man by man.

After these two introductory statements, chairman Hüsken took these points up by asking both speakers in what way Marxism could be useful in anthropology and how the results of anthropological research could contribute to Marxism.

Marxism and Anthropology

Before explaining which aspects of Marxism were of crucial importance in anthropology, Wolf called attention to some characteristics of Marx's work.

We should keep in mind that Marx's terms were in fact 'metaphors of the moment'. He tried to fashion a new language in order to be able to talk about new relationships for which as yet no words existed. Consequently many terms such as 'Überbau', 'Unterbau', 'Produktionsweise' are not clearly defined and this is why problems arise when we use them today.

Secondly we are to realize that Marx lived in an age in which the capitalist system arose and developed. This means that he saw things that to us have become so commonplace that we no longer see them. He also saw them and there is a conservative side to Marx because he feared that they would be destroyed by rising industrial capitalism. Marx was not unlike an anthropologist who studies a group that nobody knows anything about. The anthropologist also wonders whether there is a system in the seeming chaos, how we can explain the apparently unstructured and how we can show that there are regularities. This is a very productive attitude and Marx had such an attitude.

According to Wolf the theory of surplus value, although it has been much criticized, is very important for anthropologists because it carries with it a number of questions about class relations and the like that were not discussed in anthropology courses and are still not raised very often. However one might differ on the interpretation of the notion of surplus value, the idea that human labour is used for the transformation of nature is of crucial importance. That labour can be organized differently and that each way of organizing labour has consequences for the rest of society is also an important notion. If an anthropologist studies how populations are affected by various modes of production you get a totally different view of what goes on in the world. 'It changes radically the way you understand the Iroquois or the Ashanti or, I suspect, even the Baruya (. . .)'.

Godelier agreed with Wolf. At university he had not been taught about the various forms of social exploitation of man by man or the transformation of nature. According to Godelier all Marxists agree that there would be no history if people had not been able to transform nature. Chimpanzees do not have history; they have evolution. People have (make) history because they can influence and transform nature. Take for instance the domestication of plants and animals and how this changed in the course of time. And the transformation of nature is linked up with the production of societies. Marxism is not a theory of production but '(. . .) the theory of production and reproduction of society'. Subsequently Godelier gave a rather cryptic exposition of his views on myths, the development of class societies and the inequality between men and women. His argument ran more or less as follows.

In the case of myths we see, says Godelier, that people *receive* all sorts of things (i.e. knowledge about domestication of plants, animals and fire) from gods. Their own achievements are interpreted as gifts from gods. They develop an 'upside-down view' of reality. Why is this so? And what about the rise of the so-called class societies in relation to this? Under certain circumstances, in certain communities, surplus labour which aimed at reproducing the community was looked upon as labour performed for the deities. This surplus labour was done for people who represented the whole community (for example priests – JV). Thus a majority started working for a minority. This was by no means the outcome of a plan or somehow manipulated by anyone. Just as the domination of men over women is not the result of a 'plot', this domination is a self-evident 'natural' process linked up with the rise of class societies. Godelier summed up his Marxist view of society as follows:

Man is the only species able to transform nature and it is because he transforms nature that he helps history, produces history. Secondly, history is based on contradictions, or develops or involves contradictions. And the last basic idea is that the motion of societies develops (by) the exploitation of man by man.

Some twenty years ago his view had been much more rigid and also more naive. But his ideas changed and deepened thanks to, among other things, the insights of non-Marxists. 'I keep calling myself a Marxist or I keep saying that it is good to have a materialist view of history.'

Remarkably enough neither Wolf nor Godelier took up the question of how the results of anthropological research may have led to adaptations in the Marxist approaches. Both emphasized how much anthropologists may benefit from a Marxist (materialist) point of departure and left it at that. Chairman Hüsken then asked them what their ideas were about the relationship between history (or change) and structure.

STRUCTURE AND HISTORY

Wolf felt that one of the innovations in recent writings in the social sciences in a Marxist vein was that the problem of functionalism, the existence of a social structure, is being rephrased in terms of reproduction. In a functionalist model of society everything stays the same because it is assumed that everything is interrelated and that the various parts automatically check and interrelate with each other. Sometimes the term reproduction means very little, it simply refers to reproduction of the social relations. Things become more interesting when one focusses on *how* relationships are in fact reproduced, whether reproduction is complete or partial and which factors or elements play a part in this process.

Subsequently Wolf returned to a point he had briefly mentioned in his introduction: his objection to viewing society as a bounded system of ordered relations ('a kind of bounded, structured entity'). He felt that in connection with this view the study of rituals (for instance Godelier's description of initiation ritual of the Baruya[2]) were important.

> Thinking about it in crosscultural perspective, there is an awful lot of groups that we have called societies, called cultures, that are in fact marked by ritual participation. It's the participation in the ritual that recreates the social entity. And those people who are invited to participate, form part of that social ensemble or, when they no longer wish to take part in that ritual, then they fall out of that social ensemble. It turns out that rituals of this kind very often include people of different languages with very different marital systems in fact. They create entities, new webs, new networks, new extensions of social relations, that they then are instrumental in reproducing. When missionaries come in and destroy that they also destroy a central focus of the reproduction process.

When societies are no longer viewed as boxes with tops on them but rather as series of elements whose mutual relations vary, who interact with each other in the course of time, we will be able to get an insight in the dynamics of these societies (and cultures). We will be able to develop a historical view of a series of relations. But as Godelier indicated many years ago, history as such does not explain anything, it has to be explained. For knowing that one damned thing comes after the other does not mean you know how one thing led to another. If, however, you are looking for a conceptualization with regard to the continuing existence of social relations, 'while movement is going on', your perspective changes considerably . . .

After Wolf's short exposition Godelier took the floor. Instead of going into the question Hüsken had raised he picked up where Wolf had left off. He gave a brief account of a number of important themes in his work and quite honestly admitted that he had no answers to certain questions.

The Baruya (Godelier lived among them for several years) felt that they formed a kind of social entity, even though members of other tribes ('invaders') were part of that entity. In the names of parts of initiation houses this feeling was symbolically expressed ('they call the house the body of the tribe, the body of the Baruya'). The Baruya indicated that neighbouring tribes spoke the same language and had similar customs because they had stolen them. Thus they made a distinction. However, the fieldworker sees similarities. These similarities also exist between tribes who live some thousand miles apart, who never had any contact with one another, who speak a different language and whose social structures are not the same. Their kinship systems, myths and ideologies turn out to be based on the same principles.[3] As a Baruya you do not see this. Neither does the fieldworker (the pseudo-Baruya). This strikes you when you sit at your desk in Paris and read what various anthropologists have written about these populations. Then you see that there are transformations (variations on a theme), that is when you start wondering about the boundaries between societies.

In the case of the Baruya's the land, the garden and the forest they exploited formed the boundaries. They were prepared to fight over that with members of neighbouring tribes with whom they shared the same language and culture. While there were cultural similarities they opposed each other on a political and economic level. Understanding the relationship between such phenomena is a very difficult theoretical question. Moreover, these phenomena have been produced by people in the course of time.

So, if you want to understand history, you have to understand that sort of process: of dividing peoples in tribes on tracts of land and overcoming the limits in culture, in mythology. You have to understand that double

process, triple process, that multi process. Now when you live for years
with the Baruya you never see these things in fact.

Godelier associated this problem with his view on the classical problem
of the relationship between 'Grundlage' and 'Überbau', 'superstructure'
and 'infrastructure'. According to Godelier the 'Grundlage' should be
interpreted as foundations (in the sense of foundations of a building)
and the 'Überbau' as the house itself. 'Überbau' should not be translated
as 'superstructure' that would wrongly suggest that it comprises very
little while 'infrastructure' comprises virtually all. It may be true that
our society allows for a distinction between superstructure and base but
societies with 'lineages' as they exist in Africa and New Guinea, production relations and kinship relations are not neatly separated. This forces
us to conclude that kinship relations '(. . .) act at the same time as a
social matrix to act on nature, to organize labour force, to redistribute
the produce of work, social work, social labour'.[4]

We should not forget that capitalist society is exceptional in history.
In this type of society the role of the economic sphere, of material living
conditions, becomes much clearer since all sorts of institutions with specific functions arose. Marx saw that, not because he was more intelligent
than others, but because in the nineteenth century this was happening
right under his nose. However, in other societies kinship relations and
political relations function as production relations. Godelier contends
that this is why he had to fight an ethnocentric view on production relations, get rid of 'an ethnocentric Marxist view of society' Godelier speaks
of dominant relations when kinship relations, political or religious relations function at the same time as production relations.

One thing Godelier, as a Marxist, cannot explain is *why* kinship is
dominant in one society and not in the other, and how changes in these
relationships come about.[5] Another thing he cannot explain is the diversity of kinship relations in societies of hunters and gatherers.

> (. . .) even if you do understand the importance of kinship through action
> on nature there is no Marxist, I tell you, there is no Marxist, Lévi-Strauss
> included, who is able to understand the diversity of kinship systems and
> to give reasons for the existence of matrilineal, patrilineal, bilineal, and
> non-lineal societies.

Given the two sexes there are logically speaking four abstract possibilities to trace descent (via women, men, both or neither) but how this is
connected with the material base of a society is still a mystery.

At the end of his short exposition Godelier said – just as Wolf had
done earlier – that he felt that societies could not be divided up in neat
layers, one above the other. This, he said, is a naive materialist point

of view. Rather, one should think in terms of a hierarchical division of functions. Godelier calls himself a Marxist because he feels that relations that function as production relations in society are most crucial and dominate reproduction. But beyond that, as he formulated it during the debate, he was at a loss, that is, he did not know how the connection between 'the specific material base' and 'the specific identity of the social relations of production' should be viewed.

Although Godelier's account was in itself interesting enough it was a pity he did not discuss the question Hüsken had asked, but only went into one of Wolf's remarks, i.e. the problem of seeing societies as bounded entities.

Hüsken's third topic of conversation dealt with the direction in which Godelier's and Wolf's work had developed thus far. Although Wolfs units of analysis have always been larger than his research units[6] (communities in Latin America and Europe), his oeuvre clearly shows a tendency toward still larger units. In his most recent book *Europe and the People without History* (1982) Wolf takes the largest possible unit of analysis: the world. Thus we see that Wolf tends to focus his attention more and more on macro-phenomena, large contexts. Rather the opposite seems to hold for Godelier's work. As a philosopher and economist interested in general theoretical questions, he became interested in anthropology and undertook to do fieldwork in New Guinea among a recently discovered, relatively isolated tribe.

MICRO AND MACRO

Wolf said that he recognized that the anthropologist who tries to give a sketch of the development of the world should be endowed with a sort of crazy courage. There will always be colleagues who maintain that you were wrong on the Eskimo or that the Mundurucú became involved in rubber trade either a hundred years after or a hundred years prior to the date you mention. Yet because he felt more and more unhappy with traditional anthropological case histories he decided nevertheless to take the risk of such a large scale study. In order to be able to study small scale case histories within a larger context one needs a developmental perspective. In Wolf's case this perspective is largely inspired by Marx.

> You know, it is a dialectic (. . .) It is a kind of going back and forward between an intense concern with particular cases and some kind of analysis of the forces that move these cases. I know that there are methodological discrepancies and difficulties with this but I don't see these things as essentially opposed activities.

If Wolf was very brief, Godelier's answer to Hüsken's question was rather elaborate. Godelier too felt that the processes studied by anthropologists and historians should be analyzed within the larger context of the evolution of the capitalist system. He went on to say that his attempts to make general statements about problems having to do with 'infrastructure' and 'superstructure' should not be confused with Wolf's approach. He said that his long stay with the Baruya had changed his views, changed even his personality. Due to this experience he now had developed a kind of 'feeling' for social problems wherever they might occur, a 'feeling' which is not confined to the problems of the Baruya only. Nevertheless this never led him to undertake the sort of study Wolf has carried out. 'I am not interested. Maybe it is too much, too difficult in some way. What he has done is too difficult for me.'

Having said this Godelier switched to his fieldwork among the Baruya and how this influenced his thinking. He made a very detailed study of the men-women relationships among this tribe and tried to find out how they behaved toward one another in various spheres, what kind of symbolic images they had of their relationships, which initiation rites they had, how this was related to the reproduction of mutual relationships and which forms of opposition existed, for '(. . .) this structure allows resistance to the structure'. He was fascinated by this resistance. Some women refused to prepare food for their husbands and refused to sleep with them. Some even murdered their husbands. However it was remarkable that no 'counter-ideology' existed. Godelier did not observe that women either had or were developing such an ideology on the basis of which they planned to overthrow the system. During the female initiation rites – by way of exception they allowed Godelier to attend this ceremony – he noticed that '(. . .) the ideology of the women was to reproduce the same social order'. If they resisted their husbands in every day life '(. . .), there was no counter-philosophy, no programme of change'. This raises the question under which historical circumstances and contradictions in social structure lead to a 'programme of change' and collective action. Both theoretically and practically speaking this is a question of the utmost importance.

Godelier studied the ways in which the Baruya 'made blood and sperm talk', through which images the relations between the sexes took shape. For instance, on the ground of certain ideas about menstrual blood, the men were able to tell women to do certain things or to refrain from doing things and the women would obey. We know of similar practices in the West. In France we can observe '(. . .) the same process of reproducing gender inequality through theories of bodies'. A detailed case study may enable you to trace problems which have a much wider impact. On the basis of such a study it is possible to formulate questions about other, similar cases. Feminists in France are currently using the book about the Baruya because it brings to light that male domination over women did not start with the rise of capitalism but much earlier, that it is not unique to class societies, as feminists used to think. This shows that case studies can help to develop a wider view on history.

But that sort of thing, Godelier pointed out, is not the same as what Wolf does. Godelier even said he was somewhat apprehensive of the kind of macro-study Wolf had written. When Wolf pointed out that Godelier, in his study on the Baruya, had himself written about the colonial transformation, the changes which came about after the arrival of the Australians, Godelier said that this was much simpler, that it could not be compared with the kind of problems Wolf dealt with. However, Godelier agreed with Wolf that it was very useful to fit micro-studies into macro-studies but he said that that kind of analysis was not his cup of tea '(. . .) you do that, I do something else (. . .)'.

Ideology

After the break (during which the debate between the two grand masters of anthropology, but most of all the differences between Godelier's presentation of self – 'elegant', 'a trifle pedantic, perhaps?' – and Wolf's presentation – 'rather timid', 'modest' were fervently discussed), Hüsken introduced the fourth topic: the role (thought, ideas, images) of ideology and culture.[7] During the past years, Hüsken recalled, Godelier had written quite a lot about the significance of thought or, more specifically, 'l'idéel' as an active force in the production and reproduction of social relations.[8] Before he had written to this effect, Marxists prone to interpret images in terms of reflections – as a passive force. According to Hüsken, Wolf was reputed to hold a somewhat different view on ideology and culture.[9]

Wolf gave a clear exposition about the distinction that should be made between ideas on the one hand and ideology on the other and how he thought ideologies were produced. In passing he referred to the question Godelier had pointed to earlier: the nature of kinship.

Not all ideas are ideological in nature. People have an idea before they make things. They don't reinvent the shoe every time they make one. They have an image of it in their heads and on the basis of that image they can produce a shoe. In this sense it is true to say that '(. . .) the worst of architects is better than the best of bees'. Ideas, knowledge, mental skills, they all have something to do with the transformation of the material world. An *ideology*, however, is an instrument by means of which contradictions (for example between the sexes, classes, races, ethnic groups) are bridged. In that case ideas receive an extra dimension.

They begin to carry political and economic weight since they force people to accept certain relationships that they would otherwise not have accepted. '*Ideology is ideas with a weapon*' because it goes together with force and violence. Ideas that are needed in connection with the ability to identify and cook edible plants lack this extra dimension.

Different modes of production generate different ideologies, different series of images which carry power with this factor force behind them. If modes of production are based on kinship ties, notions about differences between the sexes and the way in which kinship is ordered – in short the symbolic aspects of kinship – are ideological in nature. As a matter of fact neither Marxists nor non-Marxists know what kinship is. Anthropologists who claim to be specialists in this field and have been doing 'kinship algebra' for many years do not know either.

> (. . .) what is involved in kinship, how the symbolic categories and structures originate and develop, that is a whole other issue that we don't know very much about.

In a mode of production in which power holders extract surplus production in the form of a tribute from the population another kind of ideology is generated which in itself forms 'a seedbed for more ideology'. Much more important than whether or not ideological images are false is the fact

> (. . .) that they deal with basic contradictions that come out of the way in which human beings engage nature and that the particular way in which this is done in itself is the locus of the production of ideas that carry that kind of violence or force.

In short, according to Wolf, ideology originates from the mode of production and bridges contradictions within a society and is able to do so because of the force and violence behind it.

Hüsken asked Godelier whether he agreed with Wolf's view. Godelier said he basically agreed with Wolf but not on all points. He agreed that one cannot labour or produce tools if one does not have notions and images. Ideas form part of material processes. In fact, they are a precondition for these processes. They cannot be seen as *a posteriori* legitimations. One cannot marry without an idea about kinship and marriage. Ergo, ideas are pre-conditions and form part of relations and activities. We have to abandon the thought that images only reflect. It does not get us anywhere. Ideas are phantasized realities by means of which we can change the world. We still lack a materialist theory of ideas. We do have such a theory about ideologies. Ideologies deal with ideas – false ideas more or less, that is, we think they are false – that are employed to mystify, mask, conceal and cover up relations of exploitation and domination and to get people to accept such relations. True, this often involves the use of violence but what is more, those who are being exploited and dominated share these ideas with their exploiters and dominators. There is consent or consensus. According to Godelier, the fact that women are dominated by men or that the working classes are dominated by the capitalist classes is due to *shared* ideas rather than to the use of force and violence. This sharing of ideas calls for an explanation. But this is not all. Ideologies are believed to legitimate, yet, '(. . .) ideas don't come after the process of the creation of relationships'. For example, classes could not have developed if it had not been for some kind of ideology which was there from the outset. 'It is not after the event that ideologies appear. They are present from the very beginning in some way'. In sum, two things are of fundamental importance if it comes to ideological images: they do *not* come *after* people have entered into relationships with each other but entering into these relationships presupposes the existence of ideologies and ideologies are *shared* by dominators and those who are being dominated.

Godelier explained that his term 'l'idéel' derived from the work of French philosophers who were influenced by German phenomenology. He also explained what he meant by it. To him 'l'idéel' does not mean ideal in the sense of the socialist ideal but refers to 'any kind of representation'. It is of vital importance to realize that 'l'idéel' is implicit in all sorts of phenomena (for instance, kinship, religion) and activities 'it is not a layer, not the cream at the top, but it is a condition of social life'.

Godelier summarized his rather complicated argumentation as follows:

> First we have to recognize the importance of the presence of representations ('l'idéel'). Secondly we have to understand the relation between violence and consent. They don't exclude each other as many people seem to think. No, they are both part of the process of domination.

Wolf briefly reacted to Godelier's remarks. Wolf felt that Godelier had omitted to indicate that the same metaphors may be used for different reasons. 'The same form can actually orchestrate differences.' That two or more parties maintain this form is a result of the fact that they have to deal with one another and that their lives have to somehow be organized. Moreover, the threat of violence, the fear that the world will collapse, deters people from making infractions. Wolf could not agree with Godelier that ideas rather than violence were more vital to ideologies. Sharing on one level does not necessarily mean that there cannot exist differences and contradictions on another. Godelier agreed.

Chairman Hüsken closed the debate and invited the audience to participate in the discussion.

QUESTIONS FROM THE AUDIENCE

Firstly Rod Aya asked Eric Wolf about the relationship between the theoretical chapters in his *Europe and the People without History* and the more descriptive chapters. Aya felt that it would have been possible to write the latter without making use of Marxist theory. Or, as Aya put it, if Wolf had only read *The Wealth of Nations* by Adam Smith, he could have written exactly the same history.

Wolf replied that this might be true for part of the book but he felt he could not possibly have written the whole book without Marxist theory.

Aya replied that he had been unable to make the link between the theoretical chapters and the explanations the book offers and he repeated his question: 'Could Wolf say where the Marxist theory actually served to explain the events in the historical chapters?'

Take, for instance, chapter nine, Wolf replied. Some people take the position that capitalism is identical to merchants carrying commodities from one part of the world to another, thus creating a market. If you take that definition of the capitalist mode of production then you have to conclude that capitalism is almost everywhere and probably since the beginning of the Neolithic. However, the novelty about the capitalist mode of production lies in the *combination* of wealth accumulated by merchants and the labour power that is sold on the market and harnessed to 'cost and capital and machines and resources'. Europe moves into already existing trade connections. It is out of these connections of trade that the capitalists' wealth generates.

> I think that the rise of the capitalist mode of production is a *sui generis* new kind of phenomenon. Not that the elements themselves have not existed in different parts of the world. Mercantile wealth or even wage labour, commodities, that had been there before, but this combination is what makes it go. And then once it starts it does not operate in a linear fashion. It does not 'take off' in a kind of one easy revolutionary thrust, it kind of ebbs and flows and effects different parts of the world differently. It has crises, like the present one; it is pushed forward in some sectors more than in others. So, I don't know whether that is a theory, but it comes out of a kind of Marxist approach. I could not have thought of it myself.

Someone else in the audience wondered why Wolf did not simply say that anthropologists have discovered history. It all depended, Wolf replied, what kind of a history they were supposed to have discovered and he repeated what he had pointed out earlier, that history in itself is not a category that explains anything. In order to explain certain developments and processes you need a model. His model was a Marxist inspired view of history and could not be compared to the model Von Ranke, Peter Gay or Geoffrey Barraclough employed. As far as he knew not many anthropologists worked in the same vein as he did and neither were there many Marxist historians who studied the vicissitudes of the Mundurucú. There is no such thing as world history. That which we tend to consider as such is in fact the history of continents. The interconnections do not come to light. To some extent Braudel was alive to this problem but he did not write about the people, the main interest of anthropologists, while they did form part of the mercantile networks and have often played an important part in them. Until recently these people had no history. The same holds true for the people who worked in industry or were employed at capitalist undertakings such as plantations. They do not appear in world history either. Hence the title *Europe and the People without History*.

After this answer someone remarked that the relationship between Marxism and anthropology was in fact not so new. Had not Marx himself studied the works of anthropologists? Both Godelier and Wolf reacted to this question and they clearly did not agree with each other about the significance of Marx's endeavors in anthropology.

According to Wolf his insights were dated and could not be called very spectacular. It was telling, he said, that Marx made his notes on anthropology in note-books in which he also noted down thoughts about electricity. 'I think we have learned a lot since those things were written. I am more interested in Marx's analyses of the capitalist system than I am interested in Marx as an ethnographer'.

Godelier disagreed. He felt Marx's ethnographic and archaeological studies were of some interest. Firstly, Marx had attempted, albeit making use of an evolutionist and therefore outdated model, to understand why communal modes of production and all that went with it had made way for another mode of production. Secondly, Marx's ideas about the Asiatic mode of production resulted from his studies in anthropology. Besides, not the term Asiatic mode of production but the ideas that lay behind it are of interest, namely that a state (bureaucracy) can develop while collective landownership and tribal structures continue to exist. At the end of his rather lengthy reply Godelier returned to a point Wolf had made earlier and contended that it had been easier to write world history in the nineteenth century because at the time much less was known. In fact, in his view Wolf had not written world history, for he had focussed on the developments of the capitalist mode of production and had not paid attention to the Asiatic and feudal societies.

The last question dealt with Godelier's book about rationality and irrationality in economy.[10] What did Godelier mean by this irrationality and how was it possible to invent something new if in the last instance all was determined by economy?

Godelier only went into the first part of the question. At the time of writing he was a young and naive Marxist. In the book he had wished to show, on scientific grounds, that a socialist mode of production, because it offered more possibilities to transform people's lives, was rational and superior to a capitalist mode of production which in his view was inferior and irrational. However, later Godelier concluded that economic rationality did not exist and that the notion of *homo economicus* does not hold water. Writing this book had been very meaningful for him in that it had raised his interest in economic anthropology – even though he felt that the work done in this field at the time was not very promising – and had made him decide to become an anthropologist long before he did his fieldwork among the Baruya. Now that he was older and wiser, as Godelier put it, he would never be able to write such a book again. 'I am surprised', he said, 'that the book is still sold.'

Epilogue

Boxers sometimes deal each other blows of which the effect is only felt later. Germans have a special term for this kind of delayed effect: 'Stösse mit Spätwirkung'. The debate between Godelier and Wolf had a similar effect on me. During the debate itself I was not very impressed. It annoyed me that they didn't criticize each other more sharply, that they did not try to floor each other with crystal clear arguments, that they more or less agreed with each other and often seemed to express themselves less clearly than they did in their written work. It was not until later, when I carefully listened to the tape-recordings of the debate, that I realized that during their intellectual duel Wolf and Godelier had made many intriguing remarks and observations. For instance, Godelier's exposition about the shared nature of ideological representations and the fact the representations ('l'idéel') are pre-conditions, parts of relations and activities, raises many questions whose answers can lead to new insights in (the development of) societies and cultures. The same is true of Wolf's contention that participation in ritual is crucial to social entities. The existence of economic and political ties between people is not enough. Quite a remarkable point of view for someone who uses a Marxist inspired model of history.

I was most fascinated by their both being able to admit that they did not know the answer to certain questions. For instance, both admitted they did not know what kinship was, both were able to admit to weaknesses in their Marxist approaches. It marks the 'strength' of these two intellectual strongmen. In retrospect their debate turned out to be one of the most stimulating intellectual duels I have attended in the past few years.

* The debate took place on January 25, 1984, in Amsterdam. It was one out of a series of debates between outstanding sociologists, anthropologists and historians. The debates were organized by the editors of the *Amsterdams Sociologisch Tijdschrift* to celebrate the tenth anniversary of their journal.

N<small>OTES</small>

1. Undoubtedly Wolf was referring to his teachers Julian Steward and Leslie A. White, two American anthropologists who made important contributions to the development of materialist approaches in the United States.
2. Cf. Godelier, M. (1982), *La Production des Grands Hommes*, Paris, Fayard.
3. In this context Godelier also used the phrase 'the same mental structure', which clearly shows that his work was influenced by Lévi-Strauss.
4. Cf. Godelier, M. (1978), 'Infrastructures, Societies and History', *Current Anthropology*, Vol. 19 (4), 763–69.
5. In the article mentioned in footnote 4 he said this: 'Concerning kinship, we may imagine that in primitive societies *living* labour force counts for more than labour accumulated in the form of tools, domesticated resources etc. We know that in all societies the reproduction of life is governed by different forms of kinship. It may be, then, that we should look for the ultimate reasons for kinship relations' functioning as relations of production, and hence for kinship's dominance, in some given state of the productive forces, i.e., in some *relation* between "living" (present) labour and "dead" (past) labour' (p. 766).
6. Vol. 58, No. 6. For example Wolf's famous article, 'Aspects of Group Relations in a Complex Society: Mexico', *American Anthropologist*, Vol. 58, 1065–75.
7. The terminology used at this point in the debate was rather confusing. Terms like 'thought', 'thinking', 'ideas', 'representations', 'ideology', 'culture' were employed without further explanation.
8. Cf. Godelier, M. (1978), 'La part idéelle du réel. Essai sur l'ideologique', *L,'Homme*, XVIII (3–4), 155–88, and the article mentioned in footnote 4.
9. Cf. Wolf, E.R. (1982), 'Culture: Panacea or Problem', Northeastern Anthropological Association Newsletter Fall 1982, I–II, and (1982) *Europe and the People without History*, 387–88, Berkeley: University of California Press.
10. Godelier, M. (1969), *Rationalité et irrationalité en économie*, Paris: Maspéro, Vol. 5(5), 1985.

PART II

The Debate about the Articulation of Modes of Production

In this intense and detailed discussion of Meillassoux, O'Laughlin introduces, elaborates and critiques one of the central contributions to a French-based Marxist anthropology that put economic anthropology at the centre of anthropological theory making for several years and reinvigorated historical anthropology as well as the anthropology of social change. Meillassoux's work, along with that of Emmanuel Terray, Pierre-Philippe Rey and Pierre Bonte, to mention a few of the key French authors, was central in advancing the concept of *the articulation of modes of production* and endeavouring to explain how capitalism could extract surplus from non-class-based societies. Their work had implications not only for understanding the logic of colonial rule in diverse empires (the British, French and Dutch in particular), but also for understanding new forms of labour mobilization, as in the case of plantations and mines in South Africa (see Wolpe ed., *The Articulation of Modes of Production*, 1980, for example) and in the context of the analysis of domestic labour in the core.

After a number of years' teaching African studies at Eduardo Mundo University in Maputo (where she was present when Ruth First died in 1982 from injuries sustained in the explosion of a parcel-bomb delivered by South African security forces), Dr. O'Laughlin moved to the International Institute of Social Studies in the Hague. Her 'Marxist Approaches in Anthropology' in the *Annual Review of Anthropology* (1975) is a lasting and an authoritative overview.

Chapter 3

PRODUCTION AND REPRODUCTION:
MEILLASSOUX'S *FEMMES, GRENIERS ET CAPITAUX*

BRIDGET O'LAUGHLIN

In *Femmes, Greniers et Capitaux*, Meillassoux asks why it is that social relations based on the family continue to have such great importance within a capitalist system. He provides two answers, both based on the role of the family in reproducing labour-power. First, capitalism gets extra surplus from pre-capitalist modes of production based on the domestic community, which provide capital with cheap labour-power. Secondly, in bourgeois society, the family continues to be the place where labour-power is produced and reproduced. Given these answers, it is clear that any understanding of the dynamics of capitalist development requires an analysis of domestic relations. Thus in the first half of this book, Meillassoux develops the theory of the domestic community as a productive system.

In the second half of the book, Meillassoux outlines his theory of imperialism as a mode of reproducing cheap labour through the exploitation of the domestic community. He also addresses, though much less thoroughly, the place of the family and the determinants of sexual status in bourgeois society. Since it seems to me that Meillassoux intends to contribute primarily to an analysis of the conditions of capitalist expansion, I should like to begin by fixing, in a rather general way, Meillassoux's position within contemporary work by Marxists on uneven development.

Bourgeois theory has constantly noted the dualistic structure of an underdeveloped economy; a small industrial sector is hobbled by a rapidly propagating and technologically backward traditional sector. Marxist theorists have responded by noting that if one takes the world capitalist system rather than a national economy as the basic unit of analysis, the picture which emerges is somewhat different. Instead of a series of independent economies set somewhere on a scale of traditional to modern, one sees a single unevenly developed capitalist system in which the accumulation of surplus must be by definition systemically related to the stagnation of other areas. For Marxists, then, an adequate theory of imperialism is one which strips off the dualistic appearance of the world economy to reveal the underlying contradictory dynamics of capitalist development.

Meillassoux's work fits within a tradition of analysis which presumes that in the context of a disruptively expansive capitalist system, the dynamics of capitalist development cannot be understood without reference to the dynamics of non-capitalist modes of production and to their systemic relations with capitalism.[1] This analytical position draws the work of Marxist anthropologists and historians on pre-capitalist modes of production into a central position in controversies over theories of imperialism and capitalist development.

One could argue that the dynamics of non-capitalist modes of production must be conceptualized in any concrete historical analysis of capitalist development because they shape the boundary conditions for the reproduction of capital. Meillassoux, however, makes a more specific case. The logic of capitalism requires, he argues, that capital be unable itself to reproduce labour-power. Since labour-power must nonetheless be reproduced, it may be advantageous for capital in certain historical conditions to maintain pre-capitalist modes of production as reservoirs of cheap labour-power.[2] There is, furthermore, one mode of production, that based on the domestic community, which is better exploited by capital through its preservation than by its destruction. Meillassoux's contribution to Marxist theories of imperialism is, therefore, a theory of the interrelationship of capitalism with the domestic community.

In reviewing the arguments advanced by Meillassoux in *Femmes, Greniers et Capitaux*, I shall be primarily concerned with the extent to which they provide theoretical tools which deepen our understanding of the dynamics of imperialism. The question, then, is not whether or not the domestic community has ever existed as a kind of productive system, but rather what the explanatory power of the theory of the domestic community is. For Marxists, explanation does not consist of naming and grouping social phenomena, but of laying bare the underlying relations through which social forms are reproduced. Good theories are thus tools which clarify the conditions and consequences of political struggles. In discussing the usefulness of Meillassoux's theory, I shall therefore emphasize the relevance of the theory to our understanding of the current conditions of reproduction of capital. I shall try to be very specific in locating places where Meillassoux diverges from other Marxist work on the uneven development of capitalism: my purpose in so doing is not to re-establish orthodoxy (which I am not competent to do anyway) but to clarify analytical and political consequences and alternative.

PRODUCTION AND REPRODUCTION

The fundamental argument of this review is that the central weakness in *Femmes, Greniers et Capitaux* lies in Meillassoux's ambiguous conceptualization of the relation between production and reproduction. Meillassoux is fully in accord with Marx's careful critique of Malthus: laws of population or demographic principles are always specific to particular modes of production. Meillassoux likewise agrees with Marx that the production of means of subsistence is the central condition of all production. The problem that remains outstanding, then, is the link between these two propositions. How should we think of the relationship between the reproduction of people as producers and the production of the means of subsistence? Here we confront the ambiguities of the word reproduction and the intellectual load it carries with it from evolutionist thought.

Some of this baggage came with Engels in his work on the origins of social institutions. Engels took the determining fact of history to be, in the last analysis, the production and reproduction of immediate life (Engels 1972 p71). In interpreting this basic proposition of historical materialism, however, Engels tended to treat production and reproduction as two distinct and co-ordinate aspects of the process of social production:

> This again, is of a twofold character: on the one side the production of the means of existence, of food, clothing, and shelter and the tools necessary for that reproduction: on the other side the production of human beings themselves, the propagation of the species (ibid).

This interpretation brings one very close to an evolutionist position in which the direction of social change is determined by the contribution that a particular practice makes to the biological reproduction of the group.

Engels' formulation has received a good deal of attention in contemporary work, not because of its theoretical elaboration, but because it provides one of the few extant clues to a Marxist approach to sex-roles.

In his introduction, Meillassoux defends, with perhaps some hesitancy, the usefulness of putting production of the means of subsistence and biological reproduction of producers on the same analytical level:

> Engels commettait-il une erreur en mettant sur le même plan la production des moyens d'existence et la production des hommes? C'est ce qu'exprime la note de la rédaction à l'édition publiée aux Editions sociales, selon laquelle cette assimilation serait une 'inexactitude'. C'est faire bon compte d'une production essentielle entre toutes, celle de l'énergie humaine ou, dans le système capitaliste, de la force de travail. La reproduction des hommes c'est, sur le plan économique, la reproduction

de la force de travail sous toutes ses formes. Or, le matérialisme historique,
dont on pourrait s'attendre a ce qu'il y attache une importance majeure et
bien qu'il ait été le seul à pose le probleme, n'intègre qu'imparfaitement la
reproduction de la force de travail dans son analyse (p. 8).

The difficulty here is that one cannot consistently argue both that the
production of human energy is an essential form of production and, as
Meillassoux maintains elsewhere in the book (p. 84), that the biological
reproduction of producers is subordinate to production of the means of
subsistence.

Failure to resolve this fundamental ambiguity in his conception of the
analytical primacy or determinance of production leads Meillassoux, I
think, to fall into modes of argumentation which are evolutionist, functionalist and empiricist in form. Meillassoux is a Marxist. His lapses represent ideological intrusion, not commitment. Nevertheless, confusion
over the production/reproduction problem flaws what is most innovative
in his work and undermines the explanatory power of his theoretical
constructs. In this review, my intention is to clarify this conceptual problem by a critical reading of Meillassoux's key arguments. I shall push the
logic of these arguments beyond the point to which he carries them to
emphasize inconsistencies and historical inappropriateness. My reading
of *Femmes, Greniers et Capitaux* is thus not generous, nor perhaps even
fair, but hopefully it will be theoretically clarifying.

Before proceeding to this critical reading of particular arguments, it
is helpful to juxtapose the Engels/Meillassoux formulation with Marx's
remarks on the primacy of production and reproduction of means of
subsistence in the reproduction of human society.

Whereas Engels divided production into two distinct aspects –
production of the means of subsistence and reproduction of people –
Marx used the phrase production and reproduction to describe a unitary
social process:

> Whatever the form of the process of production in a society, it must be a
> continuous process, must continue to go periodically through the same
> phases. A society can no more cease to produce than it can cease to con-
> sume. When viewed, therefore, as a connected whole, and as flowing on
> with incessant renewal, every social process of production is, at the same
> time, a process of reproduction (Marx 1967, 566).

According to this logic, the conditions of production are also those
of reproduction. Thus if production is capitalistic in form, so also is
reproduction (ibid).

Meillassoux (p. 157) specifically rejects Marx's remark on the unity of
production and reproduction, arguing that such a view is not historically

appropriate if the reproduction and maintenance of labour-power are not assured in the sphere of capitalist production. On the basis of the revisions in Marx's theory of capitalism which he thinks this anomaly requires, Meillassoux constructs his theory of imperialism as the mode of reproduction of cheap labour-power. At this point, it is important to note that Meillassoux's criticism of Marx hangs on a reinterpretation of the word reproduction to refer to the biological reproduction of labour-power.

In this reinterpretation, Meillassoux seems to me to lose that which is most incisive in Marx's critique of Malthus: the biological reproduction of people is a contingent outcome of the ways in which the production and reproduction of the means of subsistence are socially organized. Meillassoux recognizes the historical specificity of laws of population, but he still insists that the reproduction of individuals as productive agents is a functional prerequisite of all societies (p. 7). If this claim means only that human social production depends on people producing, it is tautologous. If, however, it is an analytical proposition, assigning the same determining role to the production of human energy as is assigned to production of the means of subsistence in Marxist theory, it muddies one of Marx's central insights: certain modes of production – take capitalism to name one – are organized in such a way as not to assure the biological reproduction of a given supply of workers. The quantity, quality, and value of the labour-power employed in capitalist production are constantly altering with the evolution of the technical conditions of production and the state of the class struggle. An adequate conceptualization of the relationship between production and reproduction of human energy must, therefore, be one which can admit the contingency of biological reproduction of workers.

The central issue in this review, then, is the correct theoretical interpretation of the determinance of production and reproduction in Marxist theory. In the following two sections, I shall consider difficulties in Meillassoux's discussion of capitalism and in his analysis of the 'domestic community' which arises from his treatment of reproduction. In the last section, I shall review methodological tendencies, namely functionalism and empiricism, which represent the encroachment of evolutionism in various of Meillassoux's arguments.

CAPITALISM

In *Femmes, Greniers et Capitaux* Meillassoux is concerned with the ways in which the domestic community is preserved, exploited and used by capital. Thus his discussion of the domestic community is projected upon his conception of the dynamics of a capitalist system.

Since Meillassoux suggests certain revisions of Marx's theory of the reproduction of capital, I shall invert the order of presentation followed in the book to discuss first the view of capitalism upon which the book is built. My purpose here is to show that the weakness of certain premises implicit in Meillassoux's discussion of capitalism severely restrict the usefulness of his analysis of imperialism and of the place of the family under capitalism.

According to Meillassoux, there is a basic contradiction in the logic of capitalism which prevents it from being a self-sufficient system:

> Pour que se réalise la plus-value, en effet, le salaire doit être fondé sur la durée précise du temps de travail effectivement fourni par le travailleur. Mais, pour que s'accomplisse la reproduction, il faut que les revenus du travailleur couvrent ses besoins individuels *pendant sa vie tout entière* (de sa naissance à sa mort), indépendamment de la somme effective de force de travail fournie (p. 154).

Assuming that there must be some equivalence between the wage of the individual and the length of time actually worked, Meillassoux concludes that the conditions for the production of surplus-value are not consistent with the reproduction of labour-power by capital. Implicit in this conclusion is his assumption that the reproduction of labour-power is the form taken by the reproduction of human energy under capitalism (p. 8). He makes no distinction, that is, between the reproduction of the commodity labour-power and the reproduction of labour. Yet, Meillassoux further reasons, both the production of surplus-value and the reproduction of labour-power are requirements of capitalist reproduction. The only resolution of the contradiction is the completion of the cost of reproduction of labour-power by a source exogenous to capital.

In advanced capitalist countries, suggests Meillassoux, the state provides the necessary supplement to the direct-wage through the provision of social services. Those who are barred from public welfare by discrimination and job insecurity must alternatively depend on non-capitalist modes of production for the reproduction of their labour-power as do Third World workers:

> Si l'on accepte cette analyse, on peut considerer *a contrario* que, lorsque le prolétariat ne perçoit qu'un salaire direct honaire (comme ce fut longtemps la cas en Europe et comme c'est encore le cas dans la plupart des pays sous-développés), la reproduction et l'entretien de la force de travail ne sont pas assurés dans la sphere de la production capitaliste mais nécessairement renvoyés à un autre mode de production (p. 157).

If the state enters into the reproduction of labour-power, then a share of the total product must be diverted away from potential surplus; if surplus can be extracted from non-capitalist modes of production instead, then the rate of profit will be higher than it would otherwise be.

Meillassoux sees himself correcting or supplementing Marx in two respects in this argument: first, he is showing that the form of reproduction under capitalism is not capitalist; secondly, he is demonstrating that continuing primitive accumulation (absorption of surplus from non-capitalist modes of production) is a functional requirement of the reproduction of capital. Meillassoux intends to close the gap which he takes to be the central problem in applying Marx's model of capitalism to the analysis of imperialist expansion in the 20th century – the absence of any integration of the problem of the reproduction of labour-power in the model (p. 9).

To evaluate the usefulness of Meillassoux's contribution, it is necessary first to consider the contradictory needs which he puts at the heart of capitalism: (1) the conditions of reproduction of capital require that capitalism not reproduce labour-power; (2) the reproduction of labour-power is nonetheless a boundary condition for the accumulation of capital. In each of these propositions, the reproduction of labour-power is taken to be equivalent to the reproduction of the human energy of workers. If either or both of these propositions are invalid, then Meillassoux's reasoning will not support his conclusion that capitalism must depend on other modes of production for the reproduction of labour power.

From the discussion of production and reproduction in the preceding section, it should be clear that Meillassoux's second proposition can only be valid in an *a priori* sense if one assumes, as he, does, that the reproduction of workers is always a boundary condition of social reproduction. Otherwise one must demonstrate, in an historically specific way, that the biological reproduction of workers is a condition of the production of surplus-value. The validity of both propositions, then, depends on their consistency with Marx's theory of the origin of surplus-value under capitalism.

Marx found the key to understanding the origin of surplus-value under capitalism in the conceptual distinction between labour and labour-power. Meillassoux does not use this distinction analytically; he applies the concept labour-power to pre-capitalist modes of production as well as to capitalism. For Marx, however, the distinction between labour and labour-power expresses within production the basic class relations of capitalism: labour, alienated from its means of production, has no choice but to sell its labour-power for a wage; capital, controlling the means of production, struggles to extract labour from the commodity it has purchased. The production of surplus-value depends on the ability of capital as a class to extract more value from labour in the process of production than that which is embodied in means of production consumed in production and in the commodities which make up the wage-bundle of workers.

In terms of Marx's analysis of the origin of surplus-value, there is consequently no reason whatsoever for arguing that the conditions of reproduction of capital require that capitalism not reproduce labour-power. All that is required is that the costs of reproducing labour-power and means of production remain less than the value which is produced. Nevertheless, behind Meillassoux's argument that capital cannot reproduce labour-power lies a fundamental, if mislabelled, insight into the conditions of reproduction of capital. For capital to be reproduced a class of exploitable workers must exist, they must be exploitable at a rate which permits a positive rate of surplus-value and their skills must fit the technical parameters of production. Yet capital, even with the constant intervention of the state, cannot assure that these conditions are always met. Meillassoux is thus quite correct in seeing that the internal logic of capital does not order the conditions of its reproduction; he errs, however, in his functionalist assumption that endogenous reproduction cannot therefore take place. His analysis confuses the indeterminancy of a contradictory system with functional closure.

What then of the second half of Meillassoux's contradiction: is the biological reproduction of the labour-force a necessary condition for the production of surplus-value? The answer may appear to be transparently obvious; if there are no producers, there is after all no production. I should argue, however, that the form of the proposition again precludes grasping the fundamental indeterminacy that Marx found in the demand for labour under conditions of capitalist production. Competition between capitals and the basic struggle between capital and labour are expressed in changing rates of exploitation, technical innovation, and variation in labour-requirements. We cannot therefore assume that the biological reproduction of the working-class as individuals is a pre-condition for the reproduction of capital.

If we assumed a closed system of simple reproduction of capital, without any technical change, then the commodities advanced to the worker would have sufficed for the reproduction of the family of that worker if labour, labour-power, and hence capital were to be reproduced. There is in fact a tendency in capital to drive toward the basic subsistence wage as it struggles to enlarge its share of the worker's labour-day, yet this drive is restricted both by the organized struggle of workers and by competition between capitalists.

If, as is historically more appropriate, we admit the possibility of technical change, then we can see that competition between capitalists who confront well-organized workers may lead them to cut costs by substituting machines for living labour, thus generating a reserve-army of labour. In this case, the reproduction of capital may entail the social reduction, not biological reproduction, of the labour-force. At the same time, the general adaptation of such technical changes requires an expanding scale of reproduction and hence absorption of new labour if profits are not to fall.

On the basis of Marx's understanding of the dynamics of capitalism, both of Meillassoux's propositions seem to me analytically invalid; capitalism can reproduce labour-power and the biological reproduction of workers is not a boundary condition for the accumulation of capital. Meillassoux's attempt to base a theory of imperialism on capital's need to have human energy reproduced in the domestic community is therefore vitiated by his premises. Yet the phenomena to which Meillassoux applies his theory – massive labour-migration and technical stagnation in household subsistence production – mark many Third World economies. What then are the analytical alternatives?

The beginning point must be, I think, where Lenin found it – in the contradictory, uneven and irreversible dynamics of capitalist development. In terms of Meillassoux's theory, backwardness is largely a function of the existence of the domestic community: where the domestic community existed or could be reinstated, capitalism maintained it. In fact the situation appears much more complex than that when one looks at the effects of secondary industrial development in Puerto Rico on labour-migration, or at the development of plantations and mines in colonized areas, or at the coastal concentration of urban development in the Third World, or at the development of settler colonies in Africa, Australia and the Americas. An adequate theory of imperialism should be able to recognize the consequences of competition between capitals and class struggle – the emergence of monopoly, competition between units of national capital for markets and raw materials, the growth of the reserve-army – as forces shaping the phenomenal dualism of the world capitalist economy. The theory should also be one which recognizes, as does that of Meillassoux, that the determinations of capitalist reproduction are not entirely endogenous to itself since it is a necessarily expanding and open system. The theory should also admit, as that of Meillassoux, cannot, that the reproduction of capital does not imply that capital has necessarily been able to order all exogenous determinants to its advantage.

The Domestic Community

(a) The Domestic Community as Theoretical Object

An adequate theory of imperialism cannot, then, be derived from Meillassoux's contention that the reproduction of capital depends on the existence of the domestic community for the reproduction of labour-power. Nevertheless, in any concrete historical moment, the dynamics of capitalist development are also shaped by non-capitalist modes of production. Although any *general* theory of imperialism is a theory of capitalist development, one must therefore theorize non-capitalist modes of production and their relation to capital as well. The purpose of this section is to consider the usefulness of Meillassoux's theory of the domestic community in analyzing the relation between capitalism and certain non-capitalist forms of production. Since Meillassoux's conception of the theoretical place of the domestic community is in fact much broader than capitalist/non-capitalist interaction, I shall be avoiding a number of evolutionary questions, probably of interest to anthropological readers, addressed by Meillassoux.

According to Meillassoux, the domestic community is both the basic unit of production in a distinctive pre-capitalist mode of production and a social unit encapsulated within all class societies:

> En dernier ressort, tous les modes de production modernes, toutes les sociétés de classes reposent pour se pourvoir en hommes, c'est à dire en force de travail, sur la communauté domestique, et, dans le cas du capitalisme, à la fois sur elle et sur la transformation moderne, la famille, celle-ci depourvue de fonctions productives mais toujours pourvue de ses fonctions reproductives (cf. lie partie). De ce point de vue, les rapports domestiques constituent la base organique de la féodalité, du capitalisme comme du socialisme bureaucratique (p. 10).

There are thus two problems in the analysis of contemporary capitalist development to which the theory of the domestic community is particularly relevant: (1) the reproduction of backward sectors of subsistence agriculture within a world capitalist economy; (2) the place of the family and particularly of women within the family, in the reproduction of a capitalist economy.

As a pure type of an integral mode of production, the mode of production based on the domestic community no longer exists anywhere in the world (p. 135). Defining the mode of production by the historical level of productive forces to which it corresponds, Meillassoux suggests that the domestic mode of production is a neolithic agricultural system based on seasonal cultivation and individual appropriation of tools. Long-term cooperation, deferred consumption and pooling of reserves are required for the technical reproduction of the system. Thus the basic productive units, based on filiation of kinship, are households larger than the conditions of immediate production would require.

Since the basic means of production, land and tools, are acquired through membership in the household or by individual appropriation, the reproduction of the household depends primarily on the biological reproduction of its labour-force. Given natural demographic imbalances, the process of biological reproduction requires some redistribution of resources over time. In the domestic mode of production this redistribution takes place through the transfer of people rather than product. The reproduction of the mode of production depends on the circulation of people between groups.

Kinship relations, then, are not universal, but rather the juridico-ideological expression of underlying relations of production and reproduction in the domestic community. Similarly, the exchangeability of women is not a universal, but a reflection of the fact that the orderly distribution of women's reproductive powers is a requirement of reproduction in the domestic mode of production. In showing how the importance of biological reproduction of the labour-force emerges from the organization of production in the domestic community, Meillassoux emphasizes the distinctive harmony of production and reproduction in this mode of production.

> La communauté domestique est en effet le seul système économique et social qui régente la reproduction physique des individus, la reproduction des producteurs et la reproduction sociale sous toutes ses formes par un ensemble d'institutions, et qui la domine par la mobilisation ordonnée des moyens de la reproduction humaine, c'est à dire les femmes. Ni la féodalité, ni l'esclavage, ni le capitalisme ne contiennent les mécanismes institutionnels regulateurs ou correcteurs (autres que la loi des grands nombres) de la reproduction physique des êtres humains (pp. 9–10).

In this orderly whole, the relations of reproduction are dominant, though subordinated to relations of production (p. 79).

The harmony of production and reproduction in the domestic community is reflected in two aspects of the system which are particularly important in Meillassoux's analysis of imperialism. The first of these is that the dynamic of the domestic mode of production moves it toward population growth rather than toward accumulation of surplus-product. Thus the reserves which the group holds collectively are never 'surplus' since they are maintained for the growth and reproduction of the group. Surplus-labour in the domestic community does not, therefore, take the form of surplus-product, but rather that of surplus-energy or leisure-time:

> En d'autres termes, le surtravail est la quantité d'énergie disponible au-delà des quantités appliquées à la production des subsistances nécessaires à la reproduction simple de la communauté (p. 91).

Given the seasonality of agriculture in the domestic mode of production, much of this leisure time is concentrated in a single period of the year.

The second characteristic of the domestic mode of production reflecting the harmony of production and reproduction within it is its classless structure. Male elders have privilege and power, but not the privileges and powers of class. Power accrues to male elders by virtue of their monopoly over the means of reproduction – food and women – not through control of the means of production. Land cannot be monopolized because rights to land are always implicit in access to seed and subsistence through the household. Bridewealth goods, though often monopolized by the elders, are not productive; they merely symbolize the rights in women which elders already have. As for why it is male elders who monopolize the means of reproduction, their control reflects the functions of the principles of seniority and subordination of women in the domestic community.

Seniority emerges as the basis of authority because the resources of the household must be equilibrated over time if the forms of society based on the domestic community are to be reproduced. Authority is ascribed to males because women's submission is a functional prerequisite of the reproduction of the domestic community. If society is to be reproduced, women's reproductive powers – and thus labour-power – must be distributed in an orderly manner between households over time. The power of male elders in the domestic community is therefore based on the functional compatibility of production and reproduction, not on the fundamental contradictions of class. Women and junior male siblings may indeed by exploited, Meillassoux observes, but exploitation on the basis of sex and age does not class-society make.

In the absence of class, all of the contradictions of the domestic community are latent. Since the domestic mode of production is based on production for consumption, there is an implicit contradiction in the production of bridewealth goods for exchange. Only if a group were to consciously exploit advantages gained through demographic accidents, Meillassoux argues, would this latent contradiction become manifest. There is also an implicit contradiction between the tendency toward demographic growth in the domestic community and the elders' dependence on enforcing exogamy to maintain their control over the distribution of women. Normally this contradiction is resolved through the segmentation of the group: only if a particular group monopolizing women or bridewealth goods decides to institutionalize power to their advantage will there be any radical transformation of the mode of production:

> Pour que l'apparition circonstancielle de la valeur soit à l'origine de transformations sociales et d'une inégalité structurelle qui permettrait l'accaparement de cette valeur, il faut encore que cette contradiction soit

poussée à terme, c'est- à-dire comprise dans ses implications et exploitée intentionellement au profit d'une fraction de l'ensemble social. Il faut donc que ses effets soient instiutionnalisés et greffés sur les mecanismes plus profonds de la production et de la circulation. Il faut qu'intervienne une volonté de domination pour que se fasse l'histoire (p. 113).

Unless Meillassoux really intends to promote an extremely volunta-ristic theory of social change,[3] it would appear that the domestic mode of production is somewhat like Lévi-Strauss's 'cold' societies – it can only be altered from without.

Meillassoux's attempt to break down the anthropological category of the 'primitive' society dominated by kinship and his challenge to univer-salistic theories of kinship provide much that is provocative and useful for Marxist anthropologists. By contrast, his redefinition of key Marxist categories such as surplus-labour, exploitation, class and labour-power is an extremely confusing contribution to Marxist theories of non-capitalist modes of production. Rather than reviewing these conceptual issues, however, it seems to me more important to evaluate the usefulness of the theory of the domestic community in analyzing the problems to which Meillassoux applies it: imperialism and the place of the family in an expanding capitalist system.

(b) Imperialism and the Domestic Mode of Production

The second half of *Femmes, Greniers et Capitaux*, is entitled 'The exploi-tation of the domestic community: imperialism as a mode of reproduction of cheap labour'. In reviewing contemporary Marxist and dependency theories of imperialism, Meillassoux finds two important flaws: (a) the theories do not show links between capitalist and non-capitalist modes of production which operate at the level of production itself; (b) the the-ories under-emphasize the continued existence of non-capitalist forms of production in an imperialist system. Meillassoux's alternative is to sug-gest that in certain conditions it is to the advantage of capital to maintain or preserve a domestic sector of subsistence production and thus to make primitive accumulation a continuing process (p. 148).

The advantages that capital reaps through the preservation of the domestic mode of production are the reproduction of cheap labour-power and the division of the working class:

C'est par les rapports organiques qu'il établit entre économies capitalistes et domestiques que l'impérialisme met en jeu les moyens de reproduc-tion d'une force de travail bon marché au profit du capital; procès de reproduction qui est, dans sa phase actuelle, la cause essentielle du sous-developpement en même temps que de la prosperité du secteur capitaliste.

> Socialement et politiquement, il est aussi à l'origine des divisions de la
> classe ouvrière internationale (pp. 145–6).

Workers are divided because the privileged native workers of the
advanced capitalist countries get higher direct wages and state benefits
and maintain more job stability than do migrant workers. These divisions are reinforced by the retention of ethnic and national loyalties.

The reproduction of cheap labour-power further buttresses the capitalist system by countering the tendency of the rate of profit to fall through
the 'free' transfer of an extra surplus from the domestic community:

> On peut donc établir, de façon générale, que, lorsqu'un travailleur est
> engagé à la fois dans l'agriculture d'auto-subsistance et dans un emploi
> rémunéré du secteur capitaliste, il produit à la fois une rente en travail
> et une plus-value. La première procède du tranfert gratuit d'une force de
> travail produite dans l'économie domestique vers le secteur de production
> capitaliste, l'autre de l'exploitation de la force de travail du producteur
> achetée par le capitaliste (p. 173).

Capital is therefore able to realize a profit which is an amalgam of
surplus-value produced in the capitalist sphere and of surplus-labour in the
form of a rent extracted from the domestic community. This rent consists of
the necessary costs of reproduction of the wage-worker that are not borne
by capital but by the domestic community. Capital can realize this rent by
drawing the domestic community into commercial agriculture or by organizing labour-migration of a cyclical form. It is the latter phenomenon which is
the focus of analytical attention in Meillassoux's discussion of imperialism.

What then are the historical conditions under which it will be
advantageous for capital to maintain the domestic community? Here
Meillassoux appears to be almost entirely preoccupied with the difficulties confronted by capital in certain colonized territories:

> Après diverses formules d'exploitation, travail forcé, sociétés concessi-
> onnaires, cultures obligatoires, toutes de rendement aussi médiocre que
> leur application était brutale, une politique coloniale s'élabora assez gé-
> néralement en Afrique, tirant parti et organisant les capacités productives
> de l'économie domestique. A la différence des autres modes de produc-
> tion fondés sur des rapports de classes et d'exploitation, la communauté
> domestique pouvait être en effet mieux exploitée à moyen terme par sa
> préservation que par sa destruction (p. 166).

The preservation of the domestic community under capitalism is, therefore, related to its distinctive features. First, since the domestic community is a classless collective unit of production, it is possible to exploit
the unit as a whole by exploiting the labour-power of a single member

of the group. Secondly, since the form which surplus labour takes in the domestic community is primarily that of available energy rather than surplus product, some human energy can be taken out of the unit without at first threatening its reproduction.

In terms of Meillassoux's theory, there is an extra something-for-nothing which capital gets in the wage bargain it strikes with the migrant worker. Unless one retreats to exploitation-through-exchange arguments, the problem here is the same one which Marx confronted in his analysis of the illusory freedom with which all workers sell their labour-power to capital: what are the underlying relations of production which make the extraction of surplus possible? In this case, how is it that workers who maintain access to means of production in the domestic community agree not only to their exploitation, but to their super-exploitation?

Within the sphere of capitalist production, Meillassoux finds three institutions which enforce the super-exploitation of migrant workers: intermittent migration, dual labour-markets, and discriminatory (often racist) ideologies. These institutions may explain why migrant-workers consistently get lower wages than others, but they do not explain why it is that they leave the domestic community to enter the wage-labour sphere in the first place. Meillassoux provides a number of answers to this crucial question: people need money to pay taxes or to buy goods once acquired through barter or traditional craft production; people may be forced to abandon their traditional communities because of the impoverishment wrought by continued extraction of surplus-labour, people leave because it may be possible to reproduce themselves in the capitalist sphere with less labour-time than they would be required to put in at home. Each of these possible answers is inadequate, however, since each is theoretically incomplete. All presuppose basic changes in the domestic community which are not specified by the theory of imperialism: tools are no longer individually appropriated, relations of exploitation have been established, and the law of value has come to regulate the movement of labour.

All of these basic changes were imposed, Meillassoux observes, through the involvement of the colonial state in taxation, monetization and forced labour. His theory of imperialism does not permit him, however, to analyze how the extraction of surplus by the state led to the changes in the structure of the domestic community which now lead it to ship out extra surplus in the form of migrant labour-power. The theory merely draws a picture of a process of change through which the domestic community gradually loses its autonomy:

> A l'origine, le contact est sans équivoque entre deux modes de production, l'un dominant l'autre et l'engageant dans un processus de transformation. Tant que persistent les rapports de production et de reproduction

domestiques, les communautés rurales en transformation demeurent qualitativement différentes du mode de production capitaliste. Par contre, les conditions générales de la reproduction de l'ensemble social en viennent à ne plus dépendre des déterminismes inhérents au mode de production domestique, mais de décisions prises dans le secteur capitaliste. Par ce processus, en essence contradictoire, le mode de production domestique est à la fois préservé et détruit; préservé comme mode d'organisation sociale producteur de valeur au benefice de l'imperialisme, detruit parce que prive a terme, par l'exploitation qu'il subit, des moyens de sa reproduction. Dans ces circonstances, le mode de production domestique est et n'est pas (p. 148).

Here Meillassoux captures the dialectical and contradictory nature of rural life in Africa, but theories should help us to analyze reality, not replicate it. To say that the domestic mode of production 'is and is not' is not a particularly useful theoretical formulation.

Moreover, in many ways the basic categories of the theory of the domestic community seem to me inappropriate for dealing with the problem of transition in the context of imperialism. Phenomena which Meillassoux observes to be empirically and historically relevant to the changes in rural production cannot be easily integrated analytically. The concept of an implicit surplus (excess energy), for instance, draws attention away from the disruption of dry-season craft production during the period of forced labour since it emphasizes seasonal underemployment. Similarly, depreciating the analytical importance of the means of production in the domestic community makes it difficult to understand the effects of expropriation of land and of state credit-schemes in the uneven impoverishment of rural communities. Emphasis on the elders' control over the means of reproduction could possibly explain why monetization leads to ruptures between junior men and their elders, but it does not illuminate their reasons for becoming wage-labourers rather than heads of new households. In sum, the theory of the domestic community does not contribute substantially to the theory of transition which Meillassoux's analysis of imperialism presupposes.

Meillassoux copes theoretically with the eventual destruction of the domestic community under capitalism more thoroughly than he does with the mechanisms of extraction of surplus and the nature of qualitative changes in the domestic community during the period of preservation. Under the quantitative pressure of extraction of surplus-labour, the domestic community reaches a point where it can no longer reproduce itself; its destruction is more a matter of literal demographic death than radical transformation. Such an analysis appears to have immediate reference in the history of the Sahel, yet in terms of the actual analytical content of the theory of the domestic community it is not clear why demographic catastrophe leads to destruction of the mode of production rather than to reproduction on a restricted scale.[4] Here again the inability of the theory to describe changes in use and control of the means of production renders it historically inadequate. One cannot understand, for instance, the relationship between labour-migration and famine in the Sahel without attending to the effects of cotton-schemes on the organization of the means of production.[5]

(c) The Domestic Community in Capitalist Society

Although Meillassoux is primarily concerned in the second part of *Femmes, Greniers et Capitaux* with an analysis of imperialism, he also suggests that the model of the domestic community can help us understand the place of the family in contemporary capitalist society.

The modern family is a transformation of the domestic community; robbed of its productive functions, it remains the *place* where labour-power is produced and reproduced (p. 214). This proposition has vast implications for Marxist feminists who wish to ground their understanding of movements for women's liberation in an analysis of production.

Meillassoux's analysis of the contemporary family would permit one to admit that women are not necessarily equal to men in non-class societies without presuming that sexual asymmetry is either a social or a biological universal. Meillassoux's theory suggests that the subordination of women to men in bourgeois society is not natural; rather it is the result of the social vulnerability which women, as reproducers of labour-power, inherit in all modes of production based on the domestic community. The domination of men is first established in the domestic community on the basis of women's desirability as the means of reproduction of labour-power:

> Lorsque, dans les sociétés agricoles, les femmes sont convoitées pour leurs qualités de reproductrices, elles sont davantages menacées. Comme nous l'avons vu, quelles que soient leur constitution physique ou leur capacité à se défendre, elles sont plus vulnérables parce qu'objets permanents d'aggressions d'hommes *ligués* pour les ravir. Leur préservation, leur maintien dans leur groupe d'origine – qui devient une des préoccupations majeures – réclament l'intervention organisée de tous ses membres et plus particulièrement de ceux sur qui ne pèsent pas les mêmes menaces d'enlèvement, c'est-à-dire les hommes. Ceux-ci en viennent ainsi à exercer leur protection sur elles, puis leur *domination* (p. 117)

Whereas for Lévi-Strauss women's scarcity is natural, for Meillassoux it is a social and historical construction which leads to their subordination.

As the domestic community comes to regulate peacefully the movement of women, the objective basis of their subordination alters, but they remain tied by history and function to male dominance:

> Elles héritent cependant d'un passé d'aliénation qui les prédispose à une soumission toujours nécessaire pour se prêter aux alliances et aux exils qu'implique leur condition et surtout pour renoncer à l'établissement d'une filiation avec leur progéniture (pp. 117–18).

As the domestic community has been further transformed in succeeding modes of production, it retains its functional patriarchal structure:

> Après s'être constituée comme le support de la cellule de production agricole, l'institution familiale s'est perpétuée sous des formes sans cesse modifiées, comme le support social du patrimoine des bourgeoisies marchandes, foncières, puis industrielles. Elle s'est pretée à une transmission héréditaire du patrimoine et du capital dont la confusion longtemps persistante a permis sa préservation (pp. 213–14).

Sexual equality in bourgeois society would therefore appear to be rooted in the continuing special importance of women as the means of reproduction of labour-power. Women's work in the family is, under capitalism, reproductive rather than productive for Meillassoux.

Bourgeois society is thus, like all class societies, basically molecular rather than atomistic; it is composed of households which function as units of reproduction of labour-power. The personalistic affectual ties of the family do nevertheless conflict with the contractual relations that characterize capitalism. Meillassoux sees the emergence of new family forms and the increasing role of the state in the reproduction of labour-power as arising in part from the mediation of this conflict in the interests of capital. Only with the abolition of commodity relations, however, can we expect the family to disappear.

Meillassoux's discussion of the place of the family in advanced capitalist society names a number of phenomena which are of current concern – the increasing number of employed married women, the expansion of the public sector, and the feminist movement – but I do not think that the theory of the domestic community contributes in fact any clarification of the relation between these phenomena and the contradictions of capitalist development. Consider, for instance, Meillassoux's explanation of changes in women's participation in the labour-force:

> In advanced capitalist countries, the employment of women permits recuperation of the costs of education which women have received in school or in university and which they use in the home more personally or culturally than productively (p. 215).

The distinction between productive and reproductive (personal and cultural) activities does not clarify at what point the contribution of women's labour in the capitalist sphere and the costs of their education balance the costs of expanded state involvement in child-care, nor is it clear in terms of the theory who calculates and recuperates. Furthermore the theory does not permit one to understand variation in women's participation in the labour-force, either by class or over time.

(d) The Usefulness of the Domestic Community as an Analytical Construct

The theory of the domestic community does not, therefore, appear to be a particularly useful analytical tool in understanding either imperialism or the place of the household in advanced capitalist societies. As with Meillassoux's analysis of capitalism, the central flaw is the underlying conception of the relation of production to reproduction. In this case, however, to reconceptualize this relation is in fact to destroy the unity of domestic community as a theoretical object: the household and family in advanced capitalist society do not bear the same logical relation to capital as do pre-capitalist modes of production; nor, I suspect, is it theoretically satisfactory to lump together all the pre-capitalist systems Meillassoux analyzes as forms of the domestic mode of production. In returning, then, to Marx's conception of reproduction, I shall only be able to provide scattered illustrations of the analytical alternatives to Meillassoux's position.

When Marx argued that all laws of population were historically specific to different modes of production, he meant that there are no relations of biological reproduction, either formal or functional, which exist independently of a given system of production. Precisely because human reproduction is never simply a matter of conception and birth, we can grant no analytical autonomy to any bounded set of relations of biological reproduction; thus Meillassoux is quite consistently Marxist in his rejection of the structuralist notion of universal structures of kinship (and perhaps more consistently Marxist than Marx, whose early notion of a natural division of labour within the family is incisively criticized by Meillassoux). Neither can we assume, however, that biological reproduction is a universal boundary condition for social reproduction: that is, the production of labour-power is not one essential form of production among others. Meillassoux's contention that social reproduction in the domestic community is accomplished through the orderly circulation of women is based on the presumption that the reproduction of the domestic group is a systemic imperative rather than a contingent outcome of production. It is, therefore, inconsistent with Marx's emphasis on the primacy of production of the means of subsistence in the reproduction of human social life.

Meillassoux's divergence from Marx's interpretation of the primacy of production is reflected in his placement of the means of production and the means of reproduction on the same analytical plane. According to Meillassoux, preoccupation with control of the means of production has led Marxists to neglect the importance that control over the means of reproducing people themselves, namely food and women, has in the domestic mode of production. Yet Marx's position would imply that one must always attend analytically first to the reproduction of the means of production, whether or not they are monopolized by a particular class. Contradictions may arise in agricultural systems, for instance, between patterns of land-use and the social relations that govern appropriation of land, whether or not the latter are based on conceptions of landed property. In a brief analysis of the kingship system of the Bamileke of Cameroun (p. 129), Meillassoux suggests that their 'aristocratic' society originated with the appropriation of the marriage rights of junior lineages by the senior lineage of the king. Here analytical emphasis on control of women leads Meillassoux to overlook the amount of control kings had over redistribution of land in some of the Bamileke polities (and lends a rather conspiratorial tone to his interpretation of political evolution).

If analytical attention is paid to the reproduction of the means of production in pre-capitalist modes of production, then one is better prepared to analyze the changes in rural life during the colonial period to which Meillassoux applies his theory of imperialism. Use and control of land, nets, iron-tools, livestock and seed-reserves were generally altered by taxation, forced labour, cash-crop production and expropriation of land during the colonial period. Without analysis of these changes and their effects, it is impossible to grasp the basis of capitalist domination of non-capitalist spheres of production.

If one does attend to the reproduction of the means of production, then the conceptual unity of the domestic community as a theoretical object is rent by the diversity of forms of land-use in the pre-capitalist modes of production which Meillassoux groups in a single evolutionary category. Techniques of cultivation, livestock-raising, foraging and hunting differ among subsistence cultivators as do those social relations which govern settlement patterns. These differences, as well as the logic of capital, are important if we are to understand the unevenness of capitalist development. Similarly, it is analytically inconsistent to treat the household under capitalism as a residual pre-capitalist mode of production when one recognizes the analytical priority of the reproduction of the means of production in all modes of production. Under capitalism workers are separated from their means of production; the dynamics of their household organization are not determined by the same forces as in integral pre-capitalist modes of production.

Marx's conception of the primacy of production also seems to me incompatible with the analytical distinction Meillassoux makes between work that is productive and work that is reproductive; e.g. since women bear and nurse children they are the means of reproduction. If production and reproduction are a unitary process, there can be no analytical opposition between productive and reproductive activities. All forms of human labour that produce use-values are productive whether or not certain of these – such as child-bearing and nursing – are sexually ascribed. Women are thus, like men, agents of production in all modes of production. If women are ideologically or juridically defined as means of production in certain systems, this objectification must be based in underlying contradictions in the organization of production. Grouping together all systems of exchange of women as a single mode of production – the domestic community – is therefore likely to veil considerable divergence in the organization of production in the guise of ideological unity.

Since there is no analytical opposition between productive and reproductive activities, Meillassoux's analysis of the household as the locus of reproductive activities in bourgeois society does not adequately establish the key analytical difference between public and domestic spheres under capitalism. This difference is rooted in the relation to the means of production; household-labour under capitalism, whether performed by men or women, is productive in a general sense, but not from the point of view of capital since it does not produce surplus-value. Looking at the same analytical issue from the side of capitalist production, it should be clear that wage-labour is also reproductive; it produces the commodities which go into the subsistence of workers. Production and reproduction are not mutually exclusive.

The analytical distinction between productive and reproductive activities is not, then, a useful way of sorting out the determinations of relative sexual status in any mode of production. It is of course true that whenever we are concerned with sexual status we are in fact considering the range of activities associated with functional positions in biological reproduction, but we cannot assume that these clusters contain their own determinations. The key to the position of women is therefore not to be found in the organization of the domestic community across all class societies, for there is indeed no single key. Cross-cultural comparison can therefore tell us quite a lot about what the determinants of women's positions in bourgeois society are not, but very little about what the determinants of sexual status are.

Finally, Marx's position on production and reproduction is inconsistent with still a third premise of Meillassoux's theory of the domestic community. Social reproduction consists of the reproduction of a particular system of forces and relations of production; it does not necessarily imply the biological reproduction of individuals, nor of individual units of production, nor even the reproduction of a given form of productive unit. Thus one can no more argue that social reproduction requires the reproduction of individual households in systems where labour is either recruited or reproduced on a genealogical basis than one can argue that the reproduction of capital requires the reproduction of individual firms. Meillassoux's attempt to derive the subordination of women in the domestic community from the process of social reproduction is therefore not logically tenable; sexual asymmetry, where it exists, must be based in the organization of production and is a pre-condition of the exchangeability of women between groups. Furthermore, the biological reproduction of workers and their families under capitalism and the forms which the family takes cannot be assumed to express perfectly the conditions of reproduction of capital; workers' struggles over wages and social services also shape demographic patterns.

Problems in Method: The Terms of the Question

As I read through *Femmes, Greniers et Capitaux*, I found much that was insightful and astute, yet the book remained theoretically unsatisfying. Despite a number of sharp critical points, the theoretical tools advanced for understanding the unevenness of capitalist development and the place of the family seemed to me to describe but not to explain. In trying to locate for myself the sources of difficulty in Meillassoux's arguments, I concluded that one underlying problem was his conception of the analytical meaning of the primacy of production and reproduction. In the previous sections of this review, I have therefore discussed some of the analytical problems which follow from Meillassoux's view of the production of human energy as an essential form of production.

In this section, I shall argue that Meillassoux's position on production and reproduction is consistent with an underlying pattern of evolutionist thought in his work. This evolutionism, a distinctly anthropological heritage, is incompatible with Meillassoux's basically Marxist positions. It thus leads to theoretical ambiguity in the book and to some striking inconsistencies between what Meillassoux observes in the world and that which he can explain. Methodologically, evolutionism intrudes in Meillassoux's work through the functionalist and empiricist terms in which problems are cast.

In exposing these methodological flaws, I shall be guilty of reducing the complexity of some of Meillassoux's arguments, of extending his logic beyond his own statements, and of neglecting some inconsistent formulations. I am risking distortion of the text because I think that there is a fundamental tension between historical materialism and residual evolutionism blocking advancement of work by Marxist anthropologists today.

To ferret out the methodological problems in Meillassoux's theory of imperialism, one must begin by reconstructing his implicit questions. Why, he asks, are pre-capitalist modes of production retained within a world system dominated by capital? There are two important underlying presumptions here. First, Meillassoux equates non-capitalist forms of production with non-capitalist modes of production. Secondly, he presumes that in a world capitalist system that which exists expresses a functional need of capital; Meillassoux falls, that is, into an equilibrium logic of explanation. *Femmes, Greniers, et Capitaux* is in fact riddled by functionalism and empiricism; each methodological problem is consistent with Meillassoux's underlying conception of the relation of production to reproduction and thus recurs constantly in his argumentation. I shall discuss each of these problems in turn and attempt to define the methodological alternatives that Marx's position provides for a method of analyzing imperialism and capitalist development.

When biological reproduction is taken as a boundary condition for social reproduction, the effective unit of analysis is a society, a population or group of individuals reproducing themselves in particular ways in space. Analytical space is thus assumed to correspond to the surface world of appearances; analytical categories are thought merely to summarize and organize empirical reality. Marx saw that social reality can never be adequately analyzed in such empiricist terms because the surface world of appearances provides only a fleeting and necessarily incomplete glimpse of the contradictory social relations that underlie it. Marxist categories are therefore always analytical rather than descriptive, and they are dialectical.

Perhaps the simplest example of an empiricist flaw in Meillassoux's work is contained in his mention of the analytical status of women in the theory of the domestic community:

> Dans toutes les analyses qui precédènt, la femme, malgré sa fonction irremplaçable dans la reproduction, n'intervient jamais comme vecteur de l'organisation sociale. Elle disparaît derrière l'homme; son père, son frère ou son époux (p. 116).

What is important here is that Meillassoux justifies the analytical assimilation of women to men on the basis of empirical appearances.

He further elaborates this position in a note which explains why the structurally significant political actors in the domestic community are men not women:

> Du fait que sa condition d'épouse domine toute sa vie active et que ses rapports de conjugalité l'emportent sur tous les autres, dans les analyses qui vont suivre, la femme sera cachée derrière son epoux, véhicule de toutes les relations sociales. Le produit de son travail sera assimilé à celui de ce dernier. Par 'producteur', il faut donc entendre économiquement le ménage mono- ou polygamique et, politiquement, l'époux (p. 67 n12).

Meillassoux's position here is equivalent to saying that in analyzing capitalist society we may disregard the workers because they are hidden behind capitalists in the firm. From a Marxist perspective, however, the form of the household or of the firm and the position of the capitalist or of the household head can only be understood by grasping the underlying relations of production – by making analytically apparent that which may be empirically hidden.

It is underlying methodological empiricism which leads Meillassoux, I think, to misinterpret the implications of the criticisms that A. G. Frank, among other Marxists, has addressed against bourgeois theories of dualistic development. Meillassoux reproves Frank for simply denying the existence of dualism and for assuming that under the influence of colonization all relations of production become capitalist. Instead, Meillassoux suggests, we should see a single system dominated by capital in which capital preserves and manipulates pre-capitalist modes of production to its benefit. Frank's argument is not, however, an empirical claim that all which exists is capitalist in form; rather, it is a theory which suggests that in a world dominated by capital no existing form can be assumed to be autonomous from it.

Meillassoux cannot grasp this methodological distinction because he uses the concept of mode of production in a strictly empiricist sense. The sphere of capitalist production is identified with the capitalist mode of production; inversely all forms of non-wage labour are presumed to define non-capitalist modes of production. Meillassoux thus constructs a mode of capitalist/non-capitalist articulation which replicates in its analytical categories the dualistic appearance of the world economy. In such an empiricist framework, relations between modes of production are inevitably conceptualized as things: a social formation consists of people and commodities moving between capitalist and non-capitalist modes of production which are also linked by the apparatus of the state.

To formulate an alternative to dualism, one must begin by recognizing that any concrete empirical form is the product of many determinations; hence there is never necessary homology between empirical and analytical space. Marx (cf. *Capital III*) considered it historically appropriate to apply the concept of mode of production to discrete capitalist and non-capitalist productive systems linked through the market only for the period of domination of merchant capital.[6] With the rise of industrial capital, however, he thought it necessary to drop the assumption of spatially separated modes of production; in the context of an expanding capitalist system, all non-capitalist forms lose their analytical autonomy, for all are shaped by the dynamics of the capital/labour relation. Thus instead of seeing African villagers, for instance, as settled down with their hoes in a pre-capitalist mode of production, one would assume that the movement of present village life is shaped within production by capitalist as well as pre-capitalist modes of production.

Such an approach would better permit Meillassoux to build on one of his central intuitions in the book – his contention that relations between capitalist and non-capitalist modes of production must be theorised at the level of production, not just through exchange and political organization. The empiricism of the dualist model permits one to count quantitative transfers of people and things, but it is analytically sterile as far as qualitative transformations within production are concerned. The principal logical inconsistency in Meillassoux's theory of imperialism – that it presupposes qualitative changes in production which are not accounted for in the theory – cannot be dualistically resolved. Only, for example, if we look at the ways in which the control of land by the state has altered the organization of agricultural production in rural villages as well as on plantations can we understand the increasing impoverishment of many Third World peasants which Meillassoux takes to be one of the main forces underlying labour-migration. Impoverishment is not, in this case, a result of the blockage of productive forces in a traditional system, but rather the outcome of a basic change in the relation of people to their means of production in a system in which diverse forms of labour and their inter-relations find their central dynamic in the contradiction between capital and labour. A theory of imperialism grounded in production will therefore be a good deal more complex than Meillassoux's theory of labour-transfer.

I have tried to show that in using the concept of mode of production to describe empirical populations rather than systems of forces and relations of production, Meillassoux retreats into a dualistic theory of capitalist development incapable of showing how the expansion of the capital/labour relation has in fact shaped non-capitalist forms of production. Bourgeois theories of dualism emphasize that the traditional sector eats off industry and impedes development whereas Meillassoux suggests that the real relation is inverse. Nevertheless each version of dualism has the same analytical consequences: the spatial patterning of uneven capitalist development is assumed to be a function of the existence of backward sectors of subsistence production.

Meillassoux's treatment of a mode of production as a unit of population in its unhappy analytical consequences are related, I suggested, to his view that biological reproduction of producers is a universal requisite of social reproduction. I shall further argue that Meillassoux's general conception of the relation of production to reproduction leads him not only to empiricism but to teleological forms of reasoning which are essentially functionalist in form.

If one takes a bounded population as the basic unit of social reproduction, it is consistent to argue that out of the constant flux of material life social forms which survive are those which permit the biological reproduction of the group by assuring the reproduction of labour-power. It follows that explaining social forms is taken to be equivalent to specifying the consequences which permit them to endure by contributing to the reproduction (survival) of the *body politick*. Forms of teleological reasoning that equate consequence with cause are therefore methodologically consistent with modes of explanation which take the reproduction of a given population to be a boundary condition for social reproduction. Although Meillassoux is sharply critical (p. 29) of those who fail to distinguish social groups from genetic groups, his assumption that the production of human energy is one of the determining conditions of social reproduction is quite compatible with adaptavist evolutionist reasoning. It is not, therefore, surprising that two variant forms of teleological reasoning, evolutionism and functionalism, intrude into Meillassoux's argumentation in *Femmes, Greniers et Capitaux*. Those social forms which endure, according to evolutionist thought, are those which permit society to reach a higher level of adaptive efficiency, e.g. the state evolved so that contradictory interests could be regulated. For Marxists the error of such logic is that it places the dynamics of social change outside of existing historical systems. The movement of history is rooted in the contradictions of what is, not in the advantages of what might be. Attempts to provide an historical basis for evolutionist logic have generally emphasized that adaptation is a function of success in the competitive struggle for survival. Such arguments are still ahistorical from a Marxist perspective since they presume that competition between social groups is a natural condition in all modes of production.

Meillassoux is quite aware of Marx's emphasis on the historical specificity of modes of production, yet he lapses at several points into evolutionist explanation in his discussions of surplus. He defines surplus-labour in the domestic community, for instance, as energy that could be put into labour if the system of production were something other than what it is. Similarly, the surplus which capital extracts from the domestic community under imperialism (and the source, therefore, of capital's super-profits) consists for Meillassoux of the costs of reproduction of labour-power which capital would have to bear if it had to bear them at all. In each case the theory locates surplus outside of history and the material world in which the struggle over surplus actually takes place. Meillassoux's theory of imperialism therefore provides no consistent analysis of how relations of exploitation are reproduced: the mechanisms through which this hidden surplus is extracted remain obscure.

In functionalist thought, those social forms which endure are institutions which maintain functional equilibrium in the system as a whole: e.g. witchcraft accusations occur because they resolve the tension resulting from conflict between kinship and residential ties. Those functionalists, such as Durkheim, who maintain a distinction between function and cause, are obliged to posit the existence of some kind of collective conscience defining for individual historical actors the endogenous rationality of the system. All Marxists, including Meillassoux, quickly reject the most naive forms of functionalism, for if one analyzes social systems in terms of functional equilibrium and consensual consciousness, it is impossible to see the ways in which basic contradictions constantly alter emergent social forms.

Nevertheless, many Marxists, again including Meillassoux, do accept functionalist logic when the existence of a social form is explained in terms of the contribution it makes to the reproduction of a given system of production. In non-class societies, it is simply presumed that a practice is reproduced because it is logically compatible with the requirements of the mode of production: e.g. Meillassoux (p. 56) suggests that matriliny gives way to patriliny in the domestic community because the latter is a more efficient form for the redistribution of women. In class societies, however, it is assumed that a particular social form exists because it is logically compatible with the domination of the ruling class; causes, if they are considered at all, are assumed to lie in the directing power of the ruling-class state and ruling-class ideology. Thus Meillassoux assumes that all that exists within a world capitalist system – backward subsistence sectors, government nurseries, social security programmes – exists because it fulfils some function for capital as a class.

The basic difficulty with this assumption is that it fails to recognize that all emergent social forms are the product of material contradictions which are quite different from the consequences that they have either for a particular class or for the system as a whole.[7] This point is an important one for any social theory which pretends, as Marxism does, to be a basis for political action. To act politically we must apprehend what the material pre-conditions of a particular course of action are as well as what its consequences are likely to be; adequate analysis structures political space, differentiates it, clarifies the terms of political action.

To support my argument on the incompatibility of functionalism with a dialectical and materialist theory of political action, I shall conclude this section by considering two problems addressed in a functionalist manner in Meillassoux's theory of imperialism: first, the ultimate contradictions of capitalism; second, the differential structure of wages in the world economy.

Meillassoux concludes his book with an apocalyptical and double-sided view of the death of capitalism; one side, he suggests, has already been prefigured in the concentration work-camps of Nazi Germany. Since the reproduction of capital is dependent in Meillassoux's theory on the transfer of surplus labour-power from pre-capitalist modes of production, the eventual destruction of these modes of production will bring the accumulation of capital to a halt. Capitalism will thus destroy through expansion the conditions of its own reproduction.

The outcome is not necessarily communism, however; it could equally well be elimination of recalcitrant and disposable workers through war and famine and the imposition of totalitarian rule throughout the world:

> Par cette politique d'usure et de destruction des forces productives humaines, le capitalisme se condamne lui-même, bien sur! mais, menée à son terme, l'exploitation totalitaire de l'homme par l'homme condamne avec lui l'humanité tout entière. La crise fatale et finale du capitalisme que certains attendent comme une délivrance nous entraînera vers cette barbarie que Marx avait prédite comme alternative au socialisme si le prolétariat mondial ne s'organise pas pour s'y opposer. Barbarie préfigurée par l'univers nazi et réactivée par la bourgeoisie internationale, à américainetionale, sa tête, partout où s'implantent, sous sa férule, les dictatures gardiennes de l'ordre impérialiste (p. 213).

In the terms of Meillassoux's vision of the contradictions of capitalist development, chances of achieving socialist revolution at this point would indeed appear slim. If, as Meillassoux suggests, the primary cause of the division of the international proletariat is the exploitation of pre-capitalist modes of production, the proletariat, failing a sudden infusion of consciousness, will certainly find itself fragmented at the moment of cataclysm.

The critical weakness of this theory is the absence of any analytical content in Meillassoux's use of the concept of class struggle under capitalism. In the functionalist mode so characteristic of modern systems theory, Meillassoux treats all contradictions as inter-systemic: the concept of internal contradiction is analytically avoided. Yet under capitalism the domination of capital does not set boundaries against which labour simply reacts. Rather the changing terms of the struggle between capital and labour and between capitals constantly alter the forms of capitalist hegemony. When Marx and Engels called history the history of class struggle, they were referring to peasant rebellions that failed as well as those that won, to strikes where workers lost their jobs to scabs as well as those that led to the eight-hour day. As long as the basic capital/labour relation remains, workers' victories are ephemeral, but this does not mean that their struggles are without import: 'The real fruit of their battle lies, not in the immediate result, but in the ever-expanding union of the workers' (Marx and Engels 1848:44).

If we simply analyze emergent social forms – public education, social security plans, the feminist movement – in terms of the ways in which they function to reinforce the hegemony of capital, we shall therefore understand neither the material basis of these changes, nor the forms that many-sided class struggle should take, nor the contradictory consequences of particular struggles. In Marxist terms the emergence of a self-conscious and unified proletariat is the outcome of a history of struggle: in functionalist terms one must either assume its existence from the outset or have it drop from the sky.

Functionalism cannot, then, clarify the material conditions of class struggle under capitalism. Thus, not surprisingly, functionalist explanation of one aspect of this struggle, the division between workers represented by vastly different wage-rates in the world economy, is similarly inadequate. Meillassoux argues that where workers remain tied to non-capitalist units of production, capital can pay them lower wages than it pays to other workers and thus extract a surplus from non-capitalist producers which makes the rate of profit higher than it would otherwise be. The advantage that capital obtains through this pattern of exploitation explains why non-capitalist forms of production continue to exist. First, it is clear that the state often acts consciously to promote instability in the labour-force and to assure subsistence production for the cheap provisioning of workers (cf. Wolpe 1972, Rudin 1968, Southall 1971). Secondly, Meillassoux avoids the 'bribe' formulations which interpret all successful struggles by segments of the working-class to improve their wages or working conditions as sharing in the exploitation of other workers. Nevertheless, I shall argue that because the argument is functionalist and non-dialectical in form, it provides only illusory explanation of the relationship between cheap-labour and underdevelopment.[8]

Consider the first premise of Meillassoux's argument: because workers can depend on the subsistence production of their families, capital can pay them a wage lower than that of other workers. The presumption here is that the level of the wage is determined uniquely by the technical requirements of capital; the place of working-class struggle over wages and hours and working-conditions is ignored. In a colonial context, it may be practically true that the position of workers vis-à-vis capital is so weakened by the intervention of the state that wages do reflect the minimum conditions for the reproduction of the labour-force required by capital: similarly, in advanced industrial countries the bargaining position of migrant workers – unorganized, often uneducated, excluded from unions, constantly threatened with withdrawal of work permits – may be much weaker than that of other workers. The conditions which underlie the relative powerlessness of certain workers are in any circumstances political as well as technical and cannot be understood simply in terms of the functional requirements of capital. People don't accept low wages just because they can go home to eat.

The second premise of Meillassoux's wage-theory is that when workers migrate, capital is able to extract an extra surplus from their home communities which permits the rate of profit to be higher than it would otherwise be. I have already noted the analytical difficulty of locating both this surplus and the mechanisms of its extraction. These difficulties stem, I think, from Meillassoux's underlying presumption that there is a functional normal surplus established by the technical requirements of capital. Yet the thrust of *Capital* is to show that precisely the contrary is true: the rate and conditions of exploitation are a constant focus of struggle and vary for different groups of workers and for different capitals. The exploitation of migrant-workers (for whom, incidentally, the conditions of exploitation are often not so different from that of the reserve army crowded into urban slums from birth to death) permits the rate of profit to be *what it is*. The indeterminacy of the rate of exploitation under capitalism must be grasped; otherwise it is impossible to see why there is a material basis for overcoming real competition between workers in the forging of a unified proletariat.

The final premise of Meillassoux's wage theory is that the advantages that capital gains from the maintenance of reserves of cheap labour explain the continuing existence of non-capitalist forms of production. The assumption beneath this proposition suggests that where the wage/labour relation does not exist, it must be in the interest of capital for it not to be there. In the earlier discussion of dualism, I argued that in a world system dominated by capital no non-capitalist form of production could be assumed to be autonomous from the capital/labour relation. It seems to me equally important, however, not to assume that all which exists represents the optimal functional interests of capital as a class. The task of explanation is to specify the determinations of what is; only if we assume that a social system is ordered by a single non-contradictory principle (e.g. the requirements of capital) can this task be reduced to explaining why things are not what they are not. In the case of capitalism this would be a singularly inappropriate assumption, for it is a system racked by conflict between capital and labour and by competition between capitals and national units of capital. Moreover, as a necessarily self-expanding system, the determinations of the reproduction of capitalism are not entirely endogenous to it. And here, after all, is the point where we began: any general theory of imperialism can only be a theory of capitalism, but any historical understanding of imperialism requires conceptualization of the dynamics of non-capitalist modes of production as well.

Conclusion

In this review I have tried to provide a detailed summary and criticism of the principal arguments Meillassoux makes in *Femmes Greniers et Capitaux* concerning the relationship of capitalist and non-capitalist forms of production within a single world system dominated by capital. My purpose has been to use the critique (without, I hope, undue injustice to Meillassoux) to discuss a number of methodological and theoretical issues that confront Marxists working on imperialism and capitalist development; I have also addressed some of the problems in analyzing the status of women's work and the family under capitalism which are raised by Meillassoux.

To sort out what is at stake in these issues, I have focussed on a single theoretical point – the relation of production to reproduction in Marxist thought – where it seems to me that ideology intrudes in Meillassoux's work, in the form of evolutionism. In breaking down the unitary process of production and reproduction into two coordinate aspects – production of the means of subsistence and production of labour-power – Meillassoux regresses, as Engels did, toward functionalism and empiricism. The alternatives I have posed emphasize the primacy of the production of the means of subsistence in the reproduction of human social life and demand the use of dialectical methods of analysis. The concept of class struggle therefore retains a central analytical role in explaining the uneven development of capitalism.

For me, the strength of Meillassoux's work has always been his ability to seize the whole – to bring the work and struggles of African peasants into analysis of the dynamics of capitalist development in an active way. In *Femmes, Greniers et Capitaux*, however, his political vision surpasses his theoretical control. Ironically, that which is lost is that which Meillassoux has worked hardest to provide – the meaning of the struggles of the oppressed.

Notes

1. For a useful discussion of some of the theoretical issues in capitalist/non-capitalist articulation, see Bradby 1975. Her own alternatives are flawed by a rather static conceptualization of capitalism.

2. Meillassoux invokes Wolpe's (1972) work on the labour-reserve policy in South Africa as an example of shared theoretical perspective. In general, however, Wolpe's analysis is more firmly grounded historically; it applies to particular capitals rather than capital as a whole.

3. Hindess and Hirst (1975:78) show a similar intrusion of voluntarism in Meillassoux's earlier discussion of the non-exploitative nature of the elders' redistribution of surplus in the Gouro case. They relate this slip, correctly I think, to an inadequate conceptualization of the mode of production. They also call into question the reduction of social reproduction to the reproduction of the individual labourer (ibid:63). Nevertheless, for reasons which cannot be discussed here, their conceptualization of primitive communism does not seem to me to constitute an adequate theoretical replacement for the domestic mode of production advanced by Meillassoux in the work under review.

4. Rey (1976) experiences similar theoretical difficulties in his discussion of why Gangam labour-migration no longer depends on the direct constraint of forced labour. He explains this change in terms of the intensification of the quantitative rate of migration, but the theory does not show why quantitative change should have led to one kind of qualitative change rather than another.

5. For an empirically revealing discussion of this relationship, see Comite d'information Sahel (1975).

6. This argument is based on my reading of the chapter on 'Historical Facts about Merchant's Capital', in *Capital III* (1967:323–37).

7. Duncan Foley's work on Marxist theories of the fiscal process has been particularly useful in thinking about the re-emergence of functionalism in Marxist work.

8. This discussion should also be related to the problem of the determinations of the value of labour-power, an issue which is only implicitly addressed in the criticism of Meillassoux's theory of capitalism. In particular, I should argue that Meillassoux confuses quantitative measure and qualitative determination. Cita Sen's critique of Wolpe's notion of archaic surplus-value, presented in the uneven development seminar at Stanford, clarified similar problems in Wolpe's reasoning.

References

Bradby, B. 1975. 'The destruction of natural economy', *Economy and Society* 4: 127–61.

Comite d'information Sahel. 1975. *Qui se noourit de la famine en Afrique?*, Paris: Maspero.

Engels, F. 1972. *The Origin of the Family, Private Property and the State*, New York: International Publishers.

Foley, D. n. d. 'Marxist Theories of the Fiscal Process' (preliminary draft).

Hindess, B. and Hirst, P. Q. 1975. *Pre-Capitalist Modes of Production*, London and Boston: Routledge & Kegan Paul.

Marx, K. 1967. *Capital* V. III, New York: International Publishers.

———. 1973. *Grundrisse*, Harmondsworth, England: Penguin.

———. and Engels, F. 1848. Manifesto of the Communist Party, German Workers' Educational Society: London.

———. and Engels, F. 1975. *The Manifesto of the Communist Party*, Peking: Foreign Language Press.

Rey, P-Ph. 1976. 'Les formes de decomposition des societies precapitalistes dans le Nord-Togo et le mecanisme des migrations vers les zones de capitalisme agraire' in Rey (ed.) *Capitalisme negrier*, pp. 195–209, Paris: Maspero.

Rudin, H. R. 1968. *Germans in the Cameroons 1884–1914: A Case Study in Modern Imperialism*. Hamden, Conn: Archon Books.

Southall, A. 1971. 'The Impact of Imperialism upon Urban Development in Africa', in V. Turner (ed.) *Colonialism in Africa 1870–1960, Vol. 3 Profiles of Change: African Society and Colonial Rule*, pp. 216–55, Cambridge: University Press.

Wolpe, H. 1972. 'Capitalism and cheap labour power in South Africa: From segregation to apartheid', *Economy and Society* 1:425–56.

PART III
Dependency Theory, World Systems Theory and Pre-history

The basic object of analysis in anthropology (a 'tribe', a 'people', a 'culture', a 'society' etc.) has long required much explaining away. Its usefulness as a heuristic is undeniable from a comparative point of view, but such bounded objects are also obviously embedded in larger polities such that at some levels the boundaries between such groups may seem arbitrary. Additionally, objects change over time; the logic of a particular system is necessarily subsumed under that of a larger, and historical, object.

From within anthropology, Eric Wolf has presented the most coherent model of what a world systems anthropology looks like, a model developed in parallel with Wallerstein's world systems theory (WST), which has provided one of the most fruitful conceptual frameworks in modern social theory. One of the key links between these notions of an expanded anthropological object of analysis is *dependency theory*—a theory of global economy that arose during the Cold War period and continues to underpin critical views of modernizing capitalism that is intimately associated with A. G. Frank. Dependency theory (which is actually a number of strands) presented a clear, if contested and modified, account of the way societies on the periphery—former colonies, for example—were shaped by and maintained subordinate to societies in the core/metropolis such that development and underdevelopment were aspects of the same structures and processes.

In this exchange between Frank and Wallerstein, one of the key matters at issue is precisely what it is about the distinctiveness of capitalism as a super ordinate system that marks the distinctive features of the world system that emerged in the sixteenth century. Dependency theory and world systems theory are counterposed against the prevailing political theory of modernization according to which development refers to a normative, Western form of socioeconomic change which is, formulaically, then prescribed for 'less developed' countries. The uneven development of the target countries attests to the coherence of modernization theory, but in a crucial way, the promotion of globalization as an accurate account of the development process is simply another layer of modernization theory.

Chapter 4

Transitional Ideological Modes: Feudalism, Capitalism, Socialism

Andre Gunder Frank

Introduction to Transitions and Modes in the World System

The present 'transition from socialism to capitalism' and the possible future 'shift of hegemony from the United States to Japan' are occasion to re-examine several scientific tenets of our politics and political tenets of our social science. Among these are: (1) the 'transition from feudalism to capitalism'; (2) the 'transition from capitalism to socialism'; (3) the process of 'transition' itself; (4) the notion of feudal, capitalist and socialist 'modes of production'; and (5) the hegemonic rise and decline of Europe and the West in the modern world capitalist system. The question arises as to whether any or all of the above are based on scientific analytical categories, or whether they are only derived from fond ideological beliefs. Perhaps both contemporary political reality and available historical evidence should now lead us to abandon some or even all of these positions.

My tentative conclusion is that ideological blinkers have for too long prevented us from seeing that the world political economic system greatly predated the rise of capitalism in Europe and its hegemony in the world. The rise of Europe represented a hegemonic *shift* from East to West *within* a pre-existing system. If there was any transition then, it was this hegemonic shift within the system rather than the formation of a new system. Now we are again in one of the alternating periods of hegemony and rivalry in the world system, which portends a renewed westward shift of hegemony across the Pacific. To identify the system with its dominant mode of production is a mistake. There was no transition from feudalism to capitalism as such. Neither was there (to be) an analogous transition from capitalism to socialism. If these analytical categories of 'modes of production' prevent us from seeing the real world political economic system, it would be better to abandon them altogether. These categories of 'transition' and 'modes' are not essential or even useful tools, but rather obstacles to the scientific study of the underlying continuity and essential properties of the world system in the past. They also shackle our political struggle and ability to confront and manage the development of this same system in the present and future.

A number of recent academic publications offer a good opportunity for such a re-examination of the (un?)holy canons of our historical science and contemporary politics. These publications include *The Brenner Debate* (Aston and Philpin, 1985) on the transition from feudalism to capitalism in Europe; *Before European Hegemony* on the westward shift of hegemony in the thirteenth century by Janet Abu-Lughod (1989); *The Rise and Fall of the Great Powers* by Paul Kennedy (1987); *Long Cycles in World Politics* during the last 500 years by George Modelski (1987); *On Global War* during the same period by William Thompson (1988); *Global Formation: Structures of the World-Economy* then and now by Christopher Chase-Dunn (1989a); and other works on hegemonic changes.

Several recent articles by Wallerstein also offer a particularly revealing opportunity to re-examine all of the issues posed in my opening paragraphs. Wallerstein (1989a) looked back on the last, and forward to the next, 15 years of 'World-System Analysis: The Second Phase' at the 1989 annual meeting of the American Sociological Association. Under the title 'The West, Capitalism, and the Modern World-System', Wallerstein (1989b) considers 'Why in Europe rather than China?' in a contribution to a volume edited by Joseph Needham. In two further articles, Wallerstein (1988, 1989c) hones down the definition of his 'modern-world-capitalist-system' and its *differentia specifica* from all other systems. These articles also offer good occasion for us to re-examine these issues of transitions and modes, as well as those of origins of and hegemony in the modern world capitalist system. I do so in this essay from an *historical perspective on a world system history in which Europe was only a Johnny-come-lately and temporary hegemony.*

Wallerstein (1989b) examines the possible distinctions between the 'modern world-system, the capitalist world-system and capitalism', and finds them non-existent. Examination of his argument about this distinctiveness will show that it is both internally self-contradictory and externally contradicted by the historical evidence. My own argument is that Wallerstein's interpretation is too limited, indeed, self-limiting; because he fails to take sufficient account of the world system.

I have already made a similar point about feudalism and capitalism. In a debate with Rodolfo Puiggros in 1965 I stated that 'if we are to understand the Latin American problematique we must begin with the *world system* that creates it and go outside the self-imposed optical and mental illusion of the Ibero-American or national frame' (Frank, 1965, translated in Frank, 1969:231). I now argue that the same imperative also applies to the problematique of transition between feudal and capitalist modes of production in Europe.

In the last generation, all sides of the Dobb-Sweezy (recently reprinted in Hilton, 1976) and Brenner (Aston and Philpin, 1985) debates, like generations of 'national frame' and other Eurocentric scholars before them, have sought the answer through a change in the mode of production *within* Europe. Yet if we are to understand this apparently European problematique we must also 'begin with the world system that creates it' and abandon the 'self-imposed optical and mental illusion of the [European] or national frame'. If we (re)examine Wallerstein's argument and the historical evidence from a *world system* perspective, it appears that the world system was not born in 1500; it did not arise in Europe; and it is not exclusively capitalist.

WORLD SYSTEM COMPARISONS AND SIMILARITIES

Wallerstein identifies the most essential characteristics of the 'modern-world-capitalist-system' variously in one, three, six and twelve points. The single most important and defining *differentia specifica* is:

> It is this ceaseless accumulation of capital that may be said to be its most central activity and to constitute its *differentia specifica*. No previous historical system seems to have had any comparable *mot d'ordre* of social limitlessness. . . . At the level of this central defining activity of ceaseless growth, the ceaseless accumulation of capital . . . no other historical system could have been said to have pursued such a mode of social life for more than at most brief moments. . . . The one thing that seems unquestionable, and unquestioned, is the hyperbolic growth curves—in production, population, and the accumulation of capital—that have been a continuing reality from the sixteenth century. . . . There was the genesis of a radically new system. . . . (Wallerstein, 1989b:9, 10, 26)

However, accumulation has played a central if not *the* central role in the world system far beyond Europe and long before 1500, as Gills and Frank (1990) emphasize under the title 'The Cumulation of Accumulation'. Numerous historical and theoretical objections to this thesis, including Wallerstein's, are examined in detail and rejected as unfounded in Frank (1990). A small sample of the vast evidence in support of earlier world system accumulation is presented below.

Perhaps the differences become clearer if we compare Wallerstein's 'modern-world-capitalist-system' with alternatives on more counts than just one. Elsewhere, Wallerstein distinguishes three different characteristics that supposedly set his system apart:

> . . . this descriptive trinity (core—periphery, A/B [cycle phases], hegemony—rivalry) as a pattern maintained over centuries is unique to

the modern world-system. Its origin was precisely in the late fifteenth century. (Wallerstein, 1988:108)

As it happens, and well before reading Wallerstein's above-cited article, Gills and Frank (1990) emphasized the very *same* trinity of center-periphery, A/B phased cycles, and hegemony/rivalry as the other central, defining characteristics of our world system. Certainly Chase-Dunn (1986), Abu-Lughod (1989) and Wilkinson (1987, 1988) among others have also found these same features earlier and elsewhere. Wallerstein (1989a) himself recognizes this and said so in his above-cited review at the American Sociological Association meetings.

Perhaps we should go into more detail still. Elsewhere, Wallerstein (1989c:8–10) summarizes six 'realities of the evolution of this historical system'. Wallerstein (1989a) then helps us by detailing these realities and extending the list to twelve 'characteristics presumed to be the description of the capitalist world-economy':

(1) the ceaseless accumulation of capital as its driving force;
(2) an axial division of labor in which there is a core—periphery tension, such that there is some form of unequal exchange (not necessarily as defined originally by Arghiri Emmanuel) that is spatial;
(3) the structural existence of a semi-peripheral zone;
(4) the large and continuing role of non-wage labor alongside of wage labor;
(5) the correspondence of the boundaries of the capitalist world-economy to that of an interstate system comprised of sovereign states;
(6) the location of the origins of this capitalist world-economy earlier than in the nineteenth century, probably in the sixteenth century;
(7) the view that this capitalist world-economy began in one part of the globe (largely Europe) and later expanded to the entire globe via a process of successive 'incorporations';
(8) the existence in this world-system of hegemonic states, each of whose periods of full or uncontested hegemony has however been relatively brief;
(9) the non-primordial character of states, ethnic groups, and households, all of which are constantly created and recreated;
(10) the fundamental importance of racism and sexism as organizing principles of the system;
(11) the emergence of anti-systemic movements that simultaneously undermine and reinforce this system;

(12) a pattern of both cyclical rhythms and secular trends that incarnate the inherent contradictions of the system and which accounts for the systemic crisis in which we are presently living. (Wallerstein, 1989b:3–4)

   I contend here that 240 of these 242 words describing the twelve characteristics of the world system after 1500 are equally true of the world economy/system(s) *before 1500*, whether *'capitalist' or not*. The two exceptions are under (6) 'the origins . . . probably in the *sixteenth* century' and under (7) that this world system began in '(largely *Europe*)'. Everything else Wallerstein says about the presumed characteristics of the 'capitalist world-economy' and the 'modern world-system' was *equally true* of the medieval and ancient world system.

   Thus, if we examine these separate lists, we find that *each* of them applies equally to other earlier world systems and/or the *same* world system before 1500. Of course, I do not expect the reader simply to accept this statement. He or she must undertake these comparisons personally. In doing so, however, an excellent guide can be found in Wallerstein himself. For he now has some doubts about his own position and finds 'an uncomfortable blurring of the distinctiveness of the patterns of the European medieval and modern world' (1989b:33). Indeed, Wallerstein is among those who chip away at and in fact question their own 'unquestionable' faith in various ways:

> Many of these [previous] historical systems had what we might call proto-capitalist elements. That is, there often was extensive *commodity* production. There existed producers and traders who sought *profit*. There was *investment* of *capital*. There was *wage-labor*. There was *Weltanschauungen* consonant with *capitalism*. But none had quite crossed the threshold of creating a system whose primary driving force was the incessant accumulation of capital. (1989b:35)

> We must now renew the question, why did not capitalism emerge anywhere earlier. It seems unlikely that the answer is an insufficient *technological base*. . . . It is unlikely that the answer is an absence of an *entrepreneurial spirit*. The history of the world for at least two thousand years prior to 1500+ shows an enormous set of groups, throughout multiple historical systems, who showed an aptitude and inclination for *capitalist enterprise*— as producers, as *merchants*, as *financiers*. 'Proto-capitalism' was so widespread one might consider it to be a constitutive element of all the redistributive/tributary world-empires the world has known. . . . Something was preventing it [capitalism]. For they did have the *money* and energy at their disposition, and we have seen in the modern world how powerful these weapons can be. (1989b:59–60, my emphasis)

Moreover, Wallerstein also negates the uniqueness of his 'modern-world-capitalist-system' in numerous other ways. He states, for example, that: 'All the empirical work of the past 50 years on these other systems has tended to reveal that they had much more extensive commodification than previously suspected. . . . It is of course a matter of degree' (1989b:19, 20).

After Wallerstein's own account of (proto)capitalist 'elements' in existence long before 1500, it would be tedious for me to repeat my own as set out in Frank (1990) and in more detail in Gills and Frank (1990). Suffice it to observe here that: (1) Wallerstein will readily admit that 'hyperbolic growth curves in production, population and accumulation of capital' have been *cyclical* since 1500; and (2) Wallerstein and others must also recognize that frequently, and in many places, rapid and massive growth of production, population and accumulation occurred for much more than 'brief' moments long before 1500. Wallerstein himself helps us to observe that this was true, for instance during the period 1050–1250 in Europe. The same, only much more so, also occurred *at the same time* in Sung China. Some centuries earlier, *capital accumulation* accelerated in Tang China, then in the Islamic caliphate. The same phenomenon can be observed in Gupta India and Sassanian Iran, to cite some other instances.

However, the economy and polity of the ancient and even the archaic world (system) were also characterized by the whole gamut of Wallerstein's 'elements' of (proto)capitalism (capital, money, profit, merchants, wage-labor, entrepreneurship, investment, technology, etc.) *and* the ones he synthesized for the 'modern'-world-capitalist-system (capital accumulation, core–periphery, hegemony, inter-state system, cycles, racism, sexism, social movements and the rest). Simply recall the examples best known to Westerners: Rome, China (great canals and walls), Egypt and Mesopotamia (irrigation systems and monuments). Moreover, long cyclical ups (and subsequent downs) in *accumulation* may be said to have been world systemic if not world system wide. The important fact is that they were *systemically and systematically related to each other*, e.g. in Han China, Gupta India, Parthian and then Sassanian Persia, Imperial and then Byzantine Rome, Axum East Africa and, of course, 'barbarian' Inner Asia, not to mention other parts of the world.

That is, the historical evidence also meets the more difficult test of the specificity of capitalism posed by Maurice Godelier (1990). He makes a fourfold classification of characteristics similar to Wallerstein's own efforts in that direction. Yet even Godelier remarks that the four characteristics of capitalism he identifies did *not begin* with capitalism; the necessary and sufficient conditions of a new (capitalist) economic structure are their 'combination in a new relation' and their 'mutual connection' with each other (Godelier, 1990). The historical evidence, however, shows that even the *combination and mutual relation* of Godelier's four or Wallerstein's three, six or twelve characteristics *did not begin with capitalism in 1500.*

Significantly, however, Wallerstein and the others, with the exception of Wilkinson, are talking only about some similarities with *other* 'world' systems. Following them so far, I am arguing only from the old adage that 'If it looks like a duck, walks like a duck and quacks like a duck . . . it must be a [world system] duck'. But in that case, it or they could just be one or more *other* world system ducks, as Chase-Dunn (1989b) argues. Even Wallerstein might admit this comparison, though the similarities might make him uncomfortable. So, what is this invisible and still unspecified 'something' that distinguishes the modern-world-capitalist-system? Perhaps it is only the *Weltanschauung* of *capitalism itself*, as posed by Smith and Marx then, and Wallerstein and Amin now, which retrospectively sees a qualitative break around 1500 where historically there was none. We observe below that the essential something in this *Weltanschauung* turns out to be the supposed identity of the (capitalist) mode of production *and* system. According to Smith and Marx, who led me astray in writing my own book two decades ago, the discovery of America and of the passage to the East Indies by the Cape of Good Hope were the greatest events in the history of mankind, and opened up new ground for the bourgeoisie. That is from a European point of view, of course. But from a wider world perspective these two events, as well as others within Europe, were only developments in the unfolding of world history itself. Why were these two new passages to the East and West Indies important, even for Europeans, and why did they want to get there more easily in the first place, if it was not because of what was happening there—and what was to be obtained there—before 1500?

WORLD SYSTEM TRANSITIONS AND CONTINUITY

Jacques Gernet (1985:347–8) proposes an alternative *world* perspective:

> . . . what we have acquired the habit of regarding—according to the history of the world that is in fact no more than the history of the West—as the beginning of modern times was only the repercussion of the upsurge of the urban, mercantile civilizations whose realm extended, before the Mongol invasion, from the Mediterranean to the Sea of China. The West gathered up part of this legacy and received from it the leaven which was to make possible its own development. The transmission was favored by the crusades of the twelfth and thirteenth centuries and the expansion of the Mongol empire in the thirteenth and fourteenth centuries. . . . There is nothing surprising about this Western backwardness: the Italian cities . . . were at the terminus of the great commercial routes of Asia. . . .

The upsurge of the West, which was only to emerge from its relative isolation thanks to its maritime expansion, occurred at a time when the two great civilizations of Asia [China and Islam] were threatened.

In other words, the real issue is *not* just whether there were *other* world system ducks earlier and elsewhere that had the same one, three, six or twelve characteristics as Wallerstein's world system duck. Nor is the issue one of transition *between one and the other* such ducks or systems. The real questions are whether there really was a transition to the birth of *this* world system around 1500, or whether the real historical development of *this same* ugly world system duckling reaches further back in time, and whether this system and the motive forces for its 'transitions' were based in Europe or *elsewhere in the wider world.*

I believe that what Jacques Hamel and Mohammed Sfia (1990) call a 'continuist' perspective is appropriate in answer to these questions. Such a perspective is suggested in, Godelier's (1990) and others' examinations of Wallerstein in Hamel and Sfia's (1990), *Sociologie et Sociétés.* From that perspective, the historical record suggests that *this same historical world economic and inter-state system is at least five thousand years old.* There was *more continuity* than discontinuity or even transition of *this* world (capitalist) economy as an historical system across the supposed divide of the world around 1500. More detailed support for this continuity is presented in Frank (1990) and Gills and Frank (1990). Moreover, therefore, if there really was a 'transition to capitalism' in the sixteenth century (which is also subject to debate), it took place *not in Europe nor especially due to changes within Europe* but instead in the long pre-existing world system and, importantly, due to changes in the system *outside* Europe. In other words, 'to understand the problematique . . . [of transition *in* Europe] we must begin with the world system that creates it!'

To anticipate some academic-scientific and practical political conclusions, we may well recognize the last of Wallerstein's above-cited six points about the historical system. The system may well have a life-cycle, as he says, but this cycle need not, and did not, begin with any transition from feudalism around 1500, as Wallerstein claims, and it need not, and may not, end in 2050–2100 with a transition to socialism, as he suggests. If we can identify any transitions, each is likely in reality to be a transition between a transition and a transition.

On these issues of transition and/or continuity in the world system, Wallerstein's own account is again helpful, even though—or perhaps because—its short-sighted Eurocentric perspective and internal contradictions seriously undermine his central argument and position.

Thus, like Gernet, Abu-Lughod and others, Wallerstein takes note of the Mongols and the crusades, but:

> The feudal system in western Europe seems quite clearly to have operated by a pattern of cycles of expansion and contraction of two lengths: circa 50 years [which seem to resemble the so-called Kondratieff cycles found in the capitalist world economy] and circa 200–300 years. . . . The patterns of the expansions and contractions are clearly laid out and widely accepted among those writing about the late Middle Ages and early modern times in Europe. . . . It is the long swing that was crucial. Thus 1050–1250+ was a time of the expansion of Europe (the Crusades, the colonizations). . . . The 'crisis' or great contractions of 1250–1450+ included the Black Plague. . . . (1989b:33, 34)

Thus, even according to Wallerstein, there was systematic *cyclical continuity* across his 1500 divide. Moreover, despite his comparison with China, Wallerstein omits to note that 1050–1250 was significantly, also the time of the great advances in technology, accumulation and expansion in Sung China; and that the crisis of 1250–1450 was *world* (system) wide, including China, as Abu-Lughod (1989) has rightly emphasized. Thus, the clearly laid-out 'pattern . . . of expansions and contractions', including probably that of 'demand and prices' (Wallerstein, 1989b:14) was not just (west) European, but perhaps world system wide. At the very least, their manifestation in Europe was also a function of their changing centre/periphery relations (in trade and hegemony/rivalry) with other parts of the world economy. All these factors not only merit study per se, they require analysis to make any sense out of changes in Europe—or in any other part of Eurasia and Africa, that is, the systemic relations extended far beyond Europe.

Yet even Wallerstein recognizes several additional pieces of the jigsaw puzzle outside Europe. Nonetheless, he is still unable to put it together; because he remains wedded to his old *Weltanschauung*:

> The collapse of the Mongols [was a] crucial non-event. . . . The eleventh century economic upsurge in the West that we have discussed was matched by a new market articulation in China. . . . Both linked up to a Moslem trading ecumene across the Middle East. China's commercialization reinforced this model [why not system?]. . . . the Mongol link completed the picture. What disrupted this vast trading *world-system* was the pandemic Black Death, itself quite probably a consequence of that very trading network. It hurt everywhere, but it completely eliminated the Mongol link. (1989b:57, 58 my emphasis)

For Wallerstein, the collapse of the Mongols was the last of 'four elements in an explanation' of the rise of capitalism in the West out of 'the effect of the cumulated collapses'. The other three were 'the collapse of the seigneurs, the collapse of the states, the collapse of the Church' (1989b:47). There were political economic factors behind all four collapses:

> Most governments became bankrupt . . . incapable of controlling their mercenaries. . . . The Church was a major economic actor itself, and was hurt by the economic downturn in the same way that both seigneurs . . . and states . . . were hurt. (1989b:47–55)

Yet Wallerstein resists and refuses to draw the logical—and historical—conclusions: to put the whole picture in the jigsaw puzzle together, we must liberate ourselves from the imaginary transition within the imaginary system confined to Europe. The solution to the puzzle of the four simultaneous and cumulative collapses and to the 'crisis of feudalism in Europe' itself is to be found outside the limited and optically illusory framework of 'Feudal Europe'. We must look at the real transitions in the real world system and its history as a whole. The resolution of the 'crisis of feudalism' involved changing relations within, and further expansion of, the whole world system.

REAL WORLD SYSTEM ISSUES AND PROPOSALS

To understand this and subsequent transitions therefore, we should:

(1) *Abandon the schema of a 'European' world (system)* and look outside. Wallerstein and so many others look out of the window from their European house; but they still cannot see its (still marginal) place in the world landscape. Why are the Mongols 'the link' in a Chinese—Islamic 'trading world-system' before 1500 if Wallerstein and others still refuse to accept the prior existence of this *system*?

(2) *Look at the whole **world** system*. China, the Mongols, the Islamic world and Europe, not to mention other parts of the Asiatic-Afro-European ecumene, were linked into a trading and inter-state world system in the thirteenth century, à la Abu-Lughod. Should we recognize that this was *the world system* out of whose crisis hegemonic European capitalism emerged? Posing the right question is more than half way to the right answer. Wallerstein provides another part of the right answer himself. Of course, however, since he refuses to pose the question, he also does not see the answer. Was the 'crucial cycle' limited to Europe? Most probably not. Wallerstein himself suggests some of its extra-European elements. Indeed, all four of the political economic elements of his explanation for the rise of capitalism in Europe include extra-European elements: the Mongols most obviously so, but also the financial crises of the governments,

landlords and Church in Europe. All were related to the development of the 1250–1450 crisis outside Europe and in the world system as a whole. Similarly, the 1050–1250 expansion in Europe had also been part of a world (system) wide expansion. *The crucial cycle was in the world system itself.*

(3) *Recognize long cycles of development in this world system.* Wallerstein recognizes that 'it is the long swing that is crucial: 1050–1250 upswing and 1250–1450 downswing . . . and 1450–1600 long sixteenth century' (renewed) upswing, before the renewed 'seventeenth century crisis'. Moreover, Wallerstein recognizes that it was the 'crisis' during the 1250–1450 downturn that led to 'cumulative collapse' and then to regeneration and a new 'genesis'. However, Wallerstein and others neglect to ask—and therefore to find any answer to—the crucial question: crisis, collapse, new genesis in *what system*? Of course, as George Modelski (who is also incapable of seeing *this* system; see Modelski, 1987) correctly pointed out to my seminar in person, 'in order for us to look for a cycle, we must first be clear about the *system* in which this cycle occurs'. So, there are two possibilities: the same European system predates 1500, or Europe was part of an (also the same) world system that predated 1500. Either way Wallerstein's and others' temporal and Eurocentric myopia blinds them to seeing the whole picture of systemic historical reality.

(4) *Consider the probability of a continuous cyclical process* of development in/of the *same single* world system. Of course, if there was a long cycle and it was crucial, the 1050–1250 upswing and the 1250–1400 downswing must have been the cyclical expression and development of an *already existing system*. However, in that case the 1050–1250 upswing may well have been a (re)genesis from a previous crisis/collapse/downswing, which in turn was the culmination of a previous upswing, and so on . . . how far back? Curiously, Wallerstein sees a single cycle, at least in Europe, but a variety of 'unstable' systems around the world, each of which 'seldom lasted more than 400–500 years' (1989b:35). On the other hand, Abu-Lughod (1989) sees a single world system, certainly in the thirteenth century on which she concentrates, but also in earlier periods. However, each of her world systems successively, cyclically rise (out of what?) and decline (into what?). Neither Wallerstein nor Abu-Lughod is (yet?) willing to join their insights and see both a single world system and its continuous cyclical development.

(5) *Realize that hegemony in the world system did not begin in Europe after 1500*, but that it shifted to Europe in the course of hegemonic crises in the East of the same world system. Even Wallerstein

quotes Abu-Lughod (1989) to the effect that 'Before European Hegemony, the Fall of the East preceded the Rise of the West'. Abu-Lughod is at pains to show how and why the various parts of the East declined at this time in world systemic terms. Therefore, the root causes *of the rise of the West to hegemony and the transition to capitalism in Europe cannot be found within Europe alone*, but must be sought in the course of the development of the world system—and also within its other parts—as a whole. 'If we are to understand the problematique . . . we must begin with the world system that creates it!'

(6) *Pursue the origins of the world system*—and of its development in the past half millennium—as far back in time and space as the historical evidence and our ability to analyse it allow. Wallerstein (1989b:37) writes:

> Obviously, any historical occurrence has immediate roots whose derivation can be traced back, *ad infinitum*. However, if we believe that the critical turning-point was 500–2500 years earlier, we are coming up with a cultural-genetic explanation which in effect says that the development of capitalism/'modernity' in the West, and in the West first, had been rendered 'inevitable' by this earlier 'civilizational' system.

The first sentence is true, and so is the premise in the first half of the second. However, the conclusions in the remainder are totally unwarranted and triply false. Tracing the roots of the present world system backwards in no way obliges us to come up with cultural-genetic explanations; still less with civilizational ones; and least of all with the inevitability of the present or future outcome. It is at least equally possible—and, as I argue here, preferable—to come up with a longer and wider historical systemic explanation, within which earlier civilizational factors play only a partial role, and inevitability none at all. Therefore, Wallerstein's otherwise correct rejection of causation by alternative civilizational factors and their various interpretations by others is largely beside the point.

The 'explanation' is not to be sought through the civilizational roots of the rise, nor the decline, of Rome, which Wallerstein (1989b:37–9) discusses after other authors. The same goes for his discussion (pp. 39–47) of the 'hurrah' for later culture in England and Italy schools. Instead, we should seek the explanations in the development of the world system within which Rome—and its rise *and* decline—were only regional parts (along with Parthian Iran, Gupta India, Han China, Central Asia and Africa) and transitional phases. The same goes for Italy and England. This holistic systematic analysis does not, of course, deny the importance of local, national, regional or other developments. It only places them in the systemic contexts, which also influence these developments—and are in turn influenced by them. However, the whole is more than the sum of its parts, and the problematique of no part is properly understandable in isolation from the whole of which it is but a part. Wallerstein, of course, understands this truth well—for the period since 1500. But he (still) subjectively refuses to admit it for the time before, despite the evidence he himself cites, which objectively supports it. I examine much more evidence for tracing this world system back at least 5000 years and challenge as unfounded the even greater reservations of others against so doing, in Frank (1990) and Gills and Frank (1990).

(7) *Discard the ineffective concept of 'proto-capitalism'.* The first supposed resolution of the feudalism–capitalism debate a quarter-century ago was to try to 'compromise' on 'semi-feudalism' going on to become 'semi-' 'proto-' capitalism. I thought this 'compromise' was a non-starter then; and experience has shown that the 'mode of production' debate detracted from better understanding of the world system itself. Wallerstein made his major contribution by taking this avenue himself. It is likely only to befuddle our analysis again to now argue that the essential characteristics of the modern-world-capitalist-system, quoted in 240 of the 242 words of Wallerstein's twelve-point synthesis above, are also 'proto-capitalist' 'elements', which can be found all around the world in different times and 'systems'. It is better to proceed, as Wallerstein does, with the:

> . . . effort . . . to establish a continuous pattern of scientific/technological advance, located in many different world regions (China, India, the Near [to us] East, the Mediterranean zone), into which recent western scientific efforts have fit themselves, primarily since the sixteenth century. By underlining the continuities, this argument reduces the distinctiveness of what occurred in western Europe. Furthermore, it has been argued that, in this arena as in many others, Europe had previously been a 'backward' or 'marginal' zone, implying therefore that any explanation of significant change could not be accounted for exclusively or even primarily in terms of some west European affinity . . . or tradition. (1989b:16)

Of course, this means that recourse to the idea of 'proto-capitalism' in 'different' and 'earlier' systems is not at all helpful. Instead, it is much more useful to recognize that technical change and *capital accumulation*, as well as all other characteristics of Wallerstein's 'modern world-system' also characterized earlier times and system(s). In that case indeed, 'we find an uncomfortable blurring of the distinctiveness of the patterns [of capitalism and proto-capitalism] of the medieval and modern world' (Wallerstein, 1989b:33). What is it then that makes Wallerstein and others so 'uncomfortable'? The answer is that this systemic holistic procedure threatens to pull the rug from under the very foundations of their 'scientific' edifice and their fondest ideological beliefs!

(8) *Liberate ourselves from the optical illusion of the false identity of 'system' and 'mode of production'.* Samir Amin contends that the system could not have been the same system before 1500 because it did not have the capitalist mode of production, which developed only later. Before 1500, according to Amin and others, modes of production were tributary. My answer is that the system *was the same no matter what the mode of production was.* The focus on the mode of production blinds us to the more important systemic continuity. Wallerstein makes the same confusion between 'mode' and 'system.' Indeed *the single* differentia specifica *of Wallerstein's modern-world-capitalist-system is its mode of production.* Wallerstein's identification and also confusion of 'system' and 'mode' is evident throughout his works and widely recognized by others. It is also evident in the article I am 'dissecting' here, for example:

> . . . the difference between capitalism as a mode of production and the multiple varieties of a redistributive or tributary mode of production is surely not, as often asserted . . . [in] 'extra-economic coercion'. For there is considerable extra-economic coercion in our capitalist/'modern' historical system, and markets of some kind have almost always existed in other historical systems. The most we can argue is a distinction that is more subtle. (1989b:14)

Wallerstein's system is his mode. So it is for Amin (1989), Brenner (Aston and Philpin, 1985)—and also for their ideological opponents on the right. It may be appropriate to note that our disagreement has generated long friendly discussions with Brenner and still permits collaboration in our second joint book on contemporary problems with Wallerstein and Amin (Amin et al., 1990). Moreover, both the latter have written responses to my historical arguments in Amin (1990) and Wallerstein (1990). Nonetheless, I maintain that if Wallerstein and Amin cede ground as to the distinctiveness of this mode, they also undermine the scaffolding for the construction of this system in 1500—to the point of the total breakdown of any argument about the *differentia specifica* and the beginning of Wallerstein's modern-world-capitalist-system. The one, three, six or twelve essential characteristics of the world system, and its beginning, antedate Wallerstein's period by far.

We should *separate* our notions of system and mode. Then, we could at least recognize the existence and development of the real world system over millennia. I believe it is high time to abandon the sacrosanct belief in the ideological formulations about these supposed different modes of production or the supposed transitions between them in such a world system. A transition is a transition between a transition and a transition, as I learned in Allende's Chile.

Therefore, I agree with Godelier (1990:35) when he says that there are various ways to be materialist. However, I do not agree with his opinion (1990:28) that making a theory of the articulation of modes of production or the transitions among them is now a task of the greatest urgency. On the contrary, I believe that materialism, experience and good sense urge us to abandon this quest and to seek a more fruitful approach based on the material analysis of material world system development.

(9) *Therefore, also dare to abandon (the sacrosanct belief in) capitalism* as a distinct mode of production and separate system. What was the ideological reason for my own and Wallerstein's 'scientific' construction of a sixteenth-century transition (from feudalism in Europe) to a modern-world-capitalist-economy and system? It was the belief in a subsequent transition from capitalism to socialism; if not immediately in the world as a whole, then at least through 'socialism in one country' after another. Traditional marxists and many others who debated with us, were even more intent on preserving faith in the prior, but for them more recent, transition from one (feudal) mode of production to another (capitalist) one. Their political/ideological reason was that they were intent on the subsequent transition to still another and supposedly different socialist mode of production. That was (and is?) the position of marxists, traditional and otherwise, like Brenner (Aston and Philpin, 1985) and Anderson (1974). That is still the position of Samir Amin (1990) who, like Wallerstein, now wants to take refuge in 'proto-capitalism'—and by extension 'proto-socialism'. (Before he was ousted after the Tiananmen massacre, Chinese Premier Zhao Ziyang came up with the idea that China is now only in the stage of 'primary' socialism.) If Maurice Godelier and Samir Amin, among others, would dare to undertake a 'transition' from their 'scientific' categories, they could spare themselves and their readers some of the political (dis)illusions regarding recent events in the 'second' and 'third' worlds.

Transitional Scientific and Political Conclusions

Is there a scientific/historical/academic justification to meddle with 'proto-capitalism' in such a supposed long transition from feudalism to capitalism—or from capitalism to protosocialism? *No*, definitely not, as the internal contradictions in Wallerstein's argument amply demonstrate.

So, is there still a political/ideological reason to hold on to the fond belief in a supposed 'transition from feudalism to capitalism' around 1800, or 1500, or whenever—to support the fond belief in a 'transition to socialism' in 1917, or 1949, or whenever? Is there any such reason still to continue looking for this earlier transition and its hegemonic development only in Europe, while real hegemony is now shifting (no doubt through the contemporary and near future non-hegemonic interregnum) back towards Asia? *No*, there is none.

Ironically, Reagan, Bush, Thatcher, Major, Mitterrand and all the capitalists they represent are equally, or even more, infatuated with the ideology of capitalist distinctiveness, except that they glorify it. Their opponents on the left disagree in this valuation and still want to overcome capitalism through the transition to socialism. The right, instead, want to preserve and glorify capitalism and bask in what they see as the self-destruction of marxism, socialism and the Evil Empire of the others. However, their ideological faith in the supposedly universally beneficial glories of the 'magic' of the market, of course, also lacks scientific foundation in reality. The world system-wide reality is the competitive dog-eat-dog war of all against all (à la Hobbes), in which only the few can win and the many must lose. And so it has been for millennia, thanks to the world system's unequal structure and uneven process, which Wallerstein helps us identify.

We would all do well to see the reality of the globe-embracing structure and the long historical development of the whole world system itself. It is better to recognize this system's 'unity in diversity', as Mikhail Gorbachev said at the United Nations. That would really be a 'transition' in thinking. This 'transition' would make us better placed to choose among the diversities which are really available in that world system— *Vives ces différences*! Moreover, this change in thinking could also help us to understand the real transitions that exist and guide us in the continuing struggle for what is good among these differences and against what is socially bad.

Acknowledgements

The following friends have made reflective comments: Christopher Chase-Dunn, Paulo Frank, Barry Gills especially, William McNeill and Immanuel Wallerstein. However, all have reservations, especially on point 9 and my conclusions, to which I have not ceded.

REFERENCES

Abu-Lughod, J. 1989. *Before European Hegemony: The World System* AD *1250–1350*. New York: Oxford University Press.

Amin, S. 1989. *L'Eurocentrisme: Critique d'une ideologie*. Paris: Anthropos.

———. 1990. 'Le, Système mondial contemporain et les systèmes antérieurs'. Unpublished Ms.

———. Arrighi, G., Frank, A. G., and Wallerstein, I. 1990. *Transforming the Revolution: Social Movements and the World-System*. New York: Monthly Review Press.

Anderson, P. 1974. *Lineages of the Absolutist State*. London: New Left Books.

Aston, T. H. and Philpin, C. H. E. (eds.). 1985. *The Brenner Debate*. Cambridge: Cambridge University Press.

Chase-Dunn, C. 1997. 'Rise and Demise: World-Systems and Modes of Production'. Unpublished Ms. Boulder: Westview Press.

———. 1989a. *Global Formation: Structures of the World-Economy*. Cambridge and Oxford: Basil Blackwell.

———. 1989b. 'Core/Periphery Hierarchies in the Development of Intersocietal Networks'. Unpublished Ms.

Frank, A. G. 1965. 'Con Que Modo de Produccion Convierte la Gallina Maiz en Huevos de Oro?', *El Dia*, Mexico (*in El Gallo Ilustrado*, supplement), 31 October and 25 November, pp. 2–7.

———. 1969. *Latin America: Underdevelopment or Revolution?* New York: Monthly Review Press.

———. 1990. 'A Theoretical Introduction to 5000 Years of World System History', *Review* xiii (2), Spring, pp. 155–248.

Gernet, J. 1982. *A History of Chinese Civilization*. Cambridge: Cambridge University Press.

———. 1985. *China and the Christian Impact: A Conflict of Cultures*. Cambridge: Cambridge University Press.

Gills, B. K. and Frank, A. G. 1990. 'The Cumulation of Accumulation Theses and Research Agenda for 5000 Years of World System History', *Dialectical Anthropology* 15 (2), July. Also in C. Chase-Dunn and T. Hall (eds), *Precapitalist Core–Periphery Relations*, pp. 53–81. Boulder: Westview Press, 1991.

Godelier, M. 1990. 'La Théorie de la Transition de Marx', *Sociologie et Sociétés* xxii (1), June.

Hamel, J. and Mohammed Sfia. 1990. 'Présentation', *Sociologie et Sociétés* xxii (1), June, pp. 5–14.

Hilton, R. 1976. *The Transition from Feudalism to Capitalism*. London: Verso.

Kennedy, P. 1987. *The Rise and Fall of the Great Powers*. New York: Vintage Books.

Modelski, G. 1987. *Long Cycles in World Politics*. London: Macmillan.

Thompson, W. R. 1988. *On Global War: Historical-Structural Approaches to World Politics*. Columbia, SC: University of South Carolina Press.

Wallerstein, I. 1973. *The Modern World-System 1*. New York: Academic Books.

———. 1988. 'The "Discoveries" and Human Progress', *Estudos e Ensaios,* pp. 103–14.

———. 1989a. 'World System Analysis: The Second Phase'. Paper presented at the annual meeting of the PEWS Section of the American Sociological Association in San Francisco, 13 August 1989, published in *Review* xiii (2), Spring 1990.

———. 1989b. 'The West, Capitalism, and the Modern World-System'. Prepared as a chapter in J. Needham (ed.), *Science and Civilization in China, Vol. VII: The Social*

Background, part 2, sect. 48: Social and Economic Considerations. Published as
'L'Occident, le capitalisme, et le système-mondo moderne', *Sociologie et Societés*
(Montréal), xxii (1), June 1990, pp. 15–52.
Wallerstein, I. 1989c. 'Culture as the Ideological Battleground of the Modern World-
System', *Hitotsubashi Journal of Social Studies* 21 (1), August, pp. 5–22.
———. 1990. 'Système mondiale contre système–monde: Le déparage conceptuel de
Frank', *Sociologie et Sociétés* xxii (2), October, pp. 207–222.
Wilkinson, D. 1987. 'Central Civilization', *Comparative Civilizations Review* 17
(Fall): 31–59.
———. 1988. 'World-Economic Theories and Problems: Quigley vs Wallerstein vs
Central Civilization'. Paper presented at the Annual Meeting of the International
Society for the Comparative Study of Civilizations, 26–29 May.

Chapter 5

WORLD SYSTEM VERSUS WORLD-SYSTEMS: A CRITIQUE

IMMANUEL WALLERSTEIN

I wrote my article 'The West, Capitalism and the Modern World-System' (Wallerstein, 1990)[1] before I read Andre Gunder Frank's writings, in which he insists that there was no historic transition from anything to capitalism (anywhere, and specifically not in sixteenth-century Europe) because whatever happened in Europe in the sixteenth century was simply a (cyclical?) shift *within* the framework of an already-existing 'world system', which has existed (for Frank) for several thousand years. Frank is referring primarily to a geographic zone, called by some the ecumene, which goes from eastern Asia to western Europe and southward to include at least south Asia, southwest Asia and northern Africa.

This is an interesting and important thesis, but its argument is directed at me only to the degree that it is directed at anyone and everyone who does not wish to 'abandon (the sacrosanct belief in) capitalism as a distinct mode of production and separate system'—apparently so large a group that it includes (*dixit* his Acknowledgments) even the 'friends' whom he asked to make 'reflective comments' on his paper.

My article (Wallerstein, 1990) was written not at all contra Andre Gunder Frank, but rather contra all those—from Maurice Dobb to E.L. Jones to W.W. Rostow—who believe two things simultaneously: (a) something distinctive occurred in (western) Europe which was radically new somewhere in early modern times; (b) this 'something' was a highly positive or 'progressive' happening in world history. My position is that (a) was true but that (b) was distinctly not true.

I shall not repeat the detailed arguments of my previous article. But permit me to spell out the logic of my presentation there. Basically, the paper had two parts. First, I sought to establish that most of the traditional ways of distinguishing capitalism from other previous historical systems used weak distinctions in that they did not hold up under the light of empirical investigations. These traditional versions of a *differentia specifica* included extensive commodity production, profit-seeking enterprises, wage-labor and a high level of technology.

I called all these elements 'proto-capitalism' since, without them as a
part of the whole, one couldn't have capitalism. But I argued their presence was not enough to call an historical system a capitalist system.

They were not enough because, I argued, each time the agents who
used these elements seemed as if they might be able to go further and
create a true capitalist system, they were repressed or destroyed in one
way or another. And what then distinguishes a self-sustaining long-lived
capitalist system, I asked? To which my answer was that the *differentia
specifica* was, and was *only*, that the system was based on a structural
priority given and sustained for the *ceaseless* accumulation of capital.
Not, I insist, merely for the accumulation of capital, but for the *ceaseless*
accumulation of capital.

It is my view that such a system was created, initially in Europe in
the sixteenth century, and then expanded to cover the entire world. It is
my view also that no historical system that ever existed before can be
plausibly seen as operating on the principle of structural priority to the
ceaseless accumulation of capital.

I made this argument not (I remind the reader) in order to counter
Frank but in order to counter all those who regarded such a transformation as a progressive 'miracle'. That is what brought me to the second
half of my article—the attempt to account for the peculiar *weakness(es)*
of western Europe that it permitted such a disaster to occur. I found the
weakness in the implausible contemporaneity of four collapses—those of
the seigneurs, the states, the Church and the Mongols.

Let me speak to the Mongols issue once again, since Frank reopens it.
The importance of the Mongols is negative. My argument was that the
three other 'collapses' were not enough since one might have expected
that they would have led, by occurring jointly, to the conquest of western
Europe by an external power, which would have ended the possibility
of the descent into capitalism. However, since the Mongols 'collapsed,'
this led (through several intervening steps) to the momentary collapse of
the world trading system of which Frank speaks, the weakening of its
component sectors, and hence the impossibility for anyone to conquer
western Europe at that particular moment in time. For one moment in
historical space—time, the protective anti-capitalist gates were opened
up and capitalism 'snuck in', to the loss of all of us.

Having restated my position on the 'contra-miraculous' nature of
the origins of capitalism as an historical system, let me briefly address
Frank's own views. His arguments are actually stronger than appear in
this comment, probably because he lacked the space here to elaborate
them. In another article (Frank, 1990), he makes a fuller case for the
growth over thousands of years of an interrelated trade network that
he calls the 'world system'.

I believe in fact his account is a fairly acceptable initial and partial outline of what had been happening in the world between 8000 BC (or so) up to AD 1500. I agree that there were many major nodes of political-economic activity, which I prefer to call 'world-empires,' and that these world-empires entered into long-distance trade (often? regularly?—this is still to be demonstrated) with each other. I agree too that these world-empires included in the trading network of the ecumene various zones that were not organized as 'world-empires'. I even agree that, as a consequence, there may have been some common economic rhythms between them.

However, I do not believe that this trading network at any point in time was based on an axial division of labor involving integrated production processes. And therefore, for me, by axiom they did not form a single historical system, since I use that term to mean precisely something based on an axial division of labor involving integrated production processes. Of course, we may all define terms as we wish. This is the definition I have found useful, since it is the only one that accounts for the lives of limited duration of all these various systems, and for the ways in which they have functioned historically during their lives.

I do not believe that trade alone makes a system. I have tried on at least five occasions (Wallerstein, 1973, 1982, 1985, 1989; Hopkins and Wallerstein, 1987) to spell out the distinction between trade in 'luxury' goods and trade in 'bulk' goods or 'necessities', and to indicate the consequences of the distinction. Even if it is difficult on occasion to draw the line empirically between the two kinds of trade, I continue to believe the distinction to be the key analytically. It permits us to distinguish trade *within* an historical system (primarily in 'necessities') and trade *between* separate systems (primarily in 'luxuries'). Because of the technology of transport before modern times and hence because of its high cost, 'long-distance' trade had necessarily to be in low-bulk, high-profit goods, and these had to be 'luxuries'.

Note a detail in word usage that distinguishes Frank from me. He speaks of a 'world system'; I speak of 'world-systems.' I use a hyphen; he does not. I use the plural; he does not. He uses the singular because, for him, there is and has been only one world system through all of historical time and space. For me there have been very many world-systems. For example, I do not consider that what many historians call China or the Chinese empire has been one system. There have been a number of successive systems in the geographic zone called China. The Han rose and fell. The Tang or the Ming is not the same historical system, even if the geographic location, the outward form (a 'world-empire') and some cultural features were the same. The 'modern world-system' (or the 'capitalist world-economy') is merely one system among many. Its peculiar feature is that it has shown itself strong enough to destroy all others contemporaneous to it.

This brings us to the hyphen. My 'world-system' is not a system 'in the world' or 'of the world'. It is a system 'that is a world'. Hence the hyphen, since 'world' is not an attribute of the system. Rather the two words together constitute a single concept. Frank's system is a world system in an attributive sense, in that it has been tending over time to cover the whole world. He cannot conceive of multiple 'world-systems' coexisting on the planet. Yet until the nineteenth century, or so I contend, this has always been the case.

Far from being Eurocentric, my analysis 'exoticizes' Europe. Europe is historically aberrant. In some ways this was an historical accident, not entirely Europe's fault. But, in any case, it is nothing about which Europe should boast. Perhaps Europe and the world will one day be cured of this terrible malady with which Europe (and through Europe the world) has been afflicted.

This brings us to the future. For that we have to return to a schematic view of the past. Thus far, I believe, we have had three historical eras on the planet Earth. There was the period before 8–10,000 BC, about which we still know very little. The world was probably composed of a large number of scattered mini-systems.

Then, there was the period 8–10,000 BC to circa AD 1500. There were in this period multiple instances of coexisting historical systems (of the three main varieties: world-empires, world-economies, mini-systems). None of them was 'capitalist' in that none of them was based on the structural pressure for the ceaseless accumulation of capital. Gloria Deo! As I said, I do not disagree that, among many of the major 'world-empires', there was a growing network of long-distance trade. And perhaps this 'crowding together' accounts in part for the outbreak of the malady that is capitalism, I say perhaps, because I do not like the teleological implications of this. I prefer my explanation of a fortuitous simultaneity of events. The two modes of explanation are not necessarily incompatible.

The third period began circa AD 1500. The aberrant system, our capitalist world-economy, proved aggressive, expansive and efficacious. Within a few centuries it encompassed the globe. This is where we are today. I do not think it can last too much longer (see Wallerstein, 1982). When its contradictions make it no longer able to function, there will be a bifurcation, whose outcome it is not possible to predict. This outcome, however, will be radically affected by small input, hence by our input. The world is neither continuing to inch forward to a perfect ecumene, as some might suggest, nor remaining in a relatively stable state of social imperfection. Just because our inadequate analyses based on nineteenth-century social science are now proving to have badly misled us does not mean we have to fall into a variant of eighteenth-century triumph of universal reason. Just because it is useful to probe more intelligently into the patterns of the pre-1500 era does not mean we may ignore the unpleasant and dramatic caesura that the creation of a capitalist world-economy imposed on the world. Only if we keep the caesura in mind will we remember that this historical system, like all historical systems, not only had a beginning (or genesis), but will have an end. And only then can we concentrate our attention on which kind of successor system we wish to construct.

NOTE

1. This article has appeared in French (Wallerstein, 1990). It will appear in English as a chapter in Joseph Needham, *Science and Civilization in China*, Vol. VII: *The Social Background*, part 2, section 48, 'Social and Economic Considerations' (Cambridge: Cambridge University Press, forthcoming).

REFERENCES

Frank, A.G. 1990. 'A Theoretical Introduction to 5000 Years of World System History', *Review*, XIII(2), Spring, pp. 155–248.

Hopkins, T.K. and Wallerstein, I. 1987. 'Capitalism and the Incorporation of New Zones into the World-Economy', *Review*, 10(5/6 suppl.), pp. 763–779.

Wallerstein, I. 1973, 1976. *The Modern World-System, Vols 1 and 2*. New York: Academic Press.

Wallerstein, I. 1973. 'Africa in a Capitalist World', *A Quarterly Journal of Africanist Opinion*, III(3), pp. 1–11.

———. 1982. 'Crisis as Transition', in S. Amin et al. (eds) *Dynamics of Global Crisis*, pp. 11–54. New York: Monthly Review Press, London: Macmillan.

———. 1985. 'The Three Stages of African Involvement in the World-Economy', in P.C.W. Gutkind and I. Wallerstein (eds) *Political Economy of Contemporary Africa*, pp. 35–63. Beverly Hills, CA: SAGE.

———. 1989. *The Modern World-System, Vol. 3: The Second Great Expansion of the Capitalist World-Economy, 1730–1840s*, Ch. 3. San Diego, CA: Academic Press.

———. 1990. 'L'Occident, le capitalisme, et le systéme-monde moderne', *Sociologie et Sociétés (Montréal)*, XXII (1), pp. 207–222. June.

PART IV
The Development of Peasantries under Capitalism

From the vantage points of two quite different former colonial regimes – Indonesia and Venezuela – Kahn and Roseberry address questions concerned with the characterization of capitalism in relation to peasant production, questions raised in the context of agrarian capitalism in early-modern Europe (and central to debates about the emergence of the Soviet Union) as well as within modern polities. In both cases, concern is not just with what is distinctive about the configurations of local societies (very different in terms of customary land rights, products, nature of labour regimes), but with the functional interdependence of local systems operating, in part, within non-capitalist relations of production, and through links afforded by merchant capital. Peasantries within the critical anthropology tradition were approached with a rigorous attention not only to politics, considerations of which had previously dominated anthropological discussion of rural societies, but also economic structures which maintained coexisting self-provisioning and surplus-producing activities. Key to both analyses is the complex depiction – largely ignored by modernizationist prescriptions – of coexisting forms of economic rationality and provisioning. As contributions to critical anthropology both pieces show the centrality of arguments about the determinative effect of the economy.

Joel Kahn was a major figure in the emergence of a Marxist anthropology based in detailed analysis of peasant economy and its articulation with capitalism. The late Bill Roseberry, who died tragically young, was a major contributor to the revival of the rigorous economic analysis of peasant societies.

Chapter 6

INDONESIA AFTER THE DEMISE OF INVOLUTION:
CRITIQUE OF A DEBATE

JOEL S. KAHN

The debate over Indonesia's 'agrarian question', at least among Western scholars in the last few years, has taken the form of a proliferation of writings critical of the views articulated by Clifford Geertz in his influential book *Agricultural Involution*. Beginning some ten years ago, writings critical of the involution thesis began to appear, and their volume has assumed the proportions of a flood. Refutations of Geertz's analysis have become so numerous, and an alternative model of Indonesian agrarian transformation presented with such confidence, that a reader of this literature might feel justified in assuming that not only has Geertz's analysis been totally invalidated but that we can now fully understand the major tendencies for change in Indonesian agrarian structure in terms of classical models of the social differentiation of the peasantry and the consequent development of capitalist forms of agricultural production from within the peasant economy.

The time would appear to be ripe for a debate which is no longer centred around Geertz's contribution – a contribution based on a brilliant insight, but one which must now be recognised as having been essentially misguided. It is, of course, awkward that Geertz himself remains unpersuaded by the arguments of his critics (Geertz, 1984b), whom he argues, have largely missed the point of the original book. But, it is assumed, this should not dissuade us from moving the debate onto another level altogether.

While in sympathy with the aims of a number of Geertz's critics, I want to argue in this paper that Geertz is correct at least when he maintains that:

> The problem is . . . that the placing of cultural matters outside social process as but deceptive metaphors for changing economic relationships leaves one helpless to understand even those relationships, never mind the metaphors, to which no real attention is given anyway. (ibid:520)

A 'critique of the critique' does not necessarily allow us to resurrect involution in a form that Geertz would accept, or indeed even recognise. And yet the emerging anti-Geertz consensus on Indonesian agrarian structure is, I shall argue, seriously undermined when the weaknesses of its 'objectivist' assumptions are exposed. The arguments advanced here, therefore, are offered in the spirit raising the level of the debate rather than of defending the concept of involution.

THE PROGRESSIVE DEMISE OF INVOLUTION

Following the critique of Geertz chronologically, one receives the impression of a progressive demise of the involution paradigm, beginning with the most recent period of Indonesian history and then, working backwards, to the early periods of colonial rule. A fairly exhaustive summary of the critique has appeared recently (White, 1983). My purpose here is simply to set out some of its main points by following the gradual projection of the anti-involution thesis backwards in time.

Involution and Green Revolution under Suharto's New Order

In the early 1970s a number of researchers, many of them associated with Indonesia's Agro Economic Survey, have argued that among the consequences of Java's so-called Green Revolution has been the end of village egalitarianism, the demise of village institutions that functioned to share out poverty, and the development of capitalistic forms of economic calculation in agricultural enterprises. While the writings are focussed on developments on Java, they are supported in their conclusions by an increasingly large number of critiques of the consequences for third world agrarian structures of the introduction of high yielding varieties, fertilizers, pesticides, etc. (cf. Gerdin, 1982; Konnick, et al., 1982; Griffin, 1974). Based on research findings, most of these authors point to increase in landlessness, increased inequalities in the distribution of land, a decline in the importance of full-time farming as an occupation, a fall in agricultural employment caused by the adoption of labour-saving techniques by larger landowners, unequal access to credit – in short an unequal distribution of the benefits of the new technologies. In the case of Java these and other findings have led researchers to their strong conclusion, i.e. that involution is dead. White sums it up this way:

> All of the changes . . . serve the function for the wealthy farmer of cutting the costs of rice production at the expense of landless labourers and smallholders . . . It is remarkable that these changes should have occurred within the space of a few years, and at a time when high yielding varieties

have opened the possibility of greatly increased returns to rice farming even without these cost-cutting methods. (1981:142)

William Collier describes the implication of these changes for the involution paradigm more explicitly:

> The . . . changes in cultivation practices and the contractions in labor-use associated with these transformations provides ample evidence that something other than the process of involution is acting as a prime mover in the allocation and distribution of production functions at the farm level. The concept of evolution implies the presence of certain social mechanisms and cultural norms, whereby the needs of the many maintain ascendancy over the wants of the few. Nevertheless the above evidence suggests that these mechanisms are under some stress and that the presumed equilibrium between labor supply and labor absorption is giving way to a condition where the values of efficiency and profit assume a much more pronounced role in the economy of agricultural production. (1981:161)

This brief summary in no way gives sufficient credit to the important works of researchers such as White, Collier, Stoler and others. However it serves our purpose here which is to demonstrate that the critique of involution for the period of Suharto's New Order regime rests on an argument about the way new political, economic and technological conditions have given rise to new forms of economic behaviour appropriate to a capitalist enterprise, that the economy of rural Indonesia can now be appropriated by conventional economic theory of profit-maximization, and that this finds its reflection in the simultaneous growth of a rural proletariat no longer able to survive by means of 'traditional' mechanisms which served to redistribute land, labour and the product. With some exceptions, however, this group of critics have focussed their attentions on relatively recent processes of agrarian transformation and therefore, either explicitly or implicitly, accepted the validity of Geertz's analysis for earlier historical periods. However, both because Geertz's fieldwork was carried out in the 1950s, and because he appears to have foreseen the limits of an involutional strategy under certain conditions, more telling are the critiques directed at the colonial period. Two such critics are S. Aas and G.R. Knight.

The Agrarian Land Law and the Demise of Involution

Aas (1980) argues that Dutch colonialism drastically altered the traditional structure of peasant villages by undermining the communal controls on land allocation and alienation that he assumes, along with earlier Dutch scholars, to have been a feature of pre-colonial Java. As a result, he maintains, peasant differentiation during the colonial period cannot be attributed to variation in the size of peasant households, but instead reflects underlying processes of class formation. This remained true, Aas argues, in spite of colonial policies aimed at preserving communal tenure systems. Aas maintains that this kind of 'enforced communalism' was quite different from the traditional system in that the former contained within it countervailing tendencies which encouraged the development of more individualized land rights. It is important to note that the data cited to demonstrate an increase in private property (pp. 232ff) comes entirely from the period after 1870, a point to which we shall return.

But how did the strengthening of village rights of disposal serve to increase individualism? According to Aas this happened as a result of two related processes: the destruction of household industry and the creation of the labourer.

The destruction of household industry occurred since the system of colonial extraction drew off labour surpluses form Javanese villages, hence reducing the time peasants had available for work in cottage industries. At the same time cheap imported products came on to local markets, forcing out indigenous products. The creation of the labourer took place on the one hand in response to the demand for labour on the part of colonial enterprises and the colonial State and on the other through other effects of colonialism (the breakdown of household industry itself, payments for cash crops, the demand for cash rents, and the forced training of peasants for work on government projects). This led to an increasing supply of free wage labour, such that by 1890, at least in certain regions of Java, there was a guaranteed labour market.

According to Aas, then, the evidence for increasingly individualized tenurial patterns and the increased number of wage labourers suggests that peasant differentiation in colonial Java was most probably a result of incipient class formation rather than demographic differentiation. Clearly if we accept this argument, then considerable doubt is also cast on the involution model as well.

Ignoring a number of logical problems in Aas's argument, we might here examine an important historical limit on its validity. Aas wishes to demonstrate that it was the fact of *colonialism* (since the implementation of the so-called Cultivation System in 1830) itself which undermined traditional structures of socio-economic organization on Java. However, a close reading of his article cannot support such a conclusion. Instead the data cited by Aas points to the emergence of class differentiation only in the second phase of Dutch colonialism, i.e. from the end of the Cultivation System and the passage of the Agrarian Land Law in 1870. I shall examine the implications of this point below. Suffice it to say here that with the exception of some remarks on textile imports in the early period, Aas's evidence (as opposed to his hypothesized mechanisms) comes from this later period of colonialism.

All other things being equal, then, Aas's article can be read to argue that the kinds of communal mechanisms which made involution possible existed in the pre-colonial period, persisted through the period of the Cultivation System, and really began to break down after 1870, i.e. as part of what I would argue (with Geertz) to be a capitalist transformation of the colonial economy.[2] Specifically Aas's argument does not seriously undermine the argument that agricultural involution developed as a response to the Cultivation System itself, an argument which is central to Geertz's own project. I shall now turn to precisely this kind of critique, by looking at a direct attack on the pertinence of the involution model for an analysis of socio-economic change in Javanese villages under the Cultivation System.

Javanese Peasants and the Cultivation System: Capitalism or Involution?

It is quite clear that for Geertz the process of agricultural involution is at least in part a process of the 19th century, i.e. that the intensification of paddy cultivation and associated mechanisms for sharing out the product was an adaptation of traditional village structures to the pressures on the expanding village population by the system of forced cultivation of sugar. Indeed Geertz's explanation for the persistence of involutional tendencies into the years after 1870, that is after the end of colonial extraction based on labour rents, involves the assumption that the 'mutualistic' relationship between sugar and rice cultivation continued even when the sugar industry came under the control of private foreign capital and employed ostensible free labourers.

The view that the pressures of the Cultivation System resulted in increased egalitarianism because it facilitated frequent redistribution of rice land is, of course, not new to Geertz. The observation had already been made by a number of Dutch scholars, most notably Kat Angelino the colonial historian (1931).

Therefore while the above-mentioned critiques of Geertz are of considerable interest, they do not really get to the root of the involution hypothesis. The argument that involution is at least in part a reaction to the policies of the Cultivation System has itself come in for a good deal of criticism recently. In particular a new generation of economic historians, working through the 19th century residency archives in Jakarta and Bogor, in carrying out studies of localised responses to colonialism, are becoming increasingly sceptical about the validity of Geertz's analyses of 19th century Javanese villages. While there are several such projects underway, I shall focus here on one which tackles the question of the pertinence of involution directly, i.e. the work of G.R. Knight on the coastal residency of Pekalongan (west of Semarang).

In a recent article Knight (1982) introduces his argument as a direct attack on Geertz, and it is therefore worth quoting him at some length:

> There is a widely-held view that the development of world-market pro-duction in nineteenth century Java was accompanied by (and based upon) a substantial degree of petrifaction of the existing social and economic structures of the countryside. Since these structures are at the same time conceived as having been essentially non-capitalist in character, the con-clusion has therefore been drawn that Dutch colonialism, and particu-larly the sugar industry which grew up under its aegis in the nineteenth century, both stifled the development of indigenous capitalism in rural Java and set in motion a process of 'involution'. . . . this has led to a dual-ist explanation of the 'underdevelopment' of Java. . . .
>
> Despite the influential nature of the argument, and particularly of the core concept of 'involution' as expounded by Clifford Geertz, it has not gone unchallenged. . . . The present paper seeks to sustain and develop (the) critique by focussing attention on the alleged roots of 'involution' in the nineteenth century and by developing a counter-argument for the emergence of indigenous capitalism in the countryside during the heyday of Dutch colonial rule. (1982:119f)

Knight's demonstration rests on two related arguments. The first is that 'social differentiation and commodity production were sufficiently developed in the countryside of Java prior to the Cultivation System for it to make sense to speak of a potential for capitalist development. . . .' (ibid:120); the second, that 'the changes which were taking place in Javanese society during the heyday of the Cultivation System in the mid-nineteenth century were of a capitalist rather that an "involutional" kind. . . .' (ibid). The latter argument is pursued by means of evidence that the labour rents imposed by the stipulations of the Cultivation System (Cultuurdiensten and Heerendiensten) did not fall equally on the peasantry as a whole (instead large landowners could offer the labour services of their clients in exchange for their own); that the system of land re-allocation imposed by the demands for sugar cultivation served only to distribute land among those who already owned it; that the 19th century witnessed a growing concentration of wealth and power among a small number of Javanese and that, at least after 1870, there was widespread renting of land, land sales, an increasing use of wage labour in sugar factories by the 1860s, and an important local and regional rice market.

I have of necessity reduced the discussion of the anti-involution position quite drastically, thereby no doubt passing over important differences in theoretical approach, and object of analysis as well as the existence of significant regional variation which is reflected in the different studies. However even on the basis of this limited discussion it seems possible to draw out a number of general features of the critique. All the critics of involution take issue with the non-capitalist characterization of Indonesian agrarian structure which is implied in Geertz's writing, at least for the historical period under consideration. At the same time, therefore, these writings have the effect of deconstructing the notion of a specific form of peasant economy for the period after 1965, for the period of colonial capitalism which begins in the last decades of the 19th century, or for the time of the colonial Cultivation System. What, according to the critics, emerged in these different periods was an essentially capitalist agrarian structure characterized by increased commercialization, a social differentiation of the peasantry, the rise of capitalistic economic calculation among the larger agricultural enterprises and the like. Hence in the corpus of anti-involution literature the destruction of the small peasantry, the rise of capitalist logic, the development of class relations and the like go hand in hand. Geertz, or at least the straw man Geertz constructed by his critics, can be said instead to be retaining a concept of a unique, non-capitalist agrarian structure in which subsistence-orientation is predominant, class relations are suppressed through redistributional mechanisms, and economic calculation is not to be understood by means of capitalist rationality. Finally the critics appear to have resolved the debate in their favour by the marshalling of a huge range of empirical evidence which Geertz did not have at his disposal. Had he himself had access to these data, it is presumed, he too would have abandoned his views.

Is the debate so easily-resolved? Can we accept that involution is historically and conceptually dead? Is the nature of Indonesian society now finally laid bare by Western social science, particularly in its evolutionist/positivist guise? Has 'traditional' rural economy, society and culture been swept away by the processes of modernisation or of capitalist transformation from within? The answer to all of these questions, I shall argue, is no.

ANTI-ANTI-INVOLUTION

In many ways, of course, the debate over Indonesia's agrarian question is an old debate. It has its roots in earlier debates over the nature of agrarian transformation in Europe, and specifically in the (at that time) European periphery in a period of liberal attempts at 'development'.

In both Germany and Russia, for example, nineteenth century liberals and then social democrats argued for the inevitable demise of the 'traditional' peasantry in the context of modernisation/capitalist transformation while conservatives and populists maintained, in quite different ways, that peasants as a unique social cultural and/or economic type can and should persist into the modern age. The link with Indonesia and the Indonesian debate is structural historical as well as genealogical. It is therefore important to note that both Geertz and his critics are firmly rooted in a long-standing debate over the nature of modernisation/capitalist transformation in 'peripheral' agriculture. This review is not, however, the proper context for a consideration of the significance of this fact.[1]

I want to argue here, instead, that there are three crucial problems with the anti-involution position, if it may be so characterised: the first that its empirical foundations are weak – the second that it produces an unsatisfactory account of indigenous subjectivity; and the third that it is epistemologically flawed. Together these weaknesses in the anti-involution position make it necessary, in my view, to rethink the terms of the debate to avoid an oversimplified, even dangerous characterisation of the impact of capitalism on rural Indonesia.

The Empirical Difficulty

While somewhat cautious in their positive characterisation of Indonesia after the demise of involution, most of Geertz's critics nonetheless argue implicitly, if not explicitly, for an essentially capitalist agrarian structure, manifest in the emergence of classically capitalist class relations or the presence of a rural bourgeoisie and a landless or land poor agricultural proletariat.[2] What evidence do we have that this is the case?

Even the best agricultural statistics are notoriously difficult to interpret, since they are rarely collected in terms of categories that have any social significance. Almost inevitably agricultural enterprises are classified according to criteria of size, and Indonesia is no exception to this rule. The fact that almost completely contradictory accounts of underlying socioeconomic tendencies can continue to exist even when agricultural statistics are much better than those we have for Indonesia leads one to suspect that a resolution of the involution debate cannot be sought in the 'hard facts' of the statistical evidence. If anything the Indonesian data on land distribution would tend to support Geertz rather than his critics.

Without wishing to suggest that the figures establish or can be used as a basis for establishing any definite characterisation, I have nonetheless presented some figures to compare two regions in Southeast Asia. Table 1 is based on data provided by the French geographer Pierre Gourou for the Mekong delta region in 1930, an area which is generally assumed to be one which can be characterised by the 'growth of capitalist labour relations' (Scott, 1976:67). Table 2 summarises data collected by the Agro Economic Survey for the three regions of Java in 1971.

The superficial comparison that these data allow us to make between two regions in Southeast Asia must seriously undermine the claim that Javanese village agriculture exhibits a highly developed and inegalitarian class structure. The degrees of land concentration and landlessness are

Table 1: Gourou's Data on Landownership in Cochinchina in 1930 (source: Scott, 1976:66)

Size of Holding (hectares)	% of All Households	% of Landowners	% of Cultivated Land
0	67	–	–
0–5	24	72	12.5
5–10	5	15	42.5
10–50	4	11	
50 and more	0.8	2.5	45

Table 2: Distribution of Landownership in Sample Villages on Java, 1971 (source: Agro Economic Survey, 1971)

A. Irrigated Rice Land

Size of Holding (hectares)	% of All Households in		
	Central Java	West Java	East Java
0	27.0	40.5	52.6
0.10–0.24	19.3	19.0	15.9
0.25–0.49	23.7	13.9	15.9
0.50–0.74	16.0	10.9	6.5
0.75–0.99	2.7	3.0	2.9
1.00–1.49	5.8	7.3	4.0
1.50–1.99	1.5	1.3	0.9
2.0 and more	4.0	4.2	1.3

B. Total Farm Land

0	10.4	13.6	22.0
0.10–0.24	28.5	34.6	33.6
0.25–0.49	20.3	19.2	19.3
0.50–0.74	17.7	11.2	10.1
0.75–0.99	6.3	6.3	5.6
1.00–1.49	9.3	9.1	5.2
1.50–1.99	3.0	1.8	2.4
2.0 and more	4.2	4.6	1.9

so much higher in Cochinchina already by the 1930s that they make the Javanese differences pale into insignificance. According to Gourou, 45% of all cultivated land in Cochinchina in 1930 was in the hands of land-owners owning more than 50 hectares, a group which represented less than 1% of the total population and only 2½% of all landowners. By contrast, no household on Java as late as 1971 owned more than 9½ hect-ares of land in all categories. In Cochinchina 67% of all households were completely without landed property, on Java only a maximum of 22% of households were completely landless.

This is, however, about as far as this form of argument can take us, since data which would allow for any real insight into variation in either household economic strength or forms of production in Javanese peas-ant agriculture are simply not available. All the data cited above show that given the existing aggregate statistics, or figures based on any kind of representative sampling, it is not possible to make a case either for the emergence of capitalist farming or the development of a rural proletariat.

It must also be pointed out that neither do the figures demonstrate the development/persistence of a vigorous, independent smallholding peas-antry. Indeed the data summarised in Table 2 suggests that most small-scale agricultural enterprises on Java are not viable, since we can assume that holdings of rice land below the one hectare mark are unlikely to yield even sufficient rice for the annual consumption needs of an average family.

A discussion of statistical evidence leads us to a final weakness in the argument for the demise of the Javanese peasantry and the emergence of modern/capitalist agricultural forms, a weakness manifest in the fail-ure of Geertz's critics to agree on the timing of the posited capitalist transformation of Javanese village agriculture. This quite simply is that no argument about a secular trend in agricultural development can be advanced on the basis of statistics drawn for a single period of time, a point which has been made repeatedly in the context of the European debates, but one which nonetheless seems not to have been fully appreci-ated by Geertz's critics. Even if the data in Table 2 were to testify to much higher degrees of inequality, they would, on their own, prove nothing. Put another way: the empirical arguments rely for their appeal on the picture of Javanese society before the change. It is, therefore, no accident that the critiques of Geertz have appeared in reverse chronological order, pushing the temporal boundaries of the 'traditional' economy further and further back in history. Indeed, the break with Geertz is less radical than his critics would have us believe, since almost all those attempting to demonstrate the demise of involution appear to posit an historical period in which Geertz's model, or something quite close to it, is said to be pertinent. But positing a 'traditional' economy and contrasting it with the 'fact' of commoditisation, inequalities in land distribution and the like is not the same as demonstrating a secular trend towards increased class differentiation.

This discussion of the empirical case for anti-involution has been necessarily brief. However it has been sufficient to point out that the case for a classical capitalist transformation of Java's agrarian structure cannot rest on statistical demonstration alone if at all. Quite the contrary: a comparison with other regions even in Southeast Asia suggests that in spite of everything Javanese peasant agriculture while clearly exhibiting a degree of internal inequality, is remarkable for its relative homogeneity. It might, of course, prove to be the case that if we were to take into account factors other than the distribution of land, or uncover better measurements of historical change, then Geertz's critics would be vindicated. Given the nature of the data available to us for Java now, we simply cannot say.

The Problem of Subjectivity

Classically, what might be termed the deconstructionist position in the debate over capitalism and the agrarian question has been motivated at least in part by a need to come to terms with a political situation in which claims to represent a specifically peasant point of view have had a strong foothold. Kautsky, for example, recommended that social democracy sidestep the peasant question altogether either because of the innate conservatism of particular groups of politically-active German peasants or the fact of the political cooptation of the peasantry by the forces of the right. Lenin, on the other hand, hoped that the increasingly revolutionary challenge of some sections of the Russian peasantry might be harnessed to the proletarian revolution by demonstrating the extent to which demands for the rights of peasants might be deemed to be progressive (i.e. anti-feudal but not solely bourgeois).

In spite, therefore, of the differences in the historical conjunctures of turn of the century Germany and Russia, and the political tactics advocated within these conjunctures, both Kautsky and Lenin had to come to grips with the fact of the denial, by at least some rural producers, that they could be subsumed politically as proletarians (however disguised) or capitalists (however petty).

The Indonesian deconstructionists, however, have ignored the question of the subjectivity of rural producers almost entirely. Collier may have recourse to indigenous categories when arguing that we are justified in labelling a farmer with two hectares as a large landowner, but even he had not attempted to argue that perceptions of inequalities of this order are primary political motivators in modern Indonesia.

While it would clearly take more than a simple assertion to satisfy some advocates of the anti-involution position, it could nonetheless be argued that such manifestations of political consciousness of the Indonesian masses that we, as outside observers, have access to do not point to the conclusion that rural producers either now or in past perceive economic inequalities within village agriculture to be the principal line of cleavage in Indonesian society.[3]

Since such an assertion is likely to be taken for extreme heresy let me clarify it. Firstly, I am not suggesting that what I am terming internal class differentiation has never been part of the political consciousness of Indonesian villagers, only that in many cases it is likely to prove to be secondary to the perception of other forms of class inequality. Secondly, I am far from suggesting that the characterisation of Indonesian peasants as apolitical or politically apathetic is an accurate one (although this too must not be totally denied). Instead I am arguing that there is a strong suggestion that the political mobilisation of Indonesia's rural masses – in the 1920s, in the nationalist struggles, in the post-Independence period and in recent years (with the re-emergence of regional nationalisms and of the so-called Islamic opposition) – has rarely taken place on the basis of a denial of the homogeneity of rural producers, and had usually been based on the perception of inequalities between peasants and classes defined outside the village economy.

Since the anti-involutionists have generally avoided this issue, it is hard to know how they would deal with it, but it is clearly a phenomenon that needs to be dealt with since it poses a major challenge to the characterisation of agrarian structure that emerges from the writings of Geertz's critics. And given the theoretical inadequacies of attempts to dismiss this as a consequence of 'false consciousness' in other contexts, as well as the inadequacy of the empirical evidence that would purport to show such perceptions as false in any case, it is a question which simply must be addressed by Geertz's critics before they can claim to have successfully disposed of the arguments advanced by Geertz himself.[4] Until they do, the apparent significance of apparently peasant, as opposed to a rural proletarian, forms of political consciousness in rural Indonesia will continue to represent a major challenge to the anti-involutionist position.

The Epistemological Challenge of Historicism

The intellectual project that I have termed the deconstruction of the peasantry – of which the case of the anti-involution argument is just one example – has almost always been framed in the context of another, the constitution of the peasantry as a unique form of humankind. Kautsky's theses on the demise of the peasantry in capitalist development were framed in the context of and in opposition to those influenced by the tenants of German historical economies; Lenin's arguments concerning the differentiation of the Russian peasantry were aimed at the assumptions of Russian populism; while the project of constitution in the Indonesian context has a history long before Geertz's own work.[5]

While it takes many forms, the intellectual discourse on constitution has almost always derived from certain basic postulates concerning the historical and cultural limits to 'Western' social theory – in other words a philosophy of social enquiry that in other places and other times has been termed relativist or historicist.[6] The main challenge of historicism, at least in its academic form, therefore concerns the shortcomings of an objectivist approach to the analysis of the other; whether the other be removed from the analyst in space or time and whether the analyst derives his/her positivism from the liberal or the Marxist tradition. This does not mean that objectivists are taken to task solely for their economism (and hence for ignoring other 'levels' of social existence, such as ideology), although economism has become a particular target for recent historicisms. Rather historicism must argue that the economy itself must be seen as a symbolic system, to use currently fashionable terms.

The current vogue for symbolic and subjectivist analysis is, of course, not restricted to the field of peasant studies, and indeed may be best represented outside the field. And yet its significance for the debate over the 'peasant question' is obvious, and it is on this which we shall concentrate here.

While I have no intention of taking up an historicist position here, as will become clear, it must nonetheless be said that Geertz's critics are far from posing any alternative to the challenge of the historicist argument, and their arguments are seriously undermined thereby. White, for example, appears content to dismiss the whole thing by linking Geertz's critique to the 'idealism' of postwar developmentalism, thus simply reproducing the highly misleading 'materialism : idealism' dichotomy that has proven such an obstacle in recent American anthropology (White, 1983).[7] The Alexanders relegate the concept of 'shared poverty' to the sphere of ideology, arguing that while it may have an impact of economic calculation, it is subservient to 'real' material interests of households (1982).

But what historicism argues is precisely that such dichotomies are false ones, themselves a product of Western ideology posing as science and being imposed on other societies and other cultures – for the sake of what? This out of hand rejection of the historicist argument does no credit to the work of Geertz's critics, and undermines what might otherwise be seen to be serious studies of agrarian transformation in Indonesia.

The apparent triumph of the anti-involution argument is then, in the view of this reviewer, problematic. Its empirical foundations are extremely shaky, it seems unable even to address the issue of peasant political consciousness, and it falls into an old positivist trap making it susceptible to accusations of arid formalism. Moreover it has other potential dangers, particularly for those prepared to draw too hasty conclusions from it, suggesting as it does that the major socio-economic cleavages in Indonesia today are between rich and poor peasants. This might, for example, lead to a failure to recognise the importance of crucial political struggles to the extent that they do not conform to the models of agrarian transformation suggested in the work of Geertz's critics; or a tendency to look for the causes of Indonesia's current under-development solely in the development of small-scale commercial agri-culture in rural Java. For all these reasons it would be premature to proclaim that the process of agrarian transformation in Indonesia is now fully explained.

RE-THINKING ANTI-INVOLUTION

In the concluding part of this paper I propose to make a number of sug-gestions as to how the anti-involution position needs to be modified in the light of the criticisms advanced above. I shall do this first by attempt-ing to characterise the processes of peasant differentiation in a way that appears to make more sense in the Indonesian context. I will then turn to an evaluation of the claims of historicism.

Differentiation and Commoditisation

The arguments for the existence of a class differentiated peasantry can-not rest primarily, as we have seen, on the available statistics on land distribution on Java. Instead, as I have suggested, it rests on a particu-lar theoretical assumption – that changes in the economic environment within which peasant enterprises operate generates a process of com-moditisation such that eventually peasants sort themselves out into a class of rural capitalists and a class of rural wage labourers (or in Kautsky's more careful analysis, a differentiation of agricultural enter-prises into capitalist and labour farms).

Apart from the empirical problems with such an argument, this argu-ment is flawed in two crucial ways. Firstly, by accepting, often implicitly, the pertinence of a model of 'traditional economy' at some point in the past, its advocates have been deceived into thinking that the presence of commodity circulation, individualised property rights and wage labour points to a major transformation.[8] Secondly, this mode of argument in turn lends itself to a teleological account of evolution of commodity circulation, deriving from a misleading conflation of several quite different processes of commoditisation (cf. Kahn, 1982). Differentiation becomes, therefore an inevitable evolutionary trend rather than a specific historical process each of whose component processes (commoditisation of product, land, labour, means of production) needs to be accounted for.[9]

A case in point is the Cochinchina example cited above. The highly differentiated agrarian structure, manifest in Gourou's data summarised in Table 1, did not come about solely in response to the incorporation of the Mekong delta region within an international market. First, as Scott (op. cit.) points out, the region was already characterised by quite rigid socioeconomic hierarchies even before the colonial period. Second, this form of differentiation was further accentuated because the French colonial administration created rice-growing estates through a policy of land alienation. Land, alienated from local farmers, was given then to those Vietnamese whom the French wished to reward for services and political loyalty in the period of consolidation of colonial rule.[10]

Class differentiation of rice-growing peasants or agricultural enterprises was, in this case, a direct result of colonial land appropriation, a form of primitive accumulation, and only indirectly a consequence of market incorporation. Of course, leases on large areas of rice land only became attractive to servants of the French because of the emergence of a rice market, and the comparative advantages enjoyed by producers in the Mekong Delta (as well as the new pool of landless farmers dispossessed as a consequence of colonial 'enclosures'), but such market opportunities could not, on their own, dictate the specific nature of the emerging agrarian structure.

Rejecting the teleology of the market principle as both explanation for and characterisation of a capitalist agrarian structure leads us to look for better ways of characterising particular patterns of class and enterprise differentiation as well as the specific histories of these different structures. Since this is difficult to do for an area as large and diverse as Indonesia, I can offer here only some possible approaches to these problems in terms of my own research in Southeast Asia. Addressing the problem of characterising peasant differentiation in a way quite different from that implied in the anti-involution literature, I shall describe some features of peasant enterprises in two culturally-related regions: Negeri Sembilan on the Malaysian mainland, and West Sumatra in Indonesia. It might be argued that such studies can tell us nothing about Java. However they appear in some ways to be ideal test cases since, firstly, if anything the pace of the Green Revolution has been faster in Malaysia than Indonesia (so, its effects are likely to be exaggerated) and secondly, West Sumatra can and has been considered to be more 'capitalist' than Java (even Geertz in a comparison with Java argued that in West Sumatra the process of capitalistic development was well underway). If, therefore, we can suggest that capitalist differentiation is absent in peasant agriculture even in these regions, we have grounds for rethinking the case of Java.

1. Malaysia, Technological Change and Non-capitalist Calculation

The study of Malaysian rice cultivators which I carried out in 1975/76 cannot be expected to yield results of general Malaysia-wide validity, since it was carried out not in the rice bowl regions of the northwest but instead in Negeri Sembilan which, in patterns and techniques of cultivation approximates more to those of the 'inland valleys' (see Jackson, 1972). After the 'Green Revolution' certain characteristics of this pattern can be seen to have survived, most notably the absence of a developed market in locally-produced rice. Moreover in spite of the relatively high rate of uptake of new yield-increasing and labour-saving techniques made possible in the years after the implementation of Malaysia NEP, few farmers in the region persisted with the use of HYVs, instead reverting to the cultivation of a seed introduced during the colonial period in conjunction with fertilisers, pesticides, herbicides and tractors. Table 3, however, shows just how popular these new inputs were.

In spite of these apparently high rates of uptake, there are a number of factors which might lead us to challenge the general consensus of the effects of the Green Revolution described above. Firstly, the 1970s in Negeri Sembilan does not seem to be a period of serious land concentration or increased social differentiation of peasant producers. The pattern of land distribution, tenancy rates and the like are much the same in the post 1970 period as they are before the spread of new technologies.

Secondly, although this is somewhat harder to determine given the nature of the data, there seems to have been no real increase in the productivity of the rice cultivation in the sense that average yields, average household outputs and aggregate rice output for the region as a whole appear unchanged. If anything, there is a decline in aggregate rice output, a decline which has been clearly accelerated in the years since my research.

This leads, however, to a third point, which again appears anomalous, at least when viewed from the position that agriculture has become capitalist in the region. This is that the apparent reason for this stagnation is that while rural households continue to cultivate rice, while the available technologies have the potential for increasing output, and while both before and after the introduction of the technological 'package' the

Table 3: Frequency of Use of Selected New Techniques in Survey Villages

Input	Number of Farms	% of Farms
Fertiliser (some)	91	75
Just urea	23	19
Just phosphate	5	4
Both	61	50
Bone ash	2	2
Herbicide	74	61
Before planting	29	24
After planting	31	26
Both	14	12
Pesticides		
Caterpillar	65	54
Padi fly	46	38
Rat poison	62	51
Tractor	53	44

majority of households produce less than their consumption requirements, rural producers have used the new inputs not so much to increase output as to decrease the volume of 'traditional' inputs, most notably land and labour. This is partly explained by the fact that input commoditisation in rice cultivation leads rice farmers to compare rice farming negatively to other forms of economic activity, but not totally since most households continue to cultivate to their traditional output targets (whereas a 'rational' course might well be to cease cultivation altogether).

This leads to a final point which is suggested by the results of this research. There appear to be some households which, contrary to the trend, are using the possibility of increased output to consolidate their position as truly viable 'family farms'. In other words the use of the new inputs is an adjunct to a strategy aimed at fuller employment of family labour both in rice cultivation and in other village-based economic activities. Such a strategy appears to find its parallels elsewhere in Southeast Asia, and is explicable in terms laid down by Chayanov who explained peasant use of wage labour as a means of increasing rather than decreasing the intensity of family labour at the same time (cf. Dove for a similar argument for Borneo, 1981).

These and other apparent anomalies in the reaction of the Negeri Sembilan rural economy to the introduction of new techniques suggests that it is at least possible to revive an historicist conceptualisation of peasant economy, although perhaps not as conceived by Dutch historicist writers of the colonial period or Clifford Geertz. This appears to be the case for (a region of) modern Malaysia, which suggests that similar phenomena are likely to be observed in Java.

It might, however, be justifiably argued that the picture presented above, because it focusses on only one aspect of the economic life of rural producers, is incomplete and, hence, misleading. I want therefore conclude this section by examining a case of non-agricultural production in Indonesia.

2. Blacksmiths in Minangkabau: Peasants or Petty Capitalists

The extent to which an exclusive focus on rice cultivation can produce highly misleading results is demonstrated in a recent study of the effects of the Green Revolution in West Sumatra. Here the researcher found that the use of HYVs and the accompanying technological package produced good results in the rice farming sector when compared to another region in Sulawesi, and yet he found at the same time that the increases in yields and output made only a small impact on net household incomes (see Deutser, 1981). The reason for this is quite clear, i.e. the relative unimportance of rice income as a proportion of family income even in an area of West Sumatra noted for its irrigated rice cultivation. As we have pointed out several times, this suggests the need for a more careful study of the range of income generating activities in the Indonesian peasant village.

While like the Malays from Negeri Sembilan, large numbers of Minangkabau leave their home villages to earn a cash income elsewhere, and while perhaps an increasing proportion of these migrants are becoming wage labourers, nonetheless large numbers of migrants, and an equally large proportion of village residents earn their cash incomes in very small-scale enterprises established either for production or trade. What is the nature of these enterprises, and can they be characterised as capitalist?

In a study of a localised blacksmithing industry carried out in 1970–1972, some of the features of these small enterprises emerged, and again the picture of petty capitalism suggested in the writings of Geertz's critics is by no means clearcut.

Firstly, the predominant organisational form is the individually-owned and operated unit. Wage labour exists, but it is rare, as the following figures show. (see next page)

This picture is consolidated when it is recognised that a significant proportion of wage labourers are young men whose ultimate objective is to set up either as employer, or more likely as independent producer, hence economic role is at least partly determined by the social-defined life cycle as it is by proletarianisation (see Table 5).

Table 4: Economic Relations in Smithing Breakdown by 'Class' of Total Working Population (Residents and Migrants)

Productive Role	Number of Smiths	Percent of Smiths
Owner/Worker employing 3–4 workers	24	4.7
Owner/Worker employing 1–2 workers	111	21.7
Independent producer	180	35.2
Wage worker	117	22.9
Worker with close kinsman	46	9.0
Other	34	6.6

Table 5: Breakdown by Class of Six Major Occupations (Men: Residents and Migrants)

Class	Married Men		Unmarried Men		Total Number	Total %
	Number	%	Number	%		
Wage worker	129	18.3	69	34.2	198	21.8
Works alone	365	51.8	107	53.0	472	52.0
Employer of labour	199	28.2	14	6.9	213	23.5
Wage worker with kinsman	12	1.7	12	5.9	24	2.6
Missing data	91		17		108	
Total for which data are available	705		202		907	

Secondly, these enterprises in which what I have called wage labour is employed, do not operate according to an overt profit-orientation. Instead head smiths and workers alike view the division of proceeds in cooperative terms, and describe the extra share, from which an 'objective' profit is deducted, as necessary for the reproduction of fixed capital alone (and not as payment for the capital invested by the head smith). In none of the enterprises studied in the early 1970s was the 'owner' a non-worker (with the exception of one which was tied to an unsuccessful government project), nor were merchants involved in financing production (something that did take place earlier, see Kahn, 1980).

Nonetheless the pattern described is not a strictly egalitarian one. Moreover what might be termed 'micro-class' position within the smithing industry correlates with other measures of inequality. Indeed all villagers involved in small-scale enterprises can be classified as: owner workers (and hirers of wage labour), independent owner operators, and wage labourers. These categories correlate with access to irrigated land and its principal product, viz. rice, something that emerges in the data in Table 6.

The significance of these findings for the present argument again concerns the status of land and irrigated rice cultivation in West Sumatra.

Table 6: Cross-tabulation of Class by Harvest (Excluding Farmers). Married Men, Harvest in Wife's Home

COUNT ROW PERCENTAGE
COLUMN PERCENTAGE

Size of Harvest (*Baban*)		(1) 0	(2) 1–5	(3) 6–10	(4) 11–15	(5) 16–20	(6) 21–30	(7) 31–40	(8) 41–50	(9) 51–60	(10) 61+	Row Total
Craftsman or merchant, working alone		148	112	49	20	3	2	0	0	0	0	334
	row %	44.4	33.5	14.7	6.0	0.9	0.6	0	0	0	0	45.8
	col. %	44.7	53.8	40.5	50.0	18.8	15.4	0	0	0	0	
Small-scale employer		76	43	44	13	9	7	0	0	0	0	197
	row %	38.6	24.4	22.3	6.6	4.6	3.6	0	0	0	0	27.0
	col. %	23.0	23.1	36.4	32.5	56.2	53.8	0	0	0	0	
Worker in craft or trade (wage)		60	28	13	3	2	1	0	0	0	1	108
	row %	55.6	25.9	12.0	2.8	1.9	0.9	0	0	0	0.9	14.8
	col. %	18.1	13.5	10.7	7.5	12.5	7.7	0	0	0	100.0	
Worker in craft or trade, with kinsman		7	4	3	1	1	2	0	0	0	0	18
	row %	38.9	22.2	16.7	5.6	5.6	11.1	0	0	0	0	2.5
	col. %	2.1	1.9	2.5	2.5	6.2	15.4	0	0	0	0	
White collar (includes teacher and doctor)		18	8	8	3	1	1	0	0	0	0	39
	row %	46.2	20.5	20.5	7.7	2.6	2.6	0	0	0	0	5.3
	col. %	5.4	3.8	6.6	7.5	6.2	7.7	0	0	0	0	
Manual with large enterprise		22	8	4	0	0	0	0	0	0	0	34
	row %	64.7	23.5	11.8	0	0	0	0	0	0	0	4.7
	col. %	6.6	3.8	3.3	0	0	0	0	0	0	0	
Column total		331	208	121	40	16	13	0	0	0	1	730
		45.3	28.5	16.6	5.5	2.2	1.8	0	0	0	0.1	

In spite of the fact that rice land is occasionally bought and sold, and more frequently transferred by a system of pawning sanctioned by *adat* (customary law), at least at the time of my study it would be impossible to speak of a land market, the emergence of which depends on a relatively greater 'mobility' of land as a factor of production, and a price determined by its social opportunity cost. Inequalities in access to such land, therefore, are strictly speaking a function of class, but instead a function of a form of social stratification more akin to pre-capitalist social hierarchy.

Smithing, therefore, and more importantly, successful smithing (that is larger-scale, since income is closely correlated with micro-class position) can be seen as an attempt by particular individuals/households to maintain the viability of peasant household enterprise in much the same way that the use of cash inputs in Malaysian rice cultivation can be so seen. The use of wage labour in Minangkabau enterprises, or indeed in agriculture, is therefore a peasant rather than a capitalist strategy.

Finally, it is worth re-iterating the point made earlier about the absence of a cultural category 'profit' within the village economy. This cultural outlook is further emphasised in general attitudes about social differentiation. Social-economic-class divisions emerging from within the village economy are consistently denied by the whole range of village residents, although when pressed informants will, as Collier points out, define a landholding of, say, two hectares as large.

And yet the discussion of material from both Malaysia and Sumatra suggests that the Southeast Asian peasantry is quite clearly not dead, but alive and well, both in terms of the nature of small-scale enterprise, in the aims and modes of economic calculation and in existing cultural conceptions of existing inequalities. Rather than manifesting a continued growth of capitalist enterprise in peasant agriculture, the impression given is precisely the opposite. Wage labour and new technologies seem to owe their existence, at least in part, to the desire and/or ability of particular groups of Indonesian and Malaysian villagers to maintain a viable peasant existence in the face of considerable external pressures.

In concluding this section on the empirical situation, I would like to propose a characterisation of the situation quite different from that implied in the anti-Geertz concession. The argument that the involution paradigm fails to take account of the large and growing class of landless and land-poor peasants seems to me to be indisputable. The real question concerns the way internal relations in villages are conceived. Geertz's critics describe the situation in terms of the emergence of a class of rural capitalists, and the demise of a peasantry. I would like to suggest instead that what we are witnessing is the preservation or even re-creation of a class of peasants, based on the maintenance of viable peasant enterprises, often with the assistance of what at first sight appear to be classically capitalist mechanisms, i.e. technological change and the use of wage labour. At the same time we are witnessing a growing class of rural producers and labourers who for reasons as yet not fully understood are unable to reproduce themselves as peasants. This group of petty commodity producers, rural labourers and migrant wage labourers have neither the land nor the monetary resources required to form successful peasant enterprises (defined in terms of their control of non-commodity productive inputs). In other words that a form of social differentiation has taken place is beyond doubt, that this corresponds in some way to capitalist development needs to be seriously questioned.

The Response to Involution

I have argued throughout this paper that anti-involution represents an inadequate response to the challenge posed specifically by Geertz's work and more generally by historicist writings on the 'peasant question'. Among other things, the inadequacy of the response has led Geertz's critics to a misleading characterisation of the pattern of class and enterprise differentiation within peasant villages in an attempt to demonstrate the all-pervasiveness of the logic of capital. I have not, however, intended to resurrect involution in its original form. On the contrary, my aim has been to develop the anti-involution position in such a way as to make it a more adequate response to the challenges of relativism, historicism, interpretative approaches and the like.

The anti-involutionists have set themselves what is, in my view, the impossible task of responding to Geertz by demonstrating the absence of non-capitalist logic in Indonesia over the last two centuries. In doing this they have inevitably failed, as I have attempted to argue in the preceding discussion.

The real issue, therefore, is not or should not be, whether Indonesian agrarian history can be understood in terms of the unfolding of western principles of cultural and economic rationality, but, instead, how we can best interpret the existence of non-Western cultural and economic forms (both at home and abroad). And it is the tendency in interpretive/historicist circles to treat these forms as evidence of the tenacity of traditional Indonesian culture in the face of modernisation/capitalist transformation that would appear to be the main assumption to be challenged. For only by means of this assumption can social enquiry be envisaged as a process of the subsumption of the other by an external observer. Historicist and interpretive approaches, therefore, depend for their ultimate validity on a concept of a gap between us and them, between subject and object of knowledge. This gap can fruitfully be crossed, so the argument goes, only by a sensitive observer prepared to abandon the baggage of his/her own culture, baggage that contains the whole edifice of 'Western' social theory as well as the more obvious manifestations of ethnocentrism. Those who are not prepared to abandon heir baggage before the journey are precisely those who are accused of the sins of positivism, objectivism, economism, presentism or ethnocentrism.

As long as we accept the validity of this assumption we cannot, in my view, simply brush off the challenge of historicist approaches to the study of the economy (exemplified by Agricultural Involution) or to other realms of social and cultural existence.

There is no scope in a review of this kind to explore alternative formulations in any depth. I want instead to focus briefly on two important lines of argument which have the effect of undermining the underlying claims of the involution paradigm. The first concerns the assumption that only an interpretive as opposed to a positivist mode of social enquiry allows us to escape the problem of objectification, in this case the problems posed by treating the peasantry as an object for the verification of 'Western' forms of scientific discourse. The second bears on the question of the extent to which Indonesian culture can accurately be depicted as 'other' in the sense described above.

Interpretation and Objectification

It is clear that one of the main claims made for the interpretative approach, echoing those made by earlier generations of historicists, is that it permits us to escape from the procedures of objectification so central to positivist traditions of social enquiry. How accurate is this claim?

The central issues, from the perspective of this paper, are, firstly, how interpretive ethnography is actually done and, secondly, once done, how its results are evaluated. The answer to the first lies in the meaning of the term 'ethnography'. We should not understand by this term the methods, techniques and received procedures of anthropologists in the field. Ethnography, whatever methods it employs, is a particular kind of intellectual effort, one which Geertz feels is best conveyed by Ryle's term – thick description.

Exactly how one goes about producing thick description Geertz does not, indeed perhaps understandably cannot, say exactly. But it would I think not be unfair to suggest that it refers to a process of dialogue or a reading of another culture with the help of its practitioners[11]:

> The culture of a people is an ensemble of texts, themselves ensembles, which the anthropologist strains to read over the shoulders of those to whom they properly belong. (1973:452)

To the extent that the accounts of the other are genuinely the result of an ethnographic dialogue it can be argued that interpretive anthropologists have avoided the problem of objectification, since the 'object' of knowledge is now an active participant in the construction of knowledge about itself. And yet the question now emerges: what is it that we have to show after the process of thick description has been carried out? The answer is, of course, in most cases a text. But what does this text represent? At one level the text is simply the interpretation itself. But as we can see from the passage quoted below, the text is both more and less than the interpretation of another culture:

> Nothing is more necessary to comprehending what anthropological interpretation is, and the degree to which it *is* interpretation, than an exact understanding of what it means – and what it does not mean – to say that our formulations of other peoples symbol systems must be actor-oriented.
>
> What it means is that descriptions of Berber, Jewish, or French culture must be cast in terms of the constructions we imagine Berbers, Jews, or Frenchmen to place upon what they live through, the formulae they use to define what happens to them. What it does not mean is that such descriptions are themselves Berber, Jewish, or French – that is, part of the reality they are ostensibly describing; they are anthropological – that is part of a developing system of scientific analysis. They must be cast in terms of the interpretations to which persons of a particular denomination subject their experience, because that is what they profess to be descriptions of they are anthropological because it is, in fact, anthropologists who profess them. (Ibid:15)

The text is, then, less than the interpretation of another culture because it is not, and does not claim to be, a Berber, Jewish or French interpretation. But in another sense the text is more than an interpretation of another culture. If culture is, as Geertz is honest enough to say, an anthropological construction, then the text is, in fact, the culture itself. Culture is, then, according to anthropological tradition something extrinsic to the peoples under study not because it is a superorganic phenomenon with an ontological reality in North Africa or Indonesia, but because it occupies a space, albeit a small one, in the culture from which the anthropologist comes.

The process of producing anthropological enquiry into the meaningful structures of another society, then, involves a two level operation. As a text it is an account of the way an observer proposes interpretations to his or her 'objects' of study, and judges its validity at least in part according to the degree to which the 'objects' recognise it. At the same time the text is transformed, from an account of a dialogue into an apparently objective account of the culture of the other. The procedure of verification begin when ethnography ends:

> There is no reason why the conceptual structure of a cultural interpretation should be any less formulable and thus less susceptible to explicit canons of appraisal, than that, say, of a biological observation or a physical experiment. (Ibid:24)

Doubtless, as Geertz observes, evaluation of a cultural interpretation is not a simple, straightforward process. And yet it is also clear that Geertz, in speaking of an 'interpretative science' envisions a role for the scientific community in the process of verification.

In short interpretative anthropology, even in the hands of someone as sensitive to the issue of 'actor-orientation' as Geertz, is not, and indeed cannot as Geertz points out, be genuinely free of the constraints imposed by the requirement of external verification. And this is a direct result of the assumed separateness of subject and object of knowledge, of us and them. Objectivism, dissolved by the procedures of ethnography, re-emergences in the consumption of the text. Interpretative anthropology can now be seen as the injection of a 'Western' artefact, culture, into the discourse of the non-West, the very shortcoming for which Geertz criticises the likes of White, Alexander, et al.

Indonesian Peasants: 'Other' or 'Anti-Us'?

It would seem that the above observation can lead to two quite different, conclusions. The first is to accept the inevitability of positivism at least in the study of the other, however defined. And in an important sense we might best resign ourselves to the fact. The second, not necessarily incompatible, is to seek ways of dissolving the categories of the West and the non-West in which the discipline rests.

At least for the case of Indonesia the second would seem to be a very real alternative, since it is particularly difficult in this case to treat economic, social or cultural change in Indonesia as somehow extrinsic to our own development. Indeed in much of the so-called Third World cultural perspectives and ideologies develop, and have long developed, at least within the context of cultural and intellectual transformation in the West (see Kahn, 1985). It would be a mistake, for example, to treat Indonesian political ideologies as though they developed in isolation from Western political ideologies of nationalism, communism and the like. This is not to say by any means that they simply mimic the cultural evolution of the West, indeed in many cases they have emerged as direct challenges to Western attempts at cultural domination.

Much the same can be said of rural economic transformation in
Indonesia. At least for the case of Sumatra it can be argued that the
modern agrarian structure has its roots in the period of capitalist
transformation, specifically in the impact of economic changes which
followed the passage of a new Agrarian Land Law for the Outer Islands
after 1875. Capitalist transformation did not manifest itself as a process
of peasant commercialisation or monetisation *per se*, features in any case
of the regional economy in the earlier period of colonial rule, and indeed
the pre-colonial period as well. Rather it changed the conditions under
which peasant commodity producers operated. For those affected by
land alienation by the colonial State, the changes made peasants increasingly reliant on the market for the reproduction of their market-oriented
economic activities, leading to increased specialisation and a reliance on
input/output price ratios as a guarantee of economic profitability. At the
same time the pattern of micro-differentiation described above – the creation of a division between viable and non-viable peasant enterprises –
can be seen to have its origins in regional and local variations in the
effects of the enclosures.

In short it is precisely during the capitalist transformation of Indonesia
that peasants have either been constituted from above or re-constituted
themselves in the new conditions obtaining for the reproduction of
commodity-producing enterprises.[12]

This review of the involution debate has had, as its central aim, the
demonstration of the inadequacy of the response to Geertz as manifest in the work of his large and growing body of critics. At the same
time I have continually argued that my purpose has not been a simple
resurrection of the involution thesis. Instead I have argued that the anti-
involution literature needs sharpening up not just to stave off a very real
academic challenge represented in this case by the persuasive interpretative paradigm on Clifford Geertz, but more importantly to produce a
more accurate understanding of the nature of capitalist transformation
in Indonesia in this century. To do this means to face up to the challenge
of historicism, rather than to simply reproduce the old anthropological
debate between 'materialism' and 'idealism' as though these were two
contradictory poles in the process of social enquiry.

Notes

1. This article is extracted from a book in preparation entitled *Re-Constituting the
Peasantry* in which most of these issues are treated in more detail.
2. Reference here should be made to Kautsky's more sophisticated treatment of
enterprise differentiation, between capitalist and labour farms (Kautsky, 1966).
3. This would seem to me to be self-evident, but nonetheless it has been argued
that class cleavages of the kind posited by Geertz's critics have been significant

elements of peasant subjectivity particularly in periods of PKI (Indonesian Communist Party) success – notably in the 1920s and 1960s (see for example Wertheim, 1969; Utrecht, 1972). While there is clearly an element of truth in such assertions, the argument even for these periods is based more on assertion than careful documentation. I have argued elsewhere, for example, that at least in one case (West Sumatra in 1926/7) perceptions of internal differentiation were not the main feature of communist ideology in peasant villages (Kahn, 1984).

4. I have attempted to summarise the issues elsewhere (Kahn, 1985). One seemingly fruitful line of research on this theme is to be found in the work of the 'subalternists' in India (see Arnold, 1984; Ghua, 1982).

5. Geertz's most obvious predecessor is, of course, Boeke whose notion of 'colonial economies' was at least influenced by the ideas of the German historical economists as well as Russian neo-populism in the person of Chayanov.

6. Geertz has himself rejected both labels (1984a, 1984b) – preferring to maintain that 'interpretative anthropology' is something quite different. I leave it to the reader to judge the extent to which his work falls so clearly outside such established traditions in Western social enquiry. In the area that concerns us here – the influence of Boeke is indicative of the fact the reference must at least be made to intellectual ancestors within the Western historicist tradition (nor is this something to be ashamed of).

7. This would appear to be particularly misleading in the case of Geertz. As Geertz's recent defense shows (1984b), the appeal to culture in postwar modernisation theory as a explanation for economic backwardness was part and parcel of a liberal positivism which was premised on the inevitability and desirability of the evolution of 'modern' societies throughout the world. In this case the notion of cultural lag plays a role in liberal theories analogous to that of false consciousness in certain variants of Marxism.

8. This model is implicating many of the anti-involution arguments. Aas, for example, derives his historical baseline almost entirely from Van Vollenhoven's account of the 'traditional' Javanese village (op. cit.), while most other writers accept the pertinence of Geertz's model to describe a state of affairs at some past historical period. The problems with this attempt to locate traditional society in the past are clearly pointed out, in the case of Java, by Breman (1982).

9. Dupré and Rey's critique of this mode of argument remains the definitive one (1978).

10. For a detailed discussion of the process and effects of land alienation in colonial Vietnam see Murray (1981).

11. An excellent example of an ethnography on Indonesia which shows clearly the extent to which the anthropologist's construction emerges out of an ongoing dialogue is Errington's recent book on West Sumatra (1984).

12. The notion of a re-constituted peasantry I have taken from Sidney Mintz (1974). I am grateful to Ann Stoler for drawing my attention to the relevance of this concept in the Sumatran context. I have looked at the effects of capitalist transformation in West Sumatra in another paper. It must be added that I am not advocating the argument that capitalism creates the peasantry for its own ends, the functionalism of which has been neatly exposed by Gledhill (1981).

REFERENCES

Aas, S. 1980. 'The Relevance of Chayanov's Macro Theory to the Case of Java', in E. Hobsbawm, et al., *Peasants in History*. Calcutta: Oxford University Press. Pp. 221–48.

Agro Economic Survey. 1971. *Agricultural Census in 33 Villages*. Jakarta: Economics and Finance.

Alexander, J. & P. 1982. 'Shared Poverty as Ideology: Agrarian Relationships in Colonial Java', in: *Man*, 17:597–619.

Arnold, D. 1984. 'Gramsci and Peasant Subalternity in India', in: *Journal of Peasant Studies*, 11:155–77.

Breman, J. 1982. 'The Village on Java and the Early Colonial State', in: *Journal of Peasant Studies*, 9: 189–240.

Collier, W. 1981. 'Agricultural Evolution in Java', in: Hansen (ed.), *Agricultural and Rural Development in Indonesia*. Boulder: Westview Press. Pp. 147–73.

Deutser, P. 1981. 'West Sumatra and South Sulawesi', in: Hansen (ed.), *Agricultural and Rural Development in Indonesia*. Boulder: Westview. Pp. 79–94.

Dove, M. 1981. 'Household Composition and Intensity of Labour: A Case Study of the Kantu' of West Kalimantan', in: *Bulletin of Indonesian Economic Studies*, 17 (3):86–93.

Dupré, G. and Rey, P.P. 1978. 'Reflections on the Relevance of a Theory of the History of Exchange', in: D. Seddon (ed.), *Relations of Production*. London: Cass. Pp. 171–208.

Errington, F. 1984. *Manners and Meaning in West Sumatra*. New Haven: Yale University Press.

Geertz, C. 1963. *Agricultural Involution*. Berkeley and Los Angeles: University of California Press.

———. 1973. *The Interpretation of Cultures*. London: Hutchinson.

———. 1984a. 'Distinguished Lecture: Anti-anti-relativism', in: *American Anthropologist*, 86:263–78.

———. 1984b. 'Culture and Social Change: The Indonesian Case', in: *Man*, 19:511–32.

Gerdin, I. 1982. *The Unknown Balinese: Land, Labour and Inequality in Lombok*. Gothenburg: Acta Universitatis Gothoburgensis.

Ghua, R. (ed.). 1982. *Subaltern Studies I*. Delhi: Oxford University Press.

Gledhill, J. 1981. 'Towns, Haciendas and Yeoman', in: *Bulletin of Latin American Research*, 1 (1):63–80.

Griffin, K. 1974. *The Political Economy of Agrarian Change*. London: Macmillan.

Hansen, G. (ed.). 1981. *Agricultural and Rural Development in Indonesia*. Boulder: Westview Press.

Jackson, J.C. 1972. 'Rice Cultivation in West Malaysia', in: *J Malay Br. R. Asiat. Soc.*, 45.

Kahn, J.S. 1980. *Minangkabau Social Formations: Indonesian Peasants and the World Economy*. Cambridge: Cambridge University Press.

———. 1982. 'From Peasants to Petty Commodity Production in Southeast Asia', in: *Bulletin of Concerned Asian Scholars*, 14:3–15.

———. 1984. 'Peasant Political Consciousness in West Sumatra: A Reanalysis of the Communist Uprising of 1927', in: A. Turton and S. Tanabe (eds.), *History and Peasant Consciousness in South East Asia*. Osaka: National Museum of Ethnology (SENRI Ethnological Studies, 13), pp. 293–325.

Kahn, J.S. 1985 (forthcoming). 'Peasant Ideologies in the Third World', in: *Annual Review of Anthropology*, 14, pp. 49–75.

Kat Angelino, A.D.A. de, 1931. *Colonial Policy*. The Hague: M. Nijhoff.

Kautsky, K. 1966. *La Question Agraire*. Paris: Maspero.

Knight, G.R. 1982. 'Capitalism and Commodity Production in Java', in: H. Alavi et al. (eds.), *Capitalism and Colonial Production*. London: Croom Helm, pp.119–58.

Konnick, R. De, et. al. 1982. *Agricultural Modernization, Poverty and Inequality*. Farnborough: Saxon House.

Mintz, S. 1974. *Caribbean Transformations*. Chicago: Aldine.

Murray, M. 1981. *The Development of Capitalism in Colonial Indochina (1810–1940)*. Berkeley: University of California Press.

Scott, J. 1976. *The Moral Economy of the Peasant*. New Haven: Yale University Press.

Utrecht, E. 1972. 'Some Remarks on Class Struggle and Political Parties in Indonesia'. In Association for Radical East Asian Studies and the British Indonesia Committee, in: *Indonesia's New Order*. Association et., Pp. 1–27.

Wertheim, W.F. 1969. 'From Aliran towards Class Struggle in the Javanese Countryside', in: *Pacific Viewpoint*, 10:1–17.

White, B. 1981. 'Population, Involution, and Employment in Rural Java', in: Hansen (ed.), *Agriculture and Rural Development in Indonesia*. Boulder: Westview Press. Pp. 130–46.

———. 1983. *'Agricultural Involution' and its Critics: Twenty Years after Clifford Geertz*. The Hague: ISS (Working Paper Series, 6).

Chapter 7

SOMETHING ABOUT PEASANTS, HISTORY AND CAPITALISM

WILLIAM ROSEBERRY

I am honored by Carol Smith's serious and careful review of my book.[1] She raises a number of issues, most especially about the relation and tension between universal and historically specific categories of analysis and about the relation between political questions and historical analysis, that are central to the constitution of a Marxist anthropology. As she applies these issues to an evaluation of my book and suggests ways my historical analysis might have been recast, she illuminates some of the major weaknesses of my work. Upon reflection, however, I find that I disagree with Smith's resolution of some of these central issues.

I wish to avoid the simultaneously aggressive and defensive posture normally taken in such responses and concentrate on the more general issues raised by Smith. Nonetheless, there are areas where she misinterprets what I actually say and uses those misinterpretations as points in her general argument. I therefore begin with a more straightforward response to Smith's characterization of my work.

The most significant problem arises with Smith's description of my analysis of the nineteenth century. I begin with a fundamental misinterpretation and use that discussion as a point of entry to the more general issues raised by Smith. On page 6 (of Smith, MS), she discusses my analysis of the relation between merchant capital and peasants in nineteenth century Bocono and says, 'After considerable agonizing, Roseberry decides that it was a capitalist relation of production . . . in that Bocono "peasants" are "formally" subsumed by capital.' She then points out that certain basic aspects of capitalism were absent in nineteenth century Bocono, that the presence of capital is an insufficient condition for the existence of capitalism, and that capital long preceded capitalism and existed in the Ancient World. Of course. Anyone remotely familiar with the mode of production literature or with the relevant sections of Capital, not to mention world history, recognizes this. Indeed, I make the same points in an evaluation of the literature in Chapter 2 of my book. How, then, could I have done such an abrupt about-face in Chapter 4?

The inconsistency is apparent only in Smith's review; I do not contend that relations of production in nineteenth century Bocono are capitalist.

The confusion arises, I suspect, because I did make such an argument in this journal in 1978.[2] There, under the influence of an article by Jairus Banaji[3], I examined the penetration of merchant capital into the production sphere and contended that the relationship between merchant capital and direct producers was formally similar to the relationship between industrial capital and wage labor. On that basis, I characterized the mode of production in nineteenth century Bocono as capitalist. In Chapter 4 of my book, I repeat much of this argument and then ask: 'But is an economy characterized by this type of relationship "capitalist"?' (p. 105). After pointing to the ways in which the situation does not fit rigid definitions of noncapitalist modes of production, I caution, 'But we must not jump from this observation to the conclusion that the nineteenth century coffee economy was capitalist' (p. 105). I then enter into a criticism of my 1978 article, noting that it ignored two crucial questions: (1) the distinction between absolute and relative surplus value and (2) the distinction between formal and real subsumption of labor to capital. Because the situation in Bocono was characterized by the appropriation of absolute surplus value and direct producers were only formally subsumed to capital, I reject the characterization of the economy as capitalist. I then observe:

> 'We are left, then, with the following conclusions. The investment of merchants' capital in nineteenth century Bocono signified the development of something that could not be analyzed in terms of precapitalist relations, but neither could it be analyzed in terms of capitalist relations. Bocono was more closely integrated within the capitalist world than during the colonial era, and "capital" was beginning to dominate, or to establish control, over the local economy. But "capital" was not acting in an abstract sense; it was not trying to impose "capitalism". Rather, capital was invested by particular persons who were pursuing their own interests, interests that cannot be reduced to, and might be in conflict with "capitalism" or the "worldsystem". Thus, abstract laws of capitalist development did not mechanically determine the trajectory and potential of the Bocono economy. That is, Bocono's capitalist development did not imply an inexorable movement toward industrial capitalism.' (p. 107)

Why do I go through such considerable agonizing if the results are so inconclusive? This can only be understood in terms of the structure and logic of the book. Although it is clear from Smith's review that the book alternates between fairly straight forward historical narrative and theoretical discussion of the issues raised by or relevant to particular historical periods, it is not clear how basic that structure is to the book's argument. I adopted the form for a number of reasons. First, I wanted to move beyond the false separation of 'theory' and 'history', and this seemed a useful way to effect integration. Second, I felt that one of the problems with the mode of production literature was that the basic issues were often cast at too abstract and universal a level. This was, in part, a recognition of the conflict Smith notes between universal and historically specific categories. My problem here, however, was not simply the appropriateness of categories used in the analysis of the world-system or of some other region for an analysis of Bocono. Important as that question is, my attention was directed elsewhere. My point was that the nature of the relationship of Bocono, and of dominant and subordinate classes in Bocono, to 'Venezuela', to 'capitalism', or to the 'worldsystem' was fundamentally different in the colonial period, or in the nineteenth century, or in the twentieth century. I therefore discussed the theoretical debates separately, and provided different revolutions of those debates, as I considered each historical period.

The third consequence of the book's structure follows directly from the second. Virtually every theoretical discussion in the book is inconclusive; the issues are not fully resolved. I do not adequately specify the mode of production during the colonial era; I do not categorize the nineteenth century economy as fully capitalist or fully non-capitalist; my discussion of twentieth century capitalism points to a process of peasantization within proletarianization. This is not simply the result of indecisiveness on my part. The book represents a transitional point in my own thinking, a move beyond some of the structuralist premises that informed the basic research. Thus, while I maintain that the theoretical issues raised by the mode of production literature are important, indeed crucial, I also maintain that the issues the literature raises cannot be resolved at a theoretical level. For the nineteenth century, for example, I move directly from the passage cited above to a renewed historical narrative, a discussion of the basic classes in nineteenth century Bocono, the trajectory and potential of the coffee economy, and the political struggles that were associated with the establishment of a coffee economy in the Andes. This discussion involves an examination of clientelist politics and *caudillismo*, the social, economic, political and cultural bases for peasant participation in multiclass coalitions. My discussion of these questions may be inadequate (indeed many reviewers note that the historical narrative is thin in relation to theoretical analysis), but the claim that my historical analysis ignores political questions is, I hope, misplaced. Instead, social and political analysis holds a privileged position in my resolution of theoretical debates.

This multilevel attempt to integrate theory and history was one of my basic goals in the book and one of the claims I make for the book's relevance. I take this local history not as a case for the application of universal concepts nor as a source of new concepts but as a text for a series of reflections on how we write history, how we construct theory, how we understand politics. A second goal was to provoke reflection regarding the nature of peasantries and of the concepts we use to analyze them. That goal was successfully realized in Smith's case: in a stimulating passage she takes issue with my definition of peasants, my classification of Bocono coffee producers as peasants, and my attempt to view peasants in terms of process. Here we have a straightforward and important disagreement.

It is not at all uncommon for historians or ethnographers who take one of our standard definitions of peasants to the analysis of concrete situations to find that the people they study do not fit the definition very well. Their responses to that discovery vary enormously. Perhaps the most common response is to ignore it and force their heterogeneous folk into an unproblematic category. One of the more interesting recent responses was offered in Alan Macfarlane's *Origins of English Individualism.*[4] In this work, Macfarlane constructs an outdated peasant concept and asks whether medieval and early modern English villagers fit in. His answer is that they do not, that they were quite 'individualistic' as far back as records provide relevant information. Aside from the fact that there are large gaps in Macfarlane's consideration of evidence (he never, for example, examines community forms or structures, and he ignores the literature on field systems and the cooperative practices imposed by open field agriculture), the most interesting aspect of the book is Macfarlane's stance toward the discrepancy between concept and evidence. Macfarlane simply concludes that England had no peasantry; he never turns the English evidence back toward a critical evaluation of his initial definition of peasants.

Smith's response to the Venezuelan evidence presented in my book is, in one respect, similar to Macfarlane's in England. The people I call peasants do not fit her definition of peasants, and so they are not peasants. Her own definition depends upon their placement and action as a class, that is, the existence of an objective situation such that producers live in a single class relation vis-a-vis other classes, and/or the existence of subjective conditions such that peasants *act* as a class. Yet in Bocono, 'We are talking about a heterogeneous group of people (several classes by objective criteria), who share only the fact that they engage in coffee production at some level . . . Not only did the condition of growing coffee create heterogeneity, but the social origin of the producers were themselves heterogeneous' (p. 7 Smith, MS). Of course, I agree with the characterization of Bocono producers as heterogeneous, *despite* certain basic similarities in terms of their relation to the means of production and to other classes, but heterogeneity is a central feature of my understanding of peasants. In my more theoretical passages, I take the differentiated and contradictory nature of the Bocono 'peasantry' as a starting point for a critique of less dialectical conceptualizations.

I also take the heterogeneity as a starting point for my analysis of the politics of Bocono coffee producers. Smith notes, 'I find it quite interesting that Bocono's "peasants" never acted as a class, that they always situated themselves in vertical alliances . . .' (p. 11 Smith, MS). And she suggests that I should have made this the central political and analytical theme of the book. Given my stress upon structural heterogeneity and contradictory social being, however, my analysis of the political activity of Bocono producers attempts to link this social being with changing regional and national contexts and show how peasants participated, and could be expected to participate, within a variety of vertical coalitions, regionally based in the nineteenth century, nationally based in the twentieth. I also try to indicate where there is structural space for horizontal, class based coalitions, as unlikely as I think these are for Venezuelan peasants at present. I therefore disagree with Smith's expectation of peasant class activity and her suggestion of the central political question. I would find it interesting, indeed surprising, if Bocono producers *had* acted as a class and would have treated such action as the central analytical problem, rather than reversing the emphasis as Smith suggests. My concept of peasants, and my analysis of this particular peasantry, leads me to expect peasants to act on a class basis only in the most extraordinary circumstances (Smith's research concerns an area where such circumstances now obtain). That is, aspects of their objective situation may lead to class action, under certain conditions, but they may also, and more commonly, lead to a variety of non-class forms of action. Although I stress this point in relation to peasants, however, I should note that it could be made with reference to other classes as well. If class action were a key definitional criterion, we would have to be much more selective and restrictive in our use of concepts such as 'proletarian' and 'bourgeois'.

At one level, then, our disagreement is as follows: Smith applies a definition to Bocono peasants, finds important discrepancies, and decides Bocono has no peasants; I apply other definitions to Bocono peasants, find important discrepancies, and turn those toward a critical evaluation of peasant concepts. At another level, however, our positions are reversed. Smith also criticizes concepts and finds my understanding of peasants to be hopelessly muddled. To the extent that the concept embraces heterogeneity, it is 'the most empty of analytic categories' (p. 8 Smith, MS); to the extent that it emphasizes process it repeats a truism and sidesteps the analytical dilemma. Worse, '(W)hat is the point of arguing for historical process if we have no historical product to explain?' (p. 11 Smith,

MS). As for my own approach, despite my use of the Bocono material to criticize reified understandings of peasants, I continue to use a peasant concept during an era when it has fallen out of favor.

We are dealing here with a disagreement regarding the nature and use of concepts similar to our disagreement regarding the relationship between concepts and perceived realities. Both of us recognize the multitudinous and contradictory reality encompassed by labels such as 'peasant'. Smith's preferred conceptual response seems to be one of disaggregation, the analysis of rich, middle and poor peasants, and of simple commodity producers, with separate analytical categories and class labels. In the process, 'peasant', as an empty analytical category, would be excised from Marxist discourse. The current mood among many Marxists is clearly in Smith's favor. While I share the emphasis on heterogeneity and differentiation and have tried to make it central to my theoretical and descriptive discussions, however, I resist the process of conceptual disaggregation and continue to use a 'peasant' label.

I do this for two basic reasons. First, I use concepts as provisional means to an end, useful tools for the discussion of particular processes or problems. When I wrote the book, I was struck by the fact that so many of the attributes we consider constitutive of peasant farming, especially the complex surrounding the 'family economy' of Chayanovian lore, were the product of the nineteenth century in Bocono. These characteristics' could be viewed as direct and indirect consequences of the incorporation of Bocono within an expanding world market and the creation of the 'functional commodities' of land, labor and capital. I wondered if this might be true of other peasantries elsewhere and used the Bocono example to ask questions about the historicity of peasantries and the connection between peasantization and the making of the modern world. Smith maintains that I am simply saying that all is process, that nobody disputes such a contention, and that, in any case, the contention does not release me from the requirement of a rigorous definitional exercise. I think, however, that while many will recognize historical process in an introduction or conclusion, it still holds a marginal position in most analyses. More important, my point is not simply that all is process. Rather, I argue that many of the peasantries we study may be the result of a particular kind of process and that our analyses take insufficient account of this fact. (It should be apparent that the historical process produced no historical product only if we accept Smith's definitional criteria for recognizing an historical product.) Even those writers who reject Chayanovian assumptions still view basic aspects of peasant social structure as essentially precapitalist, a legacy of our economic past. In order to question that historical vision, I needed to maintain a concept of peasant that had been placed in modern history. I was trying to view peasants, at least in part, as products of capitalist development and not simply as victims of it. This does not mean that I wish to cast the peasant label in stone in reference to Bocono coffee farmers. Indeed, as I begin to consider different questions I may find another label or set of labels more useful.

Second, I like to use concepts that embrace existential and social contradictions rather than separating out contradictory elements into mutually exclusive categories. I adopt this strategy, in part, as a personal guide. Although this results in a loss of conceptual rigor (and Smith is correct in noting this loss in the book), it also serves as a check against positivist applications of Marxist concepts and language. It forces me to try to think dialectically. It also helps me to think about and analyze politics, the relationship between contradictory social being and contradictory consciousness. The confusion analysts feel as they embrace a multitudinous reality with a concept like 'peasant' is not entirely unlike existential and political dilemmas presented to peasants as they get through daily life, plant, cultivate and harvest crops, contract debts, pay taxes, arrange marriages, work off the farm, arrange for workers on the farm, and, on occasion and under circumstances not of their own choosing, make history. As they act, they may act as cousins, compadres, clients, members of a community, poor or rich peasants, incipient proletarian or incipient bourgeois, as rank and file within larger, multi-class coalitions, or as part of a peasant class. Each of these forms of action is possible, perhaps even simultaneously, from the same group under varying conditions. My own political analysis is enhanced if I maintain a concept that is open to these varying forms rather than opting for concepts that effect premature closure.

With these considerations, my response to Smith's provocative and insightful review can conclude, and I thank Professor Smith for having stimulated me to look back over this work and defend or reconsider choices I made as I was writing. There is, however, one last issue that I wish to briefly address. Much of Smith's review concentrates on political questions, contending that I do not clarify what she considers to be the central political issues raised by the Bocono example. In my response, I have indicated that I pay a good bit more attention to politics, however inadequately and incompletely, than she suggests, and that I disagree with her definition of the central political problem (viz, why did the peasantry not act as a class?).

There is, however, another aspect to the centrality of politics in Smith's review. She charges early on that I never give sufficient reason for engaging in a historical account of this particular peasantry and indicates that such a reason should isolate the central political issues, 'which is what a historical analysis is all about' (p. 3 Smith, MS). Further, 'As he depicts it, Bocono is interesting only because it has peasants, a history, and is in the modern capitalist world-economy – and Roseberry wants to say something about peasants, history, and capitalism' (p. 4 Smith, MS). Here my disagreement could not be more complete, and I think Smith is imposing a condition upon Marxist scholarship that is stifling and unacceptable. I think a desire to say something about peasants, history, and capitalism, and to say it about particular people in a particular place, is sufficient reason to do fieldwork and to write a book. I say this, in part, because I think the history of Bocono is intrinsically interesting (many readers no doubt disagree here), and, in part, because what I have to say about peasants, history and capitalism is not being said, or said often enough or with enough force, either in Venezuelan studies or in Marxist historical and political analyses of peasants. Much of Venezuelan reflection on the agrarian past reduces it to a flat relationship between latifundistas and peones. My historical work, especially on the nineteenth century, was an attempt to recover a group that does not fit well within that image and that faced rather different historical and political limitations and possibilities. As for Marxist analysis, most of our ideas about peasant consciousness and politics depend upon a model that places them in a precapitalist past. Capitalism is seen as something that happens to them, to which they react. If my attempt to view Bocono peasants as products as well as victims of capitalist expansion is relevant to other areas, many of these ideas are in need of revision. Some of these issues could be raised in the monograph.[5] Others could not be and had to remain implicit. I hope that in both what is said and what is unsaid the book is politically consequent. But the test of political consequence applied in Smith's review is based on a narrow and simplistic understanding of the relationship between scholarly writing and political relevance. I see the relationship as much more open and multifaceted, especially in historical writing. Isolation of what the scholar considers to be the central political issues is not, I think, what 'historical analysis is all about'. It is also about the construction, or reconstruction, of an effective past in and for the present, a task that carries its own political consequences and compromises.

NOTES

1. Carol Smith, 'Anthropology and history: Look at peasants and capitalism', in: *Critique of Anthropology* 5:2 (1985), pp. 87–94.
2. 'Peasants as proletarians', in: *Critique of Anthropology* 11 (1978), pp. 3–18.
3. Jairus Banaji, 'Modes of Production in a Materialist Conception of History', in: *Capital and Class* 3 (1977), pp. 1–44.
4. Alan Macfarlane, *The Origins of English Individualism*. New York: Cambridge University Press, 1978.
5. I discuss some of these issues more explicitly in relation to the Venezuelan example in 'Images of the Peasant in the Consciousness of the Venezuelan Proletariat', in: Michael Hanagan and Charles Stephenson (eds.), *Proletarians and Protest*. Westport, Connecticut: Greenwood Press, in press.

PART V

The Crisis of Representation and *Writing Culture*

The publication of *Writing Culture: The Poetics and Politics of Ethnography* (J. Clifford and G. Marcus, eds., 1986) was a key moment in the so-called literary turn of anthropology. Scholte's critical commentary acknowledged the broad and transformative impact of that volume while highlighting some of the serious divisions in the field prompted by its publication. Tyler's brief response in defence of the postmodernist turn also indicates that, in his view, *Writing Culture* did not go quite far enough in moving away from the suffocating orthodoxy of the merely modern.

Although Geertz never claimed credit for (and certainly not leadership of) the literary, interpretive move to which his work was central, the repudiation of (even modest) scientific aims for anthropology in favour of a hermeneutic project aimed at producing text rather than research results had long been a feature of his work. In many ways, *Writing Culture* was a consolidation of a long-emergent position rather than a new position statement, but there is little disputing the galvanizing effect its publication had. Two subsequent developments in anthropology are directly related to this turn: The growing hostility between an anthropology still affiliated with a (very broadly) scientific orientation, and an anthropology happy to jettison all such associations in favour of a forthright humanities-and-hermeneutics orientation. With the emergence of evolutionary psychology, a label became available whereby a mutual demonization of the anthropology arts and anthropology science wings could be baldly stated.

The term 'ethnography', post the literary turn, came to signify a contradiction that persists: On the one hand it is indissociable from fieldwork method (and thereby harkens back to old-style, long-term, immersive fieldwork with data gathering as the primary goal), yet what is promoted in the postmodern version is a kind of anthropological rhetoric plus 'high' theory quite divorced from the rude setting of fieldwork. The latter rendering has encouraged the spread of 'the ethnographic' well outside the field of anthropology – particularly in cultural studies, and while making anthropology nominally more accessible, it has blurred yet further its disciplinary distinctiveness.

Chapter 8

THE LITERARY TURN IN CONTEMPORARY ANTHROPOLOGY *

BOB SCHOLTE

After Kuhn's demystification of scientific textbooks (Kuhn 1970), one hesitates to enumerate recent 'classics', representative 'readers', or crucial journals in contemporary anthropology. The risk of intellectual-historical reification or self-serving historiography is simply too great, the more so since the recent past is still so very near. Besides, almost every living anthropologist is an interested party to his or her own favorite movement, scientific tradition, intellectual style, etc. including their attendant textbooks, readers, classics and journals. Hence the specific choices one makes are likely to reveal current preoccupations and personal prejudgments rather than judicious disciplinary judgments or sedimented historical evaluations. Still, in order to review *Writing Culture* with a certain intellectual historical depth and philosophical sophistication, I am going to have to make provisional choices and I shall.

I would argue that the recent history of Anglo-American cultural anthropology (and I shall limit myself to that tradition) is largely defined by at least three interrelated movements. There is firstly, critical anthropology. Its representative reader is Dell Hymes' *Reinventing Anthropology* (1972); a recent classic is Eric Wolf's *Europe and the People Without History* (1982); its most prominent journals are *Critique of Anthropology* and *Dialectical Anthropology*. Secondly, there is feminist anthropology. A representative reader is Rayna Reiter's (now Rapp) *Towards an Anthropology of Women* (1975); a recent classic is Marjorie Shostak's *Nisa: The Life and Words of a !Kung Woman* (1981); an important journal is *Signs*. Lastly, there is symbolic anthropology. A representative reader is Jane L. Dolgin, David S. Kemnitzer & David M. Schneider's *Symbolic Anthropology* (1977); among its classics are Victor Turner's *The Forest of Symbols* (1967) and, more recently, Clifford Geertz's *Negara: The Theatre State in Nineteenth Century Bali* (1980). The apparently inevitable journal is now a fact: *Cultural Anthropology*.

James Clifford and George Marcus' *Writing Culture* (1986) is part and parcel of the last mouvement I mentioned: symbolic anthropology (with apologies to those whose favorite mouvements, readers, classics, and journals I left out). Not exactly a reader, the book does not attempt to cover symbolic anthropology as a whole. Its specific focus, rather, is ethnographic literacy, that is, the question of how another culture is (literally) written up. As a genre of symbolic anthropology, it may very well become a classic – though it would be premature to call it that just yet. Better to consider it, at least for now, as a specification, concretization, and delineation of that segment of the problem of meaning (a core concept in symbolic anthropology) that deals with textual and literary issues of ethnographic writing, production, construction, description, legitimacy, and authority (see Clifford 1983 for an initial formulation). Such issues are, of course, more than merely literary or textual and it is not surprising that the contributors to *Writing Culture* constantly, persistently, and perhaps inevitably meet up with proponents of the other two mouvements I mentioned: critical and feminist anthropologists. More about that meeting of the minds momentarily.

To set the intellectual-historical and philosophical scene, let me ask a deceptively obvious question: Why the recent literary turn in contemporary cultural anthropology? Clifford's 'Introduction' (pp. 2 ff.) mentions several possible factors (e.g., the 'crise de conscience' in critical anthropology, recent developments in the sociology and philosophy of science, structuralist theories of language, etc.) and related developments (e.g., historical ethnography, cultural poetics, cultural criticism, the semiotics of exotic worlds, etc.). Let me elaborate on just one or two.

The so-called semiotic revolution is in part responsible for a shift in our attention from a merely incidental concern with narrative structure, rhetorical devices, literary tropes, etc. to a decisively active interest in their constitutive effects on ethnographic description and analysis. Philosophically speaking, contemporary social scientists no longer seek a privileged or foundational discourse that is in principle adequate to describing and understanding a visible and knowable universe; rather, they experiment with multiple universes of discrete discourse that are in fact capable of expressing and illuminating those diverse possible worlds that can be meaningful to and for us. Language, in other words, has become problematic in the sense that it can no longer be considered as merely imitative or representative of reality, but must instead be considered as constitutive and expressive of that partial segment of the real that can be made intelligible and meaningful to us within the cultural confines of a specific language game (see Bernstein 1983 for a comprehensive philosophical overview; Rorty 1980 for a 'classic' formulation of a similarly motivated critique of representationalism).

This semiotic revolution (for want of a better term) has a number of implications – both concrete and abstract. Let me mention at least two abstract ones (in our actual discussion of *Writing Culture* we shall encounter them again more concretely): the epistemological consequences and the normative implications. Here, incidentally, both feminist and critical anthropology play an important role – both as historical source of inspiration and as potential source of critique of cultural anthropology's literary turn.

Briefly put, I think that the literary turn – at least from this point of view – consists of a crucial shift from an observational and empirical methodology to a communicative and dialogical epistemology (which may, of course, entail observational moments and empirical descriptions). Our conception of ethnological analysis and our activity as practicing ethnographers have changed accordingly: from a focus on the observing eye and the use of visual metaphors (as dominant in our culture as in our anthropology (see Lakoff & Johnson 1980)) to a concern with the expressive voice and the constitution of intersubjective understanding.

Much more is involved in this crucial shift than meets the eye (literally and figuratively): questions of anthropological representation, praxis and production; of analytic and dialectical modes of understanding, experiencing and interpreting; of the relation between self, other and the nature of intersubjectivity; of science, power and cooptation; of speaking, listening and writing; of objectivity, relativism and ethnocentrism; of legitimacy, authority and truth; and – perhaps most problematic of all – of social critique and political praxis. All these issues are discussed in *Writing Culture*, though some more extensively than others and, as far as I am concerned, not all of them radically enough (in the epistemological *and* political sense of the term).

In order to exemplify how such philosophic issues effect the concrete workings of the anthropologist, let me take as my point of departure the question that Clifford raises regarding the descriptive authority and analytic legitimacy of anthropological texts (see Clifford 1983 or his two contributions to *Writing Culture*). The issue here is not simply one of how to interpret an ethnographic document (e.g., Karp & Maynard 1983) nor or how to assess the ethnological reliability of a given anthropologist's work (e.g., as in the recent Shabono case (see Holmes 1983 and Pratt in *Writing Culture*) or the celebrated Freeman-Mead controversy (see Brady 1983)). Though these are certainly important issues, more fundamental still is the perennial question that Stocking singles out as cultural anthropology's most enduring problem: 'Whether anthropology offers forms of knowing that may be applied to all human subject matter even to the point of painful self-reflexivity or whether, in some profound sense historically delimited, it has simply been a way

Europeans have invented of talking about their darker brethren' (and, I would add, 'sisters') (Stocking 1982:419).

I obviously cannot attend to this issue here (I have tried to make a beginning elsewhere – see Scholte 1983), but I can at least indicate how Clifford addresses the problem. His approach is exemplary of the distinctive way in which the issue is treated by proponents of the literary approach – several contributors to *Writing Culture* deal with similar problems applied to different texts.

We need to reflect, according to Clifford, on the nature of cultural discourse, that is, on the style, rhetoric, logic, intellectualization, rationalization, etc. used by some people (mostly from the West) to describe, imagine, analyze, comprehend or co-opt other people (often the Rest). The central problem, in other words, is very similar to Stocking's, but more specifically literary: 'Are (anthropological) discourses ultimately condemned to redundancy, the prisoners of their own authoritative images and linguistic protocols?' Or can we instead '(. . . .) escape procedures of dichotomizing, restructuring, and textualizing in the making of interpretative statements about foreign cultures and traditions?' (Clifford 1980:209–210).

Clifford's question can be divided into two subsidiary ones. One is essentially literary: How are ethnographic authority and ethnological legitimacy constituted? The other is historical and, I would argue, in the last analysis political: why should anthropological viability have become so problematic recently? Why, in other words, should this specific issue have become so urgent at this particular time? While the second question hovers over every page of *Writing Culture*, it is not really addressed thoroughly. Though people like Asad, Clifford, Rabinow, and Tyler offer suggestive insights, there are few if any sustained arguments. More about this in a moment. The first question is discussed at length by all the contributors to *Writing Culture* and before I give some illustrations, let me summarize what I consider to be the most significant conclusion reached by the discussants.

The most important insight reached, I think, is precisely the fact that ethnographic authority (existential credibility, empirical comprehensiveness, descriptive adequacy, etc.) and ethnological legitimacy (scientific insight, theoretical acumen, disciplinary value, etc.) are, in fact, *constituted*, that is, they are not merely descriptive (imitative) of reality or analytic (logical) manipulations of the real, but they are also and perhaps more fundamentally literary, poetic, inventive, imaginative, and constitutive *deeds* of a meta-anthropological (political, historical, aesthetic, etc.) kind (see White 1973 for a 'classic' formulation in historiography and Hyman 1962 for a 'neglected classic' in the social sciences). They are, in this sense, constitutive of that segment of the (ethnographic, ethnological etc.) real that can be *made* meaningful, intelligible, valuable, interesting, etc. for us.

Anthropological authority and legitimacy, being constituted in a *meta-anthropological* context, is relative in at least two senses of the term: constrained and multiple. The former raises the vexing issue of the socio-cultural and political constraints on anthropological texts; the latter issue (more fully discussed in *Writing Culture* than the first one) points to the experimental and creative nature of ethnographic production. Let's discuss them briefly, taking Clifford once again as our guide.

Clifford unequivocally states: '(. . .) no sovereign scientific method or ethical stance can guarantee the truth of (anthropological) images. They are constituted – the critique of colonial modes of representation has shown at least this much – in specific historical relations of dominance and dialogue' (Clifford 1983:119). And, he adds, 'the process is complicated by the action of multiple subjectivities and political constraints beyond the control of the writer. In response to these forces ethnographic writing enacts a specific strategy of authority' (Clifford 1983:120).

Strategies of authority can take many forms, but they are essentially of two kinds; exclusive and diverse. If the former, they are said to be anchored in some specific core or privileged foundation. Clifford considers any such foundationalism or essentialism (my terms) as symptoms of '(. . .) the persistence of an ideology claiming transparency of representation and immediacy of experience' (Clifford in *Writing Culture*, p. 2). Ethnographic realism provides a concrete example. Strategies of authority can, however, also be diffuse, multiple, even experimental. That, in fact, is the position the contributors to *Writing Culture* advocate. They favor a '(. . .) mix of multiple realities written into ethnographic texts of dispersed authority' (Marcus & Cushman 1982:44). In its most dramatic form, ethnographic authority and poetic insight fuse (e.g., Prattis 1985a, 1985b). In an attempt to articulate the singularity and complexity of ethnographic experience, the anthropologist – like Wordsworth – seeks to convey 'unknown modes of being' in poetic form; a form deemed more fully appropriate to and commensurate with '(. . .) a post-hierarchical way of experiencing a multicultural world' (Rose 1983:354).

This brings us to a core theme of *Writing Culture* in particular and the literary turn in cultural anthropology in general: the post-modern (a much favored term by the advocates of this mouvement) transition from a single ideal of ethnographic authority to a multiplicity of descriptive experiments and interpretive paradigms. Foundational strategies derived from allegedly privileged sources of ethnographic authority (hard-core facts, observational data, immaculate conceptions, analytic truths, etc.) need to be replaced by multiple strategies of dispersed authority (domains of facticity, negotiated realities, cognitive intentionality, dialectical understanding, etc.).

Post-modernists consider this transition a crucial experiment in the human sciences (see Marcus & Fischer 1986). 'Traditional' modernists are more likely to see it as an involutional relativism in which any semblance to scientific consistency, credibility, verifiability, and legitimacy are recklessly thrown overboard.

At this point the reader must wonder why I have spent such an inordinate amount of time on setting the intellectual-historical scene for what was meant to be a modest review of a specific collection of diverse essays on a common theme. I have three reasons for my unorthodoxy: one, and most importantly, cultural anthropology's literary turn reflects a significant change in Western thought as a whole and some of the salient features of that reorientation need to be made explicit. Though I have merely scratched the philosophic surface (a more detailed analysis is forthcoming), I think an important conclusion can nevertheless be drawn: Critical, reflexive, and innovative intellectual developments with substantial theoretical scope and concrete descriptive results are taking place in contemporary anthropology and the literary turn is one example of that fact, irrespective of one's sympathies with or apathy towards its distinctive aims and final products. Two, I can now distill the major points of the essays in *Writing Culture* quickly and economically while still referring them to the broader intellectual issues they address – sometimes explicitly, more often implicitly. Three and finally, I can also voice some of my own misgivings without thereby detracting from *Writing Culture*'s undeniable historical interest to our discipline or compromising my genuine respect for the detailed, imaginative, and suggestive analyses found in the Clifford & Marcus volume.

The precarious balance between literary analysis and political critique that characterizes *Writing Culture* is announced right away by the editors in their 'Preface': 'Several papers stressed, and the discussions repeatedly returned to, larger contexts of systematic power inequality, worldsystem constraints, and institutional formations that could only partly be accounted for by a focus on textual production' (pp. vii–viii). With the possible exception of Asad and Rabinow, however, few contributors address the question of 'authoritative discourse' in other than structural terms, that is, as a problem of a text's internal composition. But any given discourse, including an anthropological text, is also subject to external relations of production, that is, constraints defined by people in a position to authorize the discourse on their own or someone else's behalf and/or expense (see Asad 1979; Keesing 1987; Scholte 1986). Admittedly, Clifford makes an effort to address the issue in his 'Introduction: Partial Truths' by pointing out that politics is one of the constraints operating on the process of ethnographic writing. He even adds the judicious reminder that the relation between anthropological knowledge and political power is never unilateral or unequivocal, but 'complex, often ambivalent, potentially counter-hegemonic' (p. 9). Still, his primary focus is obviously literary representation ('the evocative, performative elements of ethnography' – p. 12) rather than material production (the bourgeois academic genesis of ethnographic texts, for instance). In fairness to Clifford, it should be said that he at least leaves the door open for such material analyses, i.e., for a *specification of discourses* (p. 13) in which the question must be asked: 'Who speaks? Who writes? When and where? With or to whom? Under what institutional and historical constraints?' (p. 13).

In their 'Preliminary Report' of the seminar from which *Writing Culture* resulted, Marcus & Clifford (1985:268) single out the absence of 'papers written from a feminist standpoint' and the lack of '"Third World" or non-European perspectives'. The latter omission is more dramatically evident than the former since several contributors to *Writing Culture* raise important anthropological issues that are central to a feminist point of view as well. Mary Louise Pratts' 'Field-work in Common Places' is a good example. Her chief concern is the '(. . .) set of problematic links between ethnographic authority, personal experience, scientism, and originality of expression' (p. 29). As her dramatic examples from the classic ethnographic literature make abundantly clear, the tension between personal narrative and impersonal description has always been an intricate part of the ethnographer's dilemma. Two recent examples (the Donner affair and Marjorie Shostak's *Nisa*) reaffirm the continued importance of the existential and descriptive problem. There is, of course, another precedent not mentioned by Pratt: the frenzied debates on navel-staring surrounding critical anthropology (see Scholte 1978a). There, too, the question was and remains: Where do we draw the line between subjectivity and inter-subjectivity, between the idiosyncratic and the anthropological? That feminism must address this issue as well is clear. How, for example, would Pratt assess the *anthropological* importance of Cesara's strictly autobiographical *Reflections of a Woman Anthropologist* (1982)?

Vincent Crapanzano's 'Hermes' Dilemma: The Masking of Subversion in Ethnographic Description' raises another question dear to proponents of the literary turn: how are ethnographic texts, fashioned, created, constructed, projected, etc.? And how are such provisional ethnographic 'fictions' (not 'falsehoods' as Geertz – 1975:15 – quickly added) authenticated and legitimated? Crapanzano does not really answer the latter question either (no one in *Writing Culture* really does), but he does offer a fascinating analysis of ethnographic descriptions by Gatlin, Goethe, and Geertz in order to show how each of them, in their own distinctive way, covers up a failed attempt to convince by an unconvincing appeal to meaning (pp. 53ff.). What, according to Crapanzano, these authors should have done instead remains unclear, at least to me. His appeal to Hermes' dilemma is not really convincing: 'When Hermes took the post of messenger to the gods, he promised Zeus not to lie. He did not promise to tell the whole truth. Zeus understood. The ethnographer has not' (p. 53). True, we may never know the whole truth and we may not have the literary means to tell all that we think we know of truth, but shouldn't we nevertheless keep trying?

Renato Rosaldo's 'From the Door of His Tent: The Fieldworker and the Inquisitor' (pp. 77–97) is an excellent example of what a detailed analysis of ethnographic rhetoric can contribute to our understanding of anthropological texts. Comparing Evans-Pritchard's *The Nuer* with Ladurie's *Montaillou*, Rosaldo shows how both authors effectively circumvent and mask the relation between power and knowledge. Ladurie seems oblivious to the fact that his archival material is the written product of inquisitors with vested interests in describing, judging, and accusing powerless heretics who could neither read nor write; Evans-Pritchard adopts a studied casualness as part and parcel of '(. . .) the rhetorical work of separating the context of colonial domination from the production of ethnographic knowledge' (p. 97). In both authors, the 'pastoral mode' (pp. 96ff.) is invoked to both justify and betray '(. . .) the introductory efforts to suppress the interplay of power and knowledge' (p. 97). It would be interesting, by the way, to have more detailed analyses of the use and abuse of this 'pastoral mode' in cultural anthropology and folklore studies since it is probably one of the most prominent and appealing literary tropes implicit in our discipline (see Fabian 1983 or Clifford's essay in *Writing Culture*).

Anthropological writing as a literary genre is the explicit focus of James Clifford's 'On Ethnographic Allegory'. Echoing his colleague Haydn White's brilliant work on historical narratives (1973), Clifford calls ethnography '(. . .) a performance emplotted by powerful stories' (p. 98). And, he adds, '(. . .) these stories simultaneously describe real cultural events and make additional, moral, ideological, and even cosmological statement' (p. 98). In fact, the very act of ethnographic writing '(. . .) enacts a redemptive Western allegory' (p. 98), e.g., Shostak's *Nisa* which Pratt earlier characterized as an allegorical expression of the tension between the counter-culture of the sixties (the !Kung as victims of colonialism) and Harvard's infatuation with sociobiology during the eighties (the !Kung as primal beings outside history) (see pp. 42ff.). Clifford also points out that ethnographic narratives are not just experimental and open-ended, though it is precisely these qualities that allow for a welcome multiplicity of voices and discordant allegorical registers. Still, history and convention impose coercive strictures on the ethnographic imagination and the meaning that can be generated is in that sense always restricted and contested. The very technology of writing is problematic too – 'scriptocentrism' an anthropologist friend of mine calls it (see Lemaire 1984). I think Clifford could have gone further with the latter topic than he does, by the way. Aside from discussing Derrida's *Grammatologie*, he might have addressed the issues raised by Goody in his *Domestication of the Savage Mind* (1977) and especially Walter Ong's *Orality and Literacy* (1982) would have been germane. Ong's critique of visualism is entirely in keeping with Clifford's own emphasis on expression (as Ong – 1982:72 – says: 'Sight isolates, sound incorporates') and Ong, like Clifford, warns us that no internal analysis of narrative structure is ever sufficient ('(. . .) no text can stand by itself independent of the extratextual world. Every text builds on pretext' – Ong 1982:162). If we add up the various constraints on ethnographic writing mentioned, perhaps the ironic mode that Clifford finally advocates is indeed the only one left to choose: 'If we are condemned to tell stories we cannot control, may we not, at least, tell stories we believe to be true?' (p. 121).

Stephen Tyler's 'Post-Modern Ethnography: From Document of the Occult to Occult Document' is theoretically one of the most stimulating essays in the Clifford & Marcus collection. It is also the volume's most difficult and inaccessible contribution. If I understand Tyler correctly, post-modern ethnography is essentially post-scientific, that is, evocative and normative rather than merely analytic and descriptive. It is, in other words, poetic: '(. . .) a cooperatively evolved text consisting of fragments of discourse intended to evoke in the minds of both reader and writer an emergent fantasy of a possible world of common-sense reality, and thus to provoke an aesthetic integration that will have a therapeutic effect' (p. 125). Discourse takes precedence to text; dialogue to monologue; cooperation and collaboration to the 'ideology of the (solitary) transcendental observer' (p. 126); emergence to registration; 'perspectival relativity' (p. 127) to 'synoptic transcendence' (p. 129). Tyler's critique of scientism is unequivocal: 'The whole point of "evoking" rather than "representing" is that it frees ethnography from *mimesis* and the inappropriate mode of scientific rhetoric that entails "objects", "facts", "descriptions", "inductions", "generalizations", "verification", "experiment", "truth" and like concepts that have no parallels either in the experience of ethnographic fieldwork or in the writing of ethnographies' (p. 130). And he concludes: 'Ethnographic discourse is not part of a project whose aim is the creation of universal knowledge. It disowns the Mephistophelian urge to power through knowledge, for that, too, is a consequence of representation' (p. 131).

Though I sympathize with Tyler's point of view and share his critique of scientism (like his, in part based on Habermas' work – see Scholte 1978b), I find an exclusive appeal to aesthetics and poetry politically inadequate. On the one hand, there is no guarantee that the 'Mephistophelian urge to power' cannot also infect the poet. On the other hand, there is no guarantee that poetry by definition generates positive or desirable political consequences. The aesthetic turn made by Habermas' predecessors in the Frankfurter Schule (notably Adorno), for example, provides discouraging rather than supportive evidence. Aesthetic integration did not and could not generate a political dialogue with many voices; it was not and could not be a normative model for a non-repressive society (see Wellmer 1985:48ff.). Only critical theory and political praxis can do that.

Talal Asad's 'The Concept of Cultural Translation in British Social Anthropology' is not theoretically as ambitious as Tyler's essay, but it has the advantage that it is not only more accessible but also brings an explicitly political dimension to bear on the problem of meaning or, in this specific case, the issue of translation. Echoing a theme that Asad has previously addressed (1979), the author points out that translation (a favorite theme in British anthropology since the fifties) is not merely a question of matching sentences, but of *'learning to live another form of life'* (p. 149). And that, of course, in turn entails a political context. Specifically, in the case of translation, an 'inequality in the power of languages' (p. 160). In a critique reminiscent of Bourdieu's brilliant 'decomposition' of semiotic contemplation (1977) and as applicable to, say, Clifford Geertz as Ernest Gellner (Asad's 'bête *noire*'), the author points out that this inequality of languages and the fact that the anthropologist often translates the discourse of a non-literate and non-academic population into the written and formal language of an academic elite encourages the tendency '(. . .) to read the *implicit* in alien cultures' (p. 160). It thereby also tends to place the anthropologist in the pretentious position of the 'outside expert' who is supposed to know what the other *really* feels or knows and to 'reveal' that superior insight in a textual form often inaccessible to the person or persons spoken or written about. What Asad unfortunately does not explore are the alternatives the anthropologist has available in terms of concepts such as coevalness as developed by my colleague Fabian (1983). He restricts himself to calling for an explicit recognition of those political processes that effect '(. . .) the possibilities and the limits of effective translation' (p. 164). That is an important step, but it doesn't really solve the problem.

George Marcus' 'Contemporary Problems of Ethnography in the Modern World System' singles out a question that – as I have said – hovers over the pages of *Writing Cultures*: how can symbolic anthropology be attentive and sensitive to *both* ideational and symbolic supra-structures *and* socio-historical and politico-economic infra-structures? Marcus gives two examples of successful studies that manage to integrate the ideational (engendered) and material (encountered) worlds: the works of Raymond Williams and Paul Willis. Interestingly enough, they also exemplify the neo-Marxist tradition in recent social scientific scholarship – a fact that should have given Marcus greater food for deeper thought (. . .) According to Marcus, these studies are examples of 'mixed-genre texts' (p. 188). They reflect 'key rhetorical markers in modernist ethnography (. . .) incompleteness and indeterminateness' (p. 192). Aside from the fact that I thought contemporary experimental ethnography was meant to be *post*-modern rather than modern, I did not find Marcus' essay very original or informative. He does little more than echo what Clifford, Tyler, and others have already said more than adequately elsewhere and his 'explications des textes' of Williams and Willis can hardly substitute for the intellectual pleasure of reading the works themselves.

Michael Fischer's 'Ethnicity and the Post-Modern Arts of Memory' is more interesting, but the author again repeats much of what is already common knowledge, e.g., the recent fascination with hidden meanings, the importance of ethnographic listening, the attention to cultural criticism, or the experimentation with ethnographic writing. Fischer adds a few techniques of his own ('bifocality and reciprocity of perspectives, juxtapositioning of multiple realities, inter-textuality and interreferentiality, and comparison through families of resemblance' – p. 230), but they do not substantially add to the knowledge already gained from reading the contributions of Clifford, Tyler, and others in *Writing Culture*, *Cultural Anthropology* and elsewhere. Interesting is Fischer's subject-matter: the ethnic autobiographies of Armenian-Americans, Chinese-Americans, Afro-Americans, Mexican-Americans and Native Americans (p. 201). Fischer thereby corroborates the ethnographic significance of 'life-histories' (see also Crapanzano 1984), just as we now realize that the confessional mode has its proper role to play in ethnological reflection (see Lévi-Strauss 1955, 1963).

Paul Rabinow's 'Presentations Are Social Facts: Modernity and Post-Modernity in Anthropology' is, like Stephen Tyler's article, theoretically very provocative. I found it more accessible than the latter's 'Post-Modern Ethnography', but that may reflect on my own background in Continental philosophy and French structuralism rather than on Tyler's alleged inscrutability. However that may be, Rabinow takes Rorty's critique of epistemology as his point of departure and gives it an additional historical and sociological dimension through Hacking's specifications

(1982) and Foucault's elaborations (1976). Truth (reasoned and correct judgment, criteria of inductive and deductive logic, etc.) is, according to Rabinow, '(. . .) dependent on a prior historical event – the emergence of a style of thinking about truth and falsity that established the conditions for entertaining a proposition as being capable of being taken as true or false in the first place' (p. 237). Truth is, in that sense, context-bound rather than context-free. Rabinow's argument is, of course, a version of the relativist position in the so-called rationality debate (see Hollis & Lukes 1982, Scholte 1984 or Wilson 1971) and it is unclear to me why Foucault rather than, say, Winch (1958) is singled out, though I suspect that Rabinow's affinity with 'Pop-Foucaultism' (Darnton 1986) may have had something to do with it. In any event, truth (including dialogue) '(. . .) is nothing more and nothing less than a historically locatable set of practices' (p. 239). If so, 'anarcho-rationalism' is the only viable position for the anthropologist (and philosopher) to take: '(. . .) tolerance for other people combined with the discipline of one's own standards of truth and reason' (p. 238). Such a position, in turn, entails a re-evaluation of our epistemology and a reassessment of our priorities: if epistemology is an historical and social event rather than an internal mirror reflecting an external reality, 'we should be attentive to our historical practice of projecting our cultural practices onto the other (. . .)' (p. 241). We should be reflexive and critical, that is, 'we need to anthropologize the West: show how exotic its constitution of reality has been (. . .)' (p. 241). Furthermore (and here Rabinow echoes a familiar theme), we 'must pluralize and diversify our approaches (. . .)' (p. 241).

Rabinow does not explicitly favor one approach to another nor does he formulate specific criteria for choosing between them, but he does suggest a possible reason for the literary turn's obsession with diverse narrative structures, multiple tropes, different rhetorics, heterogeneous allegories, etc. Perhaps the method in this madness is simply '(. . .) a tactic in the field of cultural politics to be understood primarily in sociological terms' (p. 242)! That, of course, is a very dramatic and indeed embarrassing possibility (one to which Marcus returns in his 'Afterword'); that the anthropologist's apparent concern with multiple ethnographic voices is actually, in the final analysis, a disguised concern with his or her own academic career! Bring on the ethnographic narratives; they assure the university jobs! The more 'pistache' the merrier; 'representations of others' representations' (p. 250) require representatives to represent the world's 'practitioners of textuality' (p. 250). But spinning textual tapestries inspired by native designs does not, of course, guarantee a moral center. In fact, the latter threatens to disappear from anthropological praxis altogether. And there is the rub.

Politics may become merely academic – literally so. Specifically, the politics of interpretation in the academy threatens to draw a 'cordon sanitaire' (p. 257) around the interpretation of politics in society. That, I would argue, is the greatest danger of symbolic anthropology and – by implication – its literary turn.

In his 'Afterword', Marcus stresses the literary turn's interest in demystification and experimentation. Perhaps he is right, though I obviously do not think that the demystification goes far enough and I also wonder if the experimentation isn't getting too precious. I think Marcus is entirely correct in further suggesting that the literary turn in contemporary anthropology may have something to do with professional credentials in both the field and in the academy. But then he should also have asked the next obvious question: could the literary turn itself be an ethnographic illustration of 'bourgeois chique'? (see Webster 1982, 1983, & 1986). If so, wouldn't the 'ironic mode' so popular among proponents of the literary turn be an appropriate vehicle for urgent self-reflection and judicious self-understanding? And wouldn't it be ironic, too, if we had to conclude that whereas cultural anthropology began as a literary genre among gentlemen-scholars in the South of England, its professional swan song is now being composed by gentlemen-scholars from the Southern United States?

---

* Review article. *Writing Culture: The Poetics and Politics of Ethnography*. James Clifford and George E. Marcus (eds.), Berkeley & Los Angeles, University of California Press, 1986.

References

Asad, T. 1979. 'Anthropology and the Analysis of Ideology'. In: *Man*, 14:607–627.
Bernstein, R.J. 1983. *Beyond Objectivism and Relativism: Science, Hermeneutics, and Practice*. Philadelphia: University of Pennsylvania Press.
Bourdieu, P. 1977. *Outline of a Theory of Practice*. Cambridge: Cambridge University Press.
Brady, I. (ed.). 1983. 'Speaking in the Name of the Real: Freeman and Mead on Samoa'. In: *American Anthropologist*, 85, 4:908–947.
Cesara, M. 1982. *Reflections of a Woman Anthropologist: No Hiding Place*. New York: Academic Press.
Clifford, J. 1980. 'Review Essay of Edward Said's Orientalism'. In: *History and Theory*, 19, 2:204–223.
———. 1983. 'On Ethnographic Authority'. In: *Representations*, 1, 2:118–146.
———. & G.E. Marcus (eds.). 1986. *Writing Culture: The Poetics and Politics of Ethnography*. Berkeley & Los Angeles: University of California Press.
Crapanzano, V. 1984. 'Life histories'. In: *American Anthropologist*, 86, 4:953–960.
Darnton, R. 1986. 'Pop Foucaultism'. In: *The New York Review of Books*, 33, 15:15–17.

Dolgin, J. L., D. S. Kemnitzer & D. M. Schneider (eds.). 1977. *Symbolic Anthropology: A Reader in the Study of Symbols and Meanings*. New York: Columbia University Press.

Fabian, J. 1983. *Time and the Other: How Anthropology Makes its Object*. New York: Columbia University Press.

Foucault, M. 1976. *The Archaeology of Knowledge*. New York: Harper & Row.

Geertz, C. 1975. 'On the Nature of Anthropological Understanding'. In: *American Scientist*, 63:47–53.

———— 1980. *Negara: The Theatre State in Nineteenth Century Bali*. Princeton: Princeton University Press.

Goody, J. 1977. *The Domestication of the Savage Mind*. Cambridge: Cambridge University Press.

Hacking, I. 1982. 'Language, Truth, and Reason'. In: R. Hollis & S. Lukes (eds.), *Rationality and Relativism*, pp. 48–66, Cambridge, MA: MIT Press.

Hollis, R. & S. Lukes (eds.). 1982. *Rationality and Relativism*. Cambridge, MA: MIT Press.

Holmes, R.B. de 1983. 'Shabono: Scandal or Superb Social Science?' In: *American Anthropologist*, 85, 3:664–668.

Hyman, S.E. 1962. *The Tangled Bank: Darwin, Marx, Frazer and Freud as Imaginative Writers*. New York: Atheneum.

Hymes, D. (ed.). 1972. *Reinventing Anthropology*. New York: Pantheon.

Karp, I. & K. Maynard 1983. 'Reading the Nuer'. In: *Current Anthropology*, 24, 4:481–503.

Keesing, R.M. 1987. 'Anthropology as Interpretive Quest'. In: *Current Anthropology*, 28, 2:161–176.

Kuhn, Th. S. 1970. *The Structure of Scientific Revolutions*. Chicago: University of Chicago Press.

Lakoff, G. & M. Johnson 1980. *Metaphors We Live By*. Chicago: University of Chicago Press.

Lemaire, T. 1984. 'Antropologie en schrift'. In: T. Lemaire (ed.), *Antropologie en Ideologie*, pp. 103–126. Groningen: Konstapel.

Lévi-Strauss, C. 1955. *Tristes Tropiques*. Paris: Plon.

———— 1963. 'Rousseau: The Father of Anthropology'. In: *Unesco Courrier*, 16:10–14.

Marcus, G. & J. Clifford 1985. 'The Making of Ethnographic Texts: A Preliminary Report'. In: *Current Anthropology*, 26, 2:267–271.

Marcus, G. & D. Cushman 1982. 'Ethnographies as Texts'. In: Bernard J. Siegel et al. (eds.), *Annual Review of Anthropology*, Volume II, pp. 25–69. Palo Alto: Annual Reviews Inc.

Marcus, G. & M. Fischer 1986. *Anthropology as Cultural Critique: An Experimental Moment in the Human Sciences*. Chicago: University of Chicago Press.

Ong, W.J. 1982. *Orality and Literacy*. New York: Methuen.

Pratt, M-L. 1986. 'Field-work in Common Places'. In J. Clifford and G. Marcus (eds.), *Writing Culture*, pp. 27–50, Berkeley and Los Angeles: University of California Press.

Prattis, J.I. 1985a. *Reflections: The Anthropological Muse*. Washington, D.C.: American Anthropological Association.

Prattis, J.I. 1985b. 'Anthropological Poetics: Reflections on a New Perspective'. In: *Dialectical Anthropology*, 10, 1–2:107–117.

Reiter, R. (ed.). 1975. *Toward an Anthropology of Women*. New York: Monthly Review Press.

Rorty, R. 1980. *Philosophy and the Mirror of Nature*. Oxford: Basil Blackwell.

Rose, D. 1983. 'In Search of Experience: The Anthropological Poetics of Stanley Diamond'. In: *American Anthropologist*, 85, 2:345–355.

Scholte, B. 1978a. 'Critical Anthropology since its Reinvention'. In: *Anthropology and Humanism Quarterly*, 3, 1–2:4–17.

———. 1978b. 'The Ethno-centricity of Scientific Logic'. In: *Dialectical Anthropology*, 3, 2:177–189.

———. 1983. 'Cultural Anthropology and the Paradigm Concept: A Brief History of their Recent Convergence'. In: L. Graham, W. Lepenies & P. Weingart (eds.), *The Sociology of Science Yearbook*, Volume VII. Dordrecht: Reidel.

———. 1984. 'Reason and Culture: The Universal and Particular Revisited'. In: *American Anthropologist*, 86, 4:960–965.

———. 1986. 'The Charmed Circle of Geertz's Hermeneutics: A Neo-Marxist Critique'. In: *Critique of Anthropology*, 6, 1:5–15.

———. (n.d.). 'Cultural Anthropology's Literary Turn: A Philosophical and Political Critique'. In preparation.

Shostak, M. 1981. *Nisa: The Life and Words of a !Kung Woman*. Cambridge, Mass: Harvard University Press.

Stocking, G.W. Jr. 1982. 'Anthropology in Crisis?: A View from between the Generations'. In: E.A. Hoebel, R. Currier & S. Kaiser (eds.), *Crisis in Anthropology: View from Spring Hill, 1980*. New York: Garland Publishing, Inc.

Turner, V. 1967. *The Forest of Symbols: Aspects of Ndembu Ritual*. Ithaca: Cornell University Press.

Webster, S. 1982. 'Dialogue and Fiction in Ethnography'. In: *Dialectical Anthropology*, 7, 2:91–114.

———. 1983. 'Ethnography as Storytelling'. In: *Dialectical Anthropology*, 8, 3:185–205.

———. 1986. 'Realism and Reification in the Ethnographic Genre'. In: *Critique of Anthropology*, 6, 1:39–62.

Wellmer, A. 1985. 'Reason, Utopia and the Dialectic of Enlightenment'. In: Richard J. Bernstein (ed.), *Habermas and Modernity*, pp. 35–66, Cambridge: Polity Press.

White, H. 1973. *Metahistory: The Historical Imagination in Nineteenth Century Europe*. Baltimore: The Johns Hopkins University Press.

Wilson, B.R. (ed.). 1971. *Rationality*. Oxford: Basil Blackwell.

Winch, P. 1958. *The Idea of a Social Science and its Relation to Philosophy*. London: Routledge & Kegan Paul.

Wolf, E.R. 1982. *Europe and the People Without History*. Berkeley & Los Angeles: University of California Press.

Chapter 9

STILL RAYTING: RESPONSE TO SCHOLTE

STEPHEN A. TYLER

I always enjoy arguing with my old friend Bob Scholte, and am grateful that his review of *Writing Culture* provides an opportunity to renew an old and agreeable dialogue. Bob is generally sympathetic to many of the themes in *Writing Culture*, but he faults the book for avoiding politics and praxis, for failing to confront the political realities that make the context of its own Mandarin concerns with literary effect. Why worry about the organization of discourse when that worry is only a superficial symptom of underlying causes located deep within the politics of contemporary Western culture? Isn't that worry really only a cowardly retreat into a feckless literary aestheticism, a kind of psychic displacement reflecting a refusal to acknowledge the painful practicalities of power that have changed forever the conditions of fieldwork, the economics of literary production, the enabling context of academic success, the funding of research and have shattered the epistemic foundations of science by deconstructing the bourgeois fairy tale of pure research, the advancement of knowledge, and the impartial, objective quest for truth? Doesn't all this concern with how to write ethnography really reflect the impossibility of ethnography as it was constituted under the aegis of bourgeois science?

Well Bob, I agree that anthropology, along with all the rest of our discourse, has lost its old and easy legitimacy, but isn't it also the revolution in readership that has precipitated this crisis in ethnographic consciousness? Capitalist production and the inexorable spread of literacy have transformed the ethnographic audience, and capitalist communication, with its power instantly to replay destruction, death, pestilence, perversity, and peculiarity, has universalized the prurient gaze of the detached ethnographer and usurped his role as prime purveyor of pornography. And, since the ethnographic other can read, she now presumes to criticize her characterization and to clamour for the right to represent herself. Pity the poor ethnographer! His audience and message captured, co-opted, and trivialized by television and contested by newly loquacious objects, is it any wonder that his mission and mode of expression should seem flawed and problematic? *Writing Culture* then, is not really about writing at all; it is about reading because that is the silence that makes its unspeakable meaning, the absence it seeks instead to hide, not as Bob avers, by concentrating on mere literary expression, but by taking refuge in just the kind of political contextualizing he thinks it has neglected.

Where Bob finds these essays unpolitical, or evasive in their politics, or unmindful of political contexts, they strike me as being excessively political, too trapped in the discourse of RAYT – of power, politics, reason, epistemology, praxis, critique, and normative import. Even their form of literary expression is unvaryingly conservative. Tricked out in archaic rhetorical strategies and tired structures of emplotment they confirm how we are expected to RAYT when we are RAYT or seek to RAYT some wrong. Where Bob would have us believe that this volume is concerned solely with RAYTING, in contrast to critical anthropology which is concerned with the more important issue of RAYTING, I think most of the papers, particularly those of Asad and Rabinow, are altogether too eager to contextualize RAYTING to RAYTING. To me, they still spin their tales cocooned by the security of representational discourse. Still unmetamorphosed, they do not burgeon into light, nor challenge the dark hegemony of politics and epistemology, but presuppose it even in the ironies that enshroud their purposes. Like Bob, they still want quarantees, guarantees, as he RAYTS, of 'a moral center' (p. 15) and 'a positive or desirable political consequence' (p. 11). Like Bob, they have an unhealthy hankering, not for the power of truth, but for the truth of power that sets folks RAYT.

Writing Culture is not post-modern; its authors neither invert the relationship between aesthetics and epistemology nor revolutionize the three-fold hierarchy of epistemology, politics, and aesthetics (in descending order of *hierarchic* precedence). Like Bob, they are willing *only* to promote politics, to contextualize science to power, to relativize epistemology to politics, but this politicization of discourse does not change or threaten the ancient Western idea of hierarchized discourses. Instead, it preserves the myth of a privileged discourse that founds or grounds all the others.

In contrast, post-modernism grants no priority to any discourse. It aims to deconstruct the divisions that give the illusion of separate, hierarchically ordered discourses. It does not attempt to enthrone aesthetics at the pinnacle of a new hierarchy, to resuscitate the failed aesthetic program of the Frankfurt school, as Bob implies. It is a way of using these discourses against themselves neither in order to re-hierarchize them nor even to overcome them, but to realize that parodic potential which is their fullest implication.

Who now believes that politics or science works any positive transformation? Anthropology, modern science, and history have all conspired to teach us to disavow this hubris of the modern age, and now we know that change is only change, and its teleology only entropy, an ever-retreating horizon di-solving with us. But that is where post-modernism opens out as a field of dispersed possibilities resisting both the semantic totalization of symbolic anthropology and the reductionism of the exhausted master narratives of the 19th century – the fairy tales of Darwin, Marx, Freud, and Einstein.

Then too, there is boredom. Who has not wearied of those complementary modes of demystification called symbolic anthropology and critical (read Marxist, economic, political, psychological, etc.) anthropology? Must we continue to oscillate between the tropological structures of time-as-space and time-as-flow, and endlessly repeat either the allegory of memory and prefigurative duration, of a time that is always an unreachable but repetitious past structured totally as a system of hermetic symbols, or the irony of a dialectic that mystifies the past and projects an unreachable future that always escapes final totalization in the clash of conflicting interests – until – by this prattling parabasis lulled into slumber, succumbed to the rhythm of their rupture and continuity we are succussed into some new succession RAYTING still?

PART VI
Working over History: Cultural Idealism and Materialism

The manner in which Captain Cook figured in colonial Hawaii, analysed in Sahlins' *Islands of History* (1985), prompted a spirited and well-known challenge by Obeyesekere (*The Apotheosis of Captain Cook*, 1992). This debate continues to spur discussion about the relationship between anthropology and history.

In the exchange here between Sahlins and Friedman the key dispute centres on charges and counter-charges of excessive idealism or materialism. While the specifics of Sahlins' explanation for the deification or apotheosis of Cook (as Lono) are the key issues, occasionally rising from the background is another and quite different discussion about the nature of the unit of analysis; in other words, whether the case of Hawaii is contained within its own culture-logic, or whether there is a larger system at work—a Pacific world system.

The argument between Sahlins and Friedman, an early proponent of world systems theory who has had a provocative influence on historical anthropology, reveals tensions not only in terms of formulating a convincing account of what drives a culture system (idealism versus materialism, at its most reduced), but also in terms of culture analysis based, fundamentally, on historical rather than ethnographic materials. Also noteworthy is the level of invective displayed, both in charge and counter-charge. Such, at times, ill-tempered exchange (of which the succeeding pieces by Wolf/Mintz and Taussig are similar examples) indicate the level of serious disagreement about and personal investment in the course of anthropological research and writing.

Chapter 10

No History Is an Island: An Exchange between Jonathan Friedman and Marshall Sahlins*

Jonathan Friedman

I. Introduction

In the past decade, anthropology has taken a turn toward history, just as history has become increasingly anthropological. The two disciplines have mutually influenced each other in a variety of ways. From the ethnographization of history that has gained much popularity in France, dividing time into mentalities, historical equivalents of anthropological cultures, to the world-system-oriented rewriting of the history of the ethnographic present, the proliferation of historical anthropologies must certainly be reckoned as one of the major developments in the social sciences during the last few years. Within this growing field, the work of Marshall Sahlins stands at the forefront. Sahlins's theoretical transmutations have, like Picasso's art, reflected the changing configurations in Western intellectual culture. From neo-evolutionism to social structuralism to cultural structuralism; from materialism to cultural determinism—these are the vectors of the age, from the modernist postwar progressivism of a future-oriented West to the fragmented postmodernism of a declining civilization in search of its cultural roots. Sahlins began his career as a materialist and an evolutionist. Today he has repudiated most of his earlier positions. From the late, and very Parisian 1960s when he discovered that social and political relations dominate production rather than the reverse, he has moved in *Culture and Practical Reason* to a position where culture does not merely mediate[1] between material conditions and social practice, but is the 'the very organization of material production.'[2] If Marx had once turned Hegel right side up or upside down—the direction is irrelevant—Sahlins has managed the trick on himself. Why this shift has occurred, and I do not think it can be seen as a simple theoretical development independent of the goings on of our shifting reality, cannot be discussed at present.[3] Our purpose here is to discuss its content and not its context. Sahlins's current merging of cultural determinism and history within a broadly structuralist approach represents a very significant theoretical development. He has referred to it as 'structural historical anthropology,'[4] and he and Valerio Valeri, also a specialist in things Hawaiian, have done much to argue for such an approach.

II. STRUCTURAL HISTORY AND HISTORICAL STRUCTURALISM

Islands of History is about the history of islands, about their cultures and the separate histories that they supposedly engender. The book contains a number of papers and articles, all of which have either appeared previously or have been presented publically. It can, in general, be said that this work represents a refinement and development of Sahlins's other recent work *Historical Metaphors and Mythical Realities* (1981) and that it concentrates on more specific aspects of the themes in *Historical Metaphors* as well as explicitly addressing itself to some of the major theoretical issues of that earlier work.

As I am to take issue with a number of positions assumed by Sahlins, I think it only fair and necessary to stress the overall importance of this book. In a period when interpretative and post-interpretative approaches appear to be supplanting anthropological theory, it is, to say the least, refreshing and important that Sahlins continues to develop a theoretical perspective on some of the most important fundamental problems in social anthropology. More than that, he has been largely responsible for lifting the historical and ethnographic materials of Oceania to new heights, making them susceptible to the great questions of anthropological discourse: the relation between historical process and cultural order, between social structure and cosmological models, between structure and practice, the nature and symbolic constitution of political power, the relation between exchange, power, and cannibalism. The essays of this book raise all the crucial issues and abound with thought-provoking insights.

Sahlins states his view and the major organizing theme of the book from the very first line.

> History is culturally ordered, differently so in different societies, according to meaningful schemes of things. The converse is also true: cultural schemes are historically ordered, since to a greater or lesser extent the meanings are revalued as they are practically enacted. (vii)

This statement recapitulates the conclusion of *Historical Metaphors* in which history is envisaged as a 'reciprocal movement between the practice of structure and the structure of practice.'[5] Now while there are plenty of hedges and very significant references to the limits of the notion of culture (vii), Sahlins does not develop the idea. If culture is only an interpretative scheme rather than a program, the notion of real historical process posited by Sahlins becomes itself no more than a *post hoc* interpretation. I don't think that Sahlins could possibly entertain such a notion of culture and have written as he has done, but it is worth reminding ourselves that such an ephemeralization of social structures, (perhaps its culturalization) is a hallmark of certain British structuralists who take categories and mental constructs as the essential realities. In other words, I shall be assuming for the duration of this discussion, at least, that culture is meant as code, program, system of semantic categories that are implemented in the actual performance of social life and are as such essentially generative while by implication interpretative, since the meaning that organizes the world is at once its significance.

III. THEORETICAL PRELIMINARIES

In many ways, *Islands of History* represents an attempt to work out the theoretical issues that have remained more or less implicit in previous historical structural work. It is, after all, no small effort to put history into the model of cultural determinism represented in *Culture and Practical Reason* (1976) where the world is divided into historical (hot) and structural (cold) cultures. If history is already a cultural mode, then it is necessarily subsumed by culture and cannot, of course, entertain a further, external relation to it. Sahlins is implicitly, at least, quite cognizant of the problem, that is, that there is some objective temporal order within which he situates his structures, one that contains the two worlds of Captain Cook and the Hawaiian King Kamehameha and which is the locus of historical performance. But, as I shall repeatedly attempt to show, the effort to put structures into history is continuously inverted by the need to absorb history into structure.

A. Clearing the Air

The introduction and the last chapter of *Islands of History* are concerted efforts to establish firmly a theoretical framework. The introduction begins with a broadside against world-system-influenced anthropology, which supposedly assumes that since traditional societies of the hinterland are often closely articulated with larger systemic process, they can possess no 'autonomous cultural logic' (viii). His point, well taken, that 'cultural change, externally induced yet indigenously orchestrated, has been going on for millennia' (viii), has not, as far as I know, been denied by more global-oriented anthropologists who have openly accentuated the active role played by historically specific projects in the integration of populations into the peripheries of world systems. It is also true that 'so-called dominated people' did harness European wealth to the 'reproduction and even the creative transformation of their own cultural order' (viii). It is perhaps the case that Captain Cook was assimilated to the god Lono.

But it is also the case that the Hawaiian aristocracy went into bankruptcy, whether or not they so conceived it, and that an entire population of perhaps three hundred thousand was decimated, not only by disease, but by the mysterious yet undeniable consequences of a collective death wish. It has been argued that cultural changes within the global system can and must be analyzed in transformational terms. The emergence of witchcraft and cannibalism in many parts of the colonized world in the nineteenth century, the transformation of a great many powerful African kingships into divine kingships of the castrated variety, the development of American Indian confederacies, the emergence of restricted exchange in areas previously characterized by generalized exchange, and so on, have all been the focus of a global anthropology.[6] But the epithets 'so-called dominated' and 'creative transformation' seem astonishingly misplaced when one considers to just what end such articulations have invariably led. The collapse of the *kapu* system and the disintegration of Hawaiian culture are 'creative transformations' resulting from the harnessing of European wealth to the reproduction of Hawaiian society. The global position is simply that the ethnographic present is largely the historical product of the interaction of local and global processes, one which in phases of the expansion of hegemonic centers results in the integrative transformation of hinterland societies. Whether this takes the form of externally propelled if internally structured transformation or the form of direct externally dominated reorganization, it ought to be quite evident that the hinterland is caught in the grips of a process that is largely beyond its control, and which, with all due respect to cultural variation, harbours a certain sinister finality. This, in turn, implies that there are properties of reality that are not included in the cultural scheme of things, not even in the structure of practice, but in the results and conditions of practice. A great deal of my argument centers on the stubborn failure to take such structures into account.

B. Cultural Dialectics

After expelling the nemesis of the world system, Sahlins is able to concentrate on the main dialectic, one that is quite neutral with respect to such systems, since 'history is made the same general way within a given society as it is between societies' (ix). This is the dialectic we have already heard about in *Historical Metaphors*, but greatly elaborated.[7] The issue is the incongruity in interaction between the cultural order 'as constituted in society and as lived by the people' (ix), between convention and action, between denotation and connotation. The reason for the lack of fit is that practice, the lived, has its own logic independent of the cultural order which is imposed upon it. Using the Saussurean metaphor, Sahlins argues that the issue can be conceptualized as a conflict between sense and reference, between the sign defined in relation to other signs and in its reference to a reality that contains more properties than those which are salient in the sign system itself. The world of reference is the world of context, of changing material and social realities, and of a specific distribution of categories of people in an organization of power. This world of practical interest is the source of the 'revaluation of signs,' the transformation of culture. But we are never told explicitly what it is that structures 'interests,' and what it is that structures power and other social relations. If culture organizes practice, then it must also presumably organize all the rest. This principle fatally penetrates that apparently practical sphere, the performative.

C. Performance and Prescription

Some structures are prescriptive, others performative. The former, mechanical models, assimilate events to structure. As opposed to such models, performative structures adapt themselves to events, using the vicissitudes of the life stream as ever new markers and distinctions in a 'structure' whose only 'stability is a volatile history of the changing fortunes of persons and groups' (xii). Is this a restatement of the structuralist distinction between 'hot' and 'cold,' or is there, perhaps, something of the 'lukewarm' about performative structures? We are never enlightened on this matter, but it may be assumed from Sahlins's application of the concept—to Polynesians, who have as much of an anthropological reputation as African kingdoms for evolutionary in-betweenness—that lukewarm, heroic history is the intended meaning. As we shall see, these performative structures are themselves deducible from the cultural program, albeit one different in its functioning from the usual cold, or here, 'prescriptive' (x) structures of the literature. We are presented, in any case, with the bold opposition of two major types of social action—'If friends make gifts, gifts make friends' (xi). At one level, at least, the difference 'parallels the Lévi-Straussian contrast of mechanical and statistical models' (xi).

> The problem centers on the relations between social forms and appropriate acts. I raise the possibility, which seems rarely considered, that such

186 · JONATHAN FRIEDMAN

relations are reversible: that customary kinds of acts can precipitate social forms as well as vice versa. (xi)

But this is a reversibility that is itself 'structurally motivated' (xi), and the end results would appear to be very similar, at least in the end, since in the case of performance, the emergence of structure is itself predetermined by the category structure into which it must necessarily be inscribed. Performatives, after all, are only effective because of a predisposition already present for or in the actors. What are we to make of this distinction? If performative structures are structured in the same way as prescriptive structures, then they are simply another kind of cultural recipe, programmed for change rather than stereotypic reproduction. If 'social system is thus constructed out of passion, structure out of sentiment' (29), this is simply because there is already a system in the passion and a structure in the sentiment.

D. Mythopraxis and Habitus

In similar fashion, the division between societies based on mythopraxis and those based on 'habitus' is reduced to different forms of the expression of structure. 'The issue is not the absence of structure, but its inscription in *habitus* as opposed to its objectification as mythopoetics' (53).

There is a common structure in these oppositions: structure versus practice, prescription versus performance, mythopractice versus *habitus*. It is the structure outlined in *Culture and Practical Reason* that opposes culture and practice and that insists that culture is everywhere determinant. These essays represent an application of cultural determinism to historical processes, an attempt to translate all forms of historical movement into an expression of culture as a 'model for' the production of reality. There is, in other words, nothing that is not culturally generated!

Sahlins's view seems to be that first, practice consists in the implementation of received cultural categories in empirical contexts whose properties are not deducible from the received categories and that therefore may channel both practice and the results of practice in novel directions that contradict the categories. Second, culture may be implemented by prescription, that is, by the direct application of rules, or by performance, whereby cultural categories are embedded in individual motives and desires. Third, culture may be implemented via the enactment of myth or via the inscription of structure in *habitus*. Performance is not equivalent to *habitus*, in spite of its superficial similarity, since Hawaii itself offers the principal example of a mythopoetical performative culture. But a paradox immediately emerges here. For if Hawaiian practice is the willed recapitulation of the cosmogony, what is the means by which this is carried out in a nonprescriptive mode? If the ancient Hawaiians engaged in a mythopractice that did not explicitly involve the reproduction of a cosmological model, then they can only have carried it out by means of more specific individual interests, competition, and warfare, that externally reproduced the cosmological model, that is, implicitly. But this would necessarily involve something on the order of *habitus*, which, in turn, implies that mythopraxis can be equivalent to its opposite. The confusion comes about because of the totalitarian nature of cultural determinism. It stands to reason, after all, that if everything is generated by a cultural code, prescription and performance, mythopractice and *habitus*, are merely different ways of realizing the same culture in practice. In the old paradigm of 'culture of' and 'culture for', Sahlins would appear to opt for the latter, and in such a big way that 'culture of' is no more than a reflex of 'culture for.' There is, thus, a contradiction between a realization of the lack of fit between empirical historical process and abstracted cultural schemes, and the necessity of subsuming the former by the latter.

Even if the most volatile of histories can be reduced to a cultural program, there remains an exterior realm where culture is practiced in conditions that are not of its own choosing. Sahlins calls this the 'structure of the conjuncture': 'the practical realization of the cultural categories in a specific historical context, as expressed in the interested action of historic agents, including the microsociology of their interaction' (xiv). This is the realm in which the cultural categories are subject to symbolic risk and revaluation. But this place where culture is played out, which has 'reasons and forces of its own, apart from any given symbolic scheme' (xiv), is apparently not worthy of investigation or perhaps it is simply impossible to approach. What are such 'reasons' and 'interests' and to what do they owe their origin? In the present work, in any case, they do not merit the status of structure, but simply event: that which is exterior to culture. On the other hand, the closer we get to the event, the more cultural it becomes. That which gives the world form is culture. All the rest appears ephemeral, except insofar as it is imprinted by culture. Sahlins's dialectic movement between the practice of structure and the structure of practice is, in spite of claims to the contrary,[8] always presentable as a dialectical movement between cultures, that is, as culture contact. The only other conceivable externality upon which to practice culture is nature itself, in its pure materiality. While Sahlins does not indulge in such conjunctures,[9] it is worth recalling the similarity between this general framework and some earlier versions of structuralist Marxism that employed the notion of a dialectic between social form and material and/or social conditions of existence, a model of transformation via the process of social reproduction.

As the cultural dialectic is the core of Sahlins's approach, informing virtually all of the essays in this volume, we shall return to it several times in more concrete circumstances, saving a fuller discussion for the conclusion.

IV. CULTURAL ISLANDS IN A SEA OF HISTORY

Sahlins's power has always resided in his capacity to discover structure where no one suspected it. The essays in this book reveal a profundity of insight that is afforded by a truly structuralist approach. Sahlins is one of the few who has mastered the method and brought us to new worlds of understanding. The Pacific, in any case, will never be the same. If it is possible to differ on points of theory and analysis, this is thanks to the splendid clarity achieved in these texts. Much of the argument that follows will revolve around my conviction that structuralism cannot be extended to the realm of history any more than it can be imprisoned within the realm of culture. Lévi-Strauss's stringent limitations on the applicability of the concept of structure imply that the field of social reality contains structures but is not reducible to them. The 'order of orders' is not a structuralist kind of structure, nor is history, even if structuralist kinds of phenomena occur within historical processes. Sahlins's strength lies in his discovery of structures, his weakness in their combined overextension and cultural reductionism.

V. LE SEXY SAUVAGE OU LE MONDE À L'ENVERS

Chapter one, 'Supplement to the Voyage of Cook, or, *le calcul sauvage*' is about sex in ancient Hawaii. We are introduced here to the formidable corpus of Hawaiian love poetry, and to the numerous amorous incidents that brought British seamen and Hawaiian women into a relationship pregnant with the overthrow of the ancient order. Numerous phenomena are to be accounted for: the clear attraction of Hawaiian women to Captain Cook's men, the seeming importance of sexual relations in Hawaiian cosmology, the relation between male sexual prowess and political power. The unified hypothesis that is meant to connect all of this is that 'the structure of the kingdom is the sublimated form of its forces of sexual attraction.' Sexuality is not mere superstructure, then, for 'this is a political economy of love. Love is the infrastructure' (19).

What is meant by all of this? To begin with, the Hawaiian cosmogony is composed of a lengthy series of celestial unions, principal among which is that between sky, *Wakea*, and earth, *Papa*. The universe is truly united in a great genealogical network linking the original 'darkness' with inorganic, organic, and human nature by means of a metaphor of sexual reproduction. Now there is nothing particularly unusual about this kind of representation of the cosmos. But there is more to it, for many of the stories tell not merely of genealogy and reproduction as such, but of the exploits of beautiful heroes, often younger brothers and sons, even bastards, who by their superior personal qualities steal both kingdoms and women of rank from their elder rightful heirs.

It is no secret that fertility, wealth, and prosperity—the principal symbolic constituents of chiefly power—are universal phenomena in so-called theocratic chiefdoms and states, 'asiatic' states, and even more recently 'discovered' 'theater' states.[10] The 'fertility principle' so to speak is a property of stability, the legitimate authority of the priest-chief. But here that fertility is instead linked to physical prowess and political cunning, to beauty and a kind of Nietzschean aesthetic of power. But then ancient Hawaii is no peaceful theocracy, no Friendly Island. Political practice consists here in a cycle of conquest and consolidation followed by new wars of succession and conquest. The main theme is usurpation, the domination of the forces of war over those of fertility. The social structure is characterized by continual manipulation of marital alliances, 'incest and exogamy, hypergamy, and hypogamy' (22) in the great play for political and military advantage, and which is generative of an unstable web of cognatic kinship.

In all the turmoil there is no sign of anything like a corporate kin group. Commoner families are organized into political-territorial units defined by their dependency upon a rather temporary hierarchy of chiefs. It stands to reason that in this sort of a situation, marital alliances are essential acts, not only of political consolidation, but of political survival. *Marrying up* is the solution for those of low rank; 'finding a lord' procreates offspring of higher rank. It might be disputed that 'marriage' is the wrong word here, but the social recognition of the rank and connections of the children is all that is necessary. More important is the 'heroic' strategy whereby powerful youth overthrow their political seniors and both consolidate and legitimate their newly won positions by means of marriage to sacred women of senior lineages. 'We can see why Hawaiians are so interested in sex. Sex was everything; rank, power, land, and the security of all these' (26).

And of course, this applies as well to relations to Europeans, especially when they arrive in impressive ships with powerful weapons. Hypergamy again is a way of capturing the power inherent in higher rank, a way of transferring *mana*, but also its obvious manifestations in the form of wealth and military support. There is nothing particularly astonishing about this kind of phenomenon, even if, according to some very unsystematic observations by members of Captain Cook's crew, it was more intense and less mercenary than in other parts of Oceania.[11]

What are we to make of a discussion that places sexuality at the pivot of a social strategy, but then proceeds to demonstrate that this is because of the particular configuration linking the meaning of sex and fertility to the constitution of political power? Is it to provide another case study in performative structure that is 'able to reproduce a received cultural order through the free pursuit of happiness . . . by the contingencies of sexual attraction' (29)? We are presented with a large number of cases and texts in which sexual relations figure importantly, as symbols and as strategies. All of these, when analyzed by Sahlins, can be resolved into statements about the relation between fertility and power. They display the importance of biologically reproductive strategies in the accumulation of status, and the symbolic significance of the combined heroic qualities of beauty and prowess in a very competitive aristocracy. Ultimately we might expect to read something about the social foundations of these phenomena. But not so! Instead we are led in the opposite direction—toward a revival of Benedict's cultural patterns. 'As a "pattern of culture" it seems worthy of comparison with the militarism of Sioux Indians or the quietism of the Hopi—dare one place an "Aphrodisian" alongside the famous "Dionysian" and "Apollonian"?' (9). One may rightly wonder whether or not the author has been seduced by the current Geertzian fad of peddling otherness as *objet d' art*. But, of course, culturalism can easily fall prey to the 'merchants of astonishment' syndrome that has become so popular in American anthropology.[12] Whatever the case, and Sahlins, certainly, cannot be accused of the same flashy kind of narcissism that crowds all the insight out of Geertz, there is a clear pattern here. So as not to assure ourselves that this is a special case, Sahlins provides us with a consistent picture of what the performance of culturalism does to reality. After his Aphrodisian suggestions he immediately continues, 'Beyond that, the Hawaiian order is appropriately placed in that whole family of cultures, including our own, which prefer to sediment structural relations out of pragmatic actions, rather than determining the actions *a priori* from the relations' (9). What I find disappointing in all of this is that the brilliant insights into the workings of Hawaiian social life seem to be cast out, or rather recast in a cultural mold that simply reifies the original descriptions instead of getting to the heart of the matter. Rather than building on the relations between fertility, beauty, sexuality, and power that he discovers, he glosses them all into a presumed cultural paradigm ordered by sex. But we know, and he certainly knows, that sex is not infrastructure any more than warfare and tribute-taking are superstructure. And what are we to make of the crucial insight that whereas 'many Oceanic societies thus employ the aesthetic at the boundaries of the moral . . . beyond the control of kinship . . . In Hawaii, beauty is placed as it were at the center of society, as a main principle of its organization' (17)? From the point of view of culture it is merely a question of difference, of alternative ways of doing things. But from a truly structuralist perspective, there is an intricate nexus of determination to be grasped, a logic of transformation that might *account* for difference. Could it not be that a social process that constantly disturbs the stability of kinship, political and exchange structures in an anarchic struggle for a power defined by peaceful growth and god-given fertility, is likely to produce a symbolism of heroic potency, and that this situation is not just a cultural model but something that happened historically in Polynesia as elsewhere?

VI. THE MYTH OF MYTHOPRAXIS

Both Chapter 4, 'Captain Cook, or the Dying God,' and Chapter 2 deal with questions of mythopraxis. The former is a recapitulation and deepening of *Historical Metaphors* which tries more explicitly to link the confrontation between Cook and Hawaii to the structure of myth, by laying bare the correlation between specific historical events and analogous mythical episodes. But Chapter 2, 'Other Times, Other Customs: The Anthropology of History' (previously published as the Distinguished Lecture of the American Anthropological Association [1983]), is more explicitly central to the present collection. It establishes the culturalist theory of history. He begins by inviting us to consider the debate between so-called elitist versus popular history, and suggesting that the movement from the former to the latter is itself historical. 'We should recall that the passage from an elite to a more collective consciousness actually occurred in the history of Western society, as a difference in real-historical practice' (33).

We might ask here, as we shall continue to ask, what is the nature of this change in historical consciousness? Is it also the product of a specific Western culture? And if such is the case, what then of the discourse that we produce about such history and other histories? While Sahlins's own discourse is resolutely objectivist, assuming that these other histories can be understood from the outside, so to speak, it is not at all clear just where this outside is located, since at the same time it is claimed that there is no place that is not inside some culture or other. In other words, in writing about other histories as produced by other cultures in a world that is made up of nothing but culture, our own discourse about them can be nothing other than an expression of our own culture. This solipsism generated by culturalism forces us to consider the possibility that our notions of *their* heroic history are part of our own culture but not theirs.

Heroic history is the characteristic practice of a certain kind of society, hierarchical in form and inhabited by the divine, so that the action of the chief or king is simultaneously the history of the society and the recapitulation of the cosmogony. 'The chief's marriages are intertribal alliances; his ceremonial exchanges trade' (35). Thus the history of the introduction of Christianity is the story of the conversion of paramounts, followed by their subjects. The story of their wars is that of the conflicts of their chiefs. And the conversion of one chief of Mbau is the history of a total social fact in which Christianity meant success in war. The logic, of course, is common to a great many societies organized on theocratic lines. If wealth and fertility and power are divine functions, whoever possesses the former most certainly possesses the latter. Any god who can produce a better cannon is surely a more divine being. Similarly, the death of the king is a cosmic crisis that can easily cause successful armies to disband. History here is genealogy rather than chronology and the microhistory of the individual or the local group takes its temporal reference from the deeds of the sovereign. Finally the entire concrete history of a particular time period is always the expression of an ultimate cosmological drama.

A. Heroic History

From the cosmogony, through the chiefly genealogies, heroic history offers an already constituted field for the interpretation of social practice. The question is whether it is the source of social practice as well. There is a certain ambivalence here. From Sahlins's earlier work on Hawaii[13] it would appear that the Hawaiian confrontation with Captain Cook and his crew consisted in incorporating them into their cultural categories and then proceeding to treat them as participants in a scenario pre-inscribed in the Hawaiian cosmogony. Everything would have worked perfectly if the English had not had their own script. Similarly, 'For Maori, ontogeny recapitulates cosmogony' (59).

Here we are introduced to the story of Hono Heke, the Maori warrior whose rebellion against British colonization took its scenario from an origin myth. The myth tells the story of Tane, younger brother of the gods, who by 'an act likened to parricide' (60) separated Sky Father from Earth Mother, and propped up the sky with four poles, thus making it possible for his human descendants to take possession of Earth, descendants who themselves are the progeny of Tane's intercourse with his Mother Earth. This myth is explicitly connected to all acts of conquest, and the occupation of territory by the setting up of an enclosure containing one or more poles symbolizing claims to tribal lands. Thus, when the British colonists set up the flag, or more specifically, the flag pole, at their settlement, they could be understood as new conquerors from overseas, just as were the Maori themselves in a previous epoch. Now this was, of course, the case, and the ensuing battle of the flagpole is not nearly as exotic as it might appear in the text. The cultural clincher in the discussion occurs in a specific battle where a group of Maori attack the British settlement as a decoy enabling Hono Heke and a small band to mount the hill above the settlement to once more cut down the mythical flagpole.

What is implied here is that for the Maori, the flagpole is identical with their own poles, and thus signified that '"their country had gone from them"' (62). The English, of course, very obligingly set up a new flagpole every time one was cut down. Whether their action is to be conceived similarly as a case of mythopraxis or as something more mundane is not clear from the facts of the case. And if the English had seen through the Maori cultural scheme, and forgot about the flag altogether, would this have made their colonization unproblematic? It is true, of course, that the English flag is not part of an elaborate cosmology linking the origin of the world with current politics, but the symbolic raising of the colors, as a claim on territory, a claim to sovereignty, was quite sufficient for Maori mythical consumption. In this respect it might be argued that the Maori rebels must also have been acting symbolically with respect to the Union Jack. For the myth of chiefly conquest of the original people of the land also connects the setting up of the fenced altar, *tuahu*, containing the upright poles embodying the *mana* of the land. In light of the relation demonstrated by Sahlins between the poles and the act of occupation, it does not seem possible that the flagpole was the only thing that Hono Heke cared about.

B. Questions of Method

If we take mythopraxis to mean the actualization of the cosmology in human life, so that 'social structure is the humanized form of cosmic order' (58), a relation between the script and the performance, then I think it is safe to say that the concept is *identical* to simple cultural determinism. It is Durkheim inverted, for whom cosmic order was the sacred expression of social structure. In either case there is a serious reductionism, one that empties the dependent term of the equation of all properties. The problem can be stated simply: Are there any societies whose members act out their origin myths? It is commonly assumed that ritual action is an organization of action by means of a mythical scheme. But there is more to social life than ritual. Mythopraxis would appear to be ritual writ large, as the entirety of social activity. In other words, mythopoetical societies are literally texts in action. In this they can be and are opposed to a cultural order characterized by *habitus*, a term used by Bourdieu to highlight the structured nature of social practice, not merely in so-called individualist societies, but in any social formation.[14] The concept represents an attempt to transcend rule reductionist models of human action that pervade both functionalist and structuralist literature. Even if it might be argued that the concept of *habitus* fails to overcome the structuralist impasse, insofar as it reinstates structure as a principle that generates action, Bourdieu does make it quite clear that social practice, which is always an *individual* practice, does not consist in *the application* of rules or cultural schemes, but in the 'intentionless invention of regulated improvisation'[15] in a social field that provides the conditions of existence of a given structure of practice over time. Sahlins, however, not content with the *absolutely generalist* argument made by Bourdieu, remodels it to fit into his culturalist scheme. In a series of interpretative remarks *habitus* is presented as culture as 'lived.'

> Their lives are run on an unconscious mastery of the system, something like Everyman's control of the grammatical categories, together with the homespun concepts of the good that allow them to improvise daily activities on the level of the pragmatic and matter-of-fact. (51)

The association of *habitus* with what can only be interpreted as linguistic competence is not, I think, what Bourdieu has in mind, especially in light of his critique of modern linguistics as an archetype of rule reductionism.[16] After all, the notion of an 'unconscious mastery of the system' is not significantly different from the cognitivist reduction of culture to grammar. In Sahlins's interpretation, mythopraxis and *habitus* are merely two expressions of the same cultural determinism.

> Here is a main distinction of structures, crosscutting the others to which I alluded: between those that are practiced primarily through the individual subconscious and those that explicitly organize historical action as the projection of mythical relations.

Culture can either be 'inscribed' directly in unconscious motivations, or objectified in an explicit system of rules. For Bourdieu, of course, culture is not *inscribed*, but representational schemes are produced and reproduced on the basis of the emergent social forms that crystallize for longer or shorter periods into structures of *habitus*. And the emergence of structures is beyond culture as such. Bourdieu might even be criticized for the opposite of cultural determinism, since he conceives of a realm of pure practice, in which culture is merely an instrument, a symbolic capital in a struggle for power.

Now if Bourdieu can be made to stand on his head with such ease, what then of the Maori, the Fijians, the Hawaiians? Let me make a few suggestions here. Mythopraxis is best conceived not as a generative scheme, but as an interpretative or definition space within which practice finds its meaning. Social practice is organized around currently meaningful situations and strategies, all of which are defined in terms of a context of contemporary social relations. The fact that a usurper of the throne can find a mythical significance to his activities in an origin myth does not detract from the fact that the immediate content of his strategy and the definition of the social situation in which he finds himself may be quite unlike that described or supposed by the myth. Even if the situation is comparable, this could very well signify that the repetition of the cosmogony is rooted in a continuity in social structure rather than in the attempt to carry out an identical program. In a system where the categories of social relation are identical with those of the cosmology, social praxis always finds its immediate meaning in the cosmic order, which does not necessarily imply that the latter determines the former. Mythopraxis is, thus, a modern myth, a product of a culturalist bias that assumes by definition that the categories of social practice are an imprint, an inscription of a system of representations. In the example of Hono Heke, we might suggest the following internal logic:

1. For the Maori, the British flagpole is a sign of a claim to territory.
2. The Maori have nothing against British settlement as such, since it brings prestige-goods, weapons that are highly valued by those who are able to obtain them in their own social relations.
3. Hono Heke rebels against the claim to sovereignty by the British but not to their presence. Hence, his focus on the flagpole itself rather than in the British presence in general.
4. The Maori rebel interpretation is supported by the reaction of the colonists who stubbornly resurrect the pole each time it is cut down, thus demonstrating their claims to more than the right merely to be present.

Now all of this can be referred back to an original myth which supplies a larger cosmological rationale for the Maori struggle, but which is not its cause. The fact that the rationale is constantly invoked by the Maori says more about the congruence between their practice and the myth than about the ultimate cause of their behaviour.

The same kind of argument might be made for the death of Captain Cook. Was the broken mast of his ship and the return to his hosts a mythical threat to the Hawaiians, in the sense that the god Lono had decided to reconquer Hawaii, or did he mess up an entire ritual protocol upon which the chiefs depended? We can never know what the motives of the Hawaiians were at this point since there is no direct report. What we do know is that Cook's crew was asked to leave so that the Makahiki ritual could be closed and that their return was not relished. But we also know that Cook's usual procedure of kidnap-the-chief-when-the-going-gets-rough was the immediate cause of his death. In other words, there is reason enough on the Western side to account for Cook's death without having recourse to the inevitability of a mythical scenario, even if the latter provided the explicit and immediately given interpretation of the outcome.

Our claim, then, is that mythopraxis is itself a myth, one that results from the conflation of an interpretative scheme with a plan of action, of historical text with historical action. The only way that mythopraxis can be saved is by demonstrating that it is somehow equivalent to a social movement,[17] a project that has become the core of a group's identity, organizing its historical action in terms of an explicit model aimed at the transformation of reality, a ritual become historical. Now while there might be certainly some truth to this, there is little in the historical material that would indicate that it is the case, and Sahlins has not seen fit to take up the problem in such terms.

VII. STRUCTURALISM AND SOVEREIGNTY

'The Stranger King: or, Dumézil among the Fijians' is a broadly comparative essay on the nature of chiefly and royal power. Its argument is a development of some of the relatively unknown theses that have emerged in the work of Luc de Heusch during the last two decades, on the nature of the appearance of state power in kinship based society.[18] While there is certainly a tradition here, stretching back to Hocart and Frazer and including the seminal work of Dumézil on the symbolism of kingship among the Indo-Europeans, de Heusch is the first to attempt a structuralist synthesis of the relations linking kinship organization, the definition of incest, and the symbolism of power.

Sahlins invokes, as does de Heusch,[19] the political philosophy of the late Pierre Clastres, to the effect that the state is a foreign body that had to be imposed upon society. The origin of power is seen as an act of violence and of the transgression of the rules of the kinship order. For Clastres this is a problem of world historical proportions, one that is not bound to culturally specific symbolic configurations. And Sahlins, in spite of his theoretical cultural relativism, adheres, in this case, to a classic structuralist universalism.[20]

He is not so concerned with Clastres's 'controversial thesis of populist resentment' (76), as with the structure of state power that it identifies:

> The political dimensions of the structure in question, the ideology of external domination and social usurpation, are well known to anthropological

studies of archaic states and proto-states. The famous work of Sir James Frazer and A.M. Hocart on divine kingship document a worldwide distribution of the same basic scheme of power, from the Fiji Islands and the Americas through India and the classical world. (77)

This essay carries on the discussion embarked upon by de Heusch, Adler, and other 'neo-Frazerians.' The latter opposed the supposed ethnocentrism and functionalism of the political conflict school represented by Evans-Pritchard, whom they have criticized for reducing divine kingship to a mere ideological expression of power politics in lineage society.[21] Divine kingship is seen here as a symbolic structure of power that can be understood entirely in terms of its internal properties. The king is a stranger who comes from another country, from overseas. He is a warrior whose function is to usurp the kingship from its legitimate heirs, the autochthons, 'original people of the land.' He is a transgressor of sacred tabus, associated with both incest and cannibalism. He represents politics, violence, war, and destruction as opposed to peace, the sacred, and fertility. He is as male is to female. The relation between the king and the indigenous people takes the form of an alliance between the foreign man and a daughter of the ranking elder lineage of the people. A certain dualism inheres in this relation, one that opposes political chief to religious chief, younger to elder, wife-taker to wife-giver, mother's brother to sister's son.

Traces of this scheme of things can be found throughout the history and ethnography of the world, from the myth of the founding of Rome or the dualism of *Mitra-Varuna*[22] to the royal rituals of Central and South Africa. These traces, are, of course, embedded in different contexts, some of which would significantly alter the commonalities of the universal scheme that Sahlins underlines. Dumézil himself located the dualism of sovereignty within the famous tripartite scheme that he thought was peculiarly Indo-European. While it is certainly true that the mythology of the Indo-Europeans contains a great deal of the kind of dualism that is common to both Fiji and Central Africa, the social distributions of political authority are quite different insofar as in the latter two cases, a dualism of male/female, fertility/warfare, autochthons (land people)/invaders (sea people), wife-givers/wife-takers provides the *global symbolic structure* of a polity that is divided into three in Dumézil's scheme.

Sahlins's insightful discussion of the diarchic myths of the foundation of Greek and Roman kingdoms raises important questions since these myths display such strong resemblances to their Oceanic and African counterparts. The various myths of the foundation of Rome recount the often violent establishment of dual sovereignty between invading warriors and local agricultural people (for example, the Latins) cemented by the gift of women from the latter to the former. Similarly, it might be argued that the Indian pair *Mitra-Varuna*, representing the same kind of division of power between violence and peace, politics and ritual, expresses a comparable dualist definition of the state. But such myths are not incorporated into the social organizations of India and Rome in the same way as they are in Fiji. They might indeed refer to an earlier social structure, and Dumézil himself suggests a former 'couple *raj-brahman*.'[23] But in the historic material, *Mitra-Varuna* form a unity and are both associated with the priestly class, in opposition to the kings, whose authority is secular and whose god, *Indra*, while replicating many of the warlike traits of *Varuna*, is of absolutely inferior status. While one might wish to argue that an original Indo-European social and cultural system similar to those of Polynesia, Africa, and perhaps the rest of the world may someday come to light, it is quite clear that the Indo-European universe from which Dumézil gathers his data, while containing elements comparable to the Fijian case, is as different as is dualist from tripartist cosmology and divine kingship from *brahmannical* rule.[24]

The analysis of Fijian kingship is developed from the major works of Hocart on the subject.[25] The archetypal Eastern Fijian chief or king is supposed to be a fair-skinned stranger who arrives on a shark and is taken in by a local chief whose daughter he marries, engendering in this way the future line of paramounts. In the report of a chiefly installation, the successor arrives by sea and is led along the path of bark cloth, the 'path of the god' (85). He is symbolically put to death by his hosts by means of kava. The 'sea chief' is thus captured by the indigenous people of the land and converted into a paramount via his submission. The paramount represents the foreign patriline, wife-taker to the people, and, consequently, their sister's son as well. 'The line of conquering chiefs becomes the sister's sons of the conquered people' (8).[26] Thus the duality and the ambiguity of chiefly identity, descendent in the patriline of the invader warriors, and descendent in the matriline of the fertility gods of the land, lays the ground for the transformation that characterizes the Fijian variations on sacred kingship. Sahlins posits two transformations that define a final base structure of sovereignty. The first inverts the initial relation between warrior and priest: In the ritual of installation, the chief, 'brought from the periphery of society to the center' is now 'marked off by sacred *tabus* . . . where he "just sits"' while 'the ancient inhabitants become his war dogs' (87). The domestication of the warrior provokes the inversion of the original structure. While it is easy to get the impression from Sahlins's discussion that there is only one chief, embodying two opposing principles, it is quite clear from Hocart that diarchy is prevalent in the Lau Islands, and while the Northern States display triadic forms, these are all reducible to transformations of dual power that he links to the dislocations of nineteenth-century warfare. The basic model is one in which there are two ruling lines, chiefs of the land and chiefs of the sea at every segmentary level, that maintains several different variants of alliance and succession, all of which are compromises between elementary structures of kinship and a shifting balance of power. There are also notable variations in the symbolic configurations of the chiefship, from a simple ritual/political dualism to complex divisions of functions and inversions of signs.

But Sahlins, in his Hegelian fascination with the number three, pursues his dialectic of duality through a final permutation in his attempt to show that 'The logic of the whole lies in the generative development of the categories, by which alone may be motivated all static and partial expressions of it' (103). The conjunction of sea and land, chief and people, produces a synthesis, 'the sovereign power.' 'The fully constituted global structure is a tripartite pyramidal scheme, composed of the same three functions Dumézil determines for Indo-European civilizations, if not exactly in the same arrangement' (99). In this final fusion, the chief comes to represent both male and female and all the other opposed principles of the diarchy. His immobilization introduces the necessity for a third part, a new 'sea people' who can carry out the function of warfare that the chief has relinquished. But what and where is this necessity? Have we not just been informed that the land people have become the sacred chief's 'war dogs'? While it is true that an opposition between people of the land and the nobility is a common representation, there are invariably chiefs of both land and sea. And unless the data are severely misleading, single paramounts would appear to be singularly rare occurrences, molten products of the heat of war. Now the heat of war is certainly a feature of mid-nineteenth-century Fiji, but it too is reduced to a *cultural* force in Sahlins's discussion.

A. Cannibalism as Will and Idea

The origin of the chief, we recall, was the warrior, who in this case turns out to be more violent than at first assumed. For he is a man-eater! Whether this is an extended metaphor on the definition of power as eating or something very much more specific is not as important as the fact that in the period formative of our image of traditional society, cannibalism was rife, a principle constituent of Fijian warfare. Most interesting here is the way in which cannibal victims figure in the exchange relations among chief and people. If the triadic structure suggested by Sahlins consists of a flow of wives from land people to chief to sea people, there is, apparently, a distinct flow of cannibal victims in the opposite direction. Now there is a significant and, as far as I know, little investigated relation between the symbolic constitution of exchange and tribute, sacrifice and cannibalism, such that cannibal victims are prestige-goods of last resort, often figuring in origin myths of exchange and tribute. But the chain of symbolic substitutes does not account, except purely intellectually, for the actual practice of systematic cannibalism.[27]

Sahlins posits this tripartite cannibalistic structure as the ultimate Fijian model, a deep structure.[28] But is this not an exaggeration of culture? In the ordinary dualistic representation of Fijian chiefdoms, the 'face of the land' is opposed the 'edge of the land,' as inner is to outer, land to sea, chief to *sau* (second chief). The dual relation is that which is dominant, no matter how many titles there are. Hocart is quite explicit about the fact that Northern Fiji is characterized by a dualism overlaid by a triadic structure, but one which is brought about by dichotomization rather than by a Dumézilian trichotomization of functions. The dual division between the immobile chief and the active warrior, between peace and war, fertility and destruction is reproduced on all segmentary levels—thus the equivalence of the oppositions, divine king (sea)/war king (land), people of the land (peace)/people of the sea (war). The triad, divine king (sea)/warrior king (land)/people of the land is of course, simply a double dichotomy, as Sahlins has himself remarked;[29] in spite of the ambivalent relation between sacred chiefs and war chiefs, the opposition sea/land is continuously replicated in the polarities of political and ritual power and nobility and people.[30] This is equally true of Sahlins's example of sea chief/land chief/sea warriors, where the latter opposition is reducible to the couple chiefs (land)/warriors (sea).

I don't wish to appear fanatical about dualism here, and I certainly would not argue that it is a question of the social expression of mental principles, as Needham does.[31] On the contrary, I have suggested that the asymmetric and ambivalent dualism of Fijian and even Tongan diarchic forms is related to the nature of hierarchic generalized exchange that plays such an important role in the political organization of these societies.[32] The wife-taker/wife-giver asymmetry that founds the diarchy and, in the case of male mobility, splits the local group into a female-indigenous side and a male-foreign side, defines the necessary relation between generalized exchange and dualism. The hierarchy, of course, favors concentric tendencies, and it is here that the magic triad is always immanent.[33] In other words, turning two into three is not called for by the mechanisms involved. And the mechanisms themselves would appear to be more historical than cultural. The dislocations that multiply the oppositions seem to lie in the external realm of nineteenth-century military conflicts. The stories of shifting alliances, nobility on the run, and the elimination of divine kings and their clans may be culturally organized, but certainly not culturally determined, not the mere working out of the temporal structure of the self-determining code.

B. The Logic of Culture and the Logic of Practice

It is worth elaborating on this problem by way of some parallels. First consider the logic of the domestication of the foreign king. The king moves from periphery to center. He is poisoned and reborn as a god of the land. His violent essence is thus pacified and he, immobilized. This implies a necessary inversion whereby sea chiefs take on the function of feasting, wealth, and fertility while land chiefs take on the functions of war. But this is only one of an array of possibilities. Sea chiefs might well remain war chiefs in a balanced relation to the chiefs of the land. They might combine the elements of divine kingship and political supremacy, while the priest chief functions more as a combination of religious representative of the land, prime minister under the king, and interregnum regent. The indigenous chief might function as the divine ruler leaving the political functions to the stranger king. An historical example from Central Africa sheds some light on the universal variations I have in mind. The Kongo kingdom at the time of European contact shows striking similarities to Fiji, even though its scale is far greater, perhaps on the order of Tonga. It has a diarchic structure, represented as the conquest of the indigenous people of the land by a foreign group of men whose leader is unable to take power until the indigenous king bestows the sacred relics of the land upon him. The king, represented as a beautiful younger son, a conqueror, is ritually defeated by the priest-chief of the land, his elder, as a central part of the coronation. He is also, traditionally, wife-taker to the indigenous people.[34] At contact, the king would appear to be a very powerful and active personage, directly involved in all three political affairs. The priest chief functions as *chef de terre*, royal proxy and interregnum regent. The divinity of the king is not in question, but it is associated with activity rather than passivity. In the fifteenth and sixteenth centuries, at least, there would seem to be a rather clear balance of power between the two sides of the diarchy. But two centuries later, after the fall of the kingdom, or rather its fragmentation into warring chiefdoms, the situation is very different. Here amidst the ravages of the slave trade and with the rise of a new class of enriched warrior aristocrats, the king has become the classic model of the passive, even pacified, divinity.[35] He is isolated, surrounded with massive taboos and is quite the equivalent of the Fijian chief 'that just sits.' The historical transformation suggests a possible interpretation of the Fijian material in which fragmentation and warfare, perhaps because of and most certainly exacerbated by European trade, may have provoked a particular configuration of power that takes the form of an inversion of an earlier dualism. There is some evidence that chiefdoms that were autonomous and at war in the mid-nineteenth century may have been organized in larger hegemonic networks in the more distant past,[36] networks that might even have been more peaceful. If there is a certain 'deductive' coherence in the kinds of transformations suggested above, it cannot be understood in mere cultural terms, for there is a logic in the relation between cultural change in conditions of existence that are not themselves included in the cultural order. The sacred immobility of a divine king in relation to his active double is not the outcome of the application of a model, but rather a set of properties of a social form, a unity of cultural practice. In this sense cannibalism cannot be understood as simply culture any more than as simply a consumption of protein. Sahlins is again clear about the structural relations linking the cannibal act and exchange, sacrifice, and the totality within which such acts find their meaning. Power as people-eating, the accumulation of 'soul force,' all of which maintains the necessary cosmologically defined cycle of social reproduction, is a truly widespread representational configuration. But the physical realization of the metaphor, the enactment of the origin myth is something else again. The Arapesh represent the origin of the exchange of pigs as a 'civilized' substitute for an earlier exchange of sons and daughters to eat,[37] but they certainly do not practice the sport. There are examples from the Kongo Kingdom of aristocrats offering themselves to the king to be eaten and cannibalism is a definite part of the cosmology. But the large scale market for 'meat that talks' in the late nineteenth century, where the consumption of cannibal victims was strongly felt to be a necessity for spiritual and physical survival in a disintegrated social world, is a specific phenomenon that can only be grasped in its historical context. Even in Fiji, cannibalism would seem to be a prerogative of those most ferociously engaged in war.[38]

Yet we are told that 'the exchange of raw women against cooked men is paradigmatic of the entire chiefdom economy.'[39] In other words, cannibalism is not merely a possibility, a realization in specific conditions and in a specific form of an underlying structure, but a cultural program. And the cultural program is itself a set of categories. Are we being reductionist in sensing that the cannibal act is not the mere acting out of a semantic recipe, but a practice predicated on a structure of desire and not of categories? Could it be that the constitution of experience is not of the same order as the structure of language?

If I have dwelled at such length on 'The Stranger King . . .' it is precisely because it begins to lay bare the fundamental problems of the entire approach. The chapter is full of structuralist insights but they are consistently integrated into a culturalism that is, in my opinion, diametrically opposed to Lévi-Strauss's insistence that the fundamental totality for the sciences of man is praxis.[40] It is true, of course, that Lévi-Strauss has consciously specialized in 'superstructures,' but he has not, and would not, I think, presume to treat them as some kind of historical totality. When he, for example, accounts for the distribution of mythical variants and not merely their existence, he proceeds by way of the dialectical relation between social practices and mythical representations.[41] This should be all the more so when we are dealing with representations of political author-ity, where it is not a mere question of discourses in their context, but of symbolic forms that are *embedded* in social relations, that is, as properties of practice. Sahlins tends, instead, to embed social relations in symbolic forms. It is in this way that warfare, cannibalism, variations in diarchy or even its suppression can be understood as expressions or moments in the 'generative development of the categories . . . the internal diachrony of structure' (103), whose properties are cultural-symbolic and not social.

VIII. FINALE: MARX IN CULTURALIST CLOTHING

Sahlins winds up this collection with a theoretical exploration of the major issue of the previous essays, the relation between 'structure and history,' a well-worn theme of the Parisian 1960s. The chapter begins straightaway with a play on Hawaiian categories, and on the historically established and mythostructured analogy: Chiefs:commoners::British:Hawaiians (139). The Hawaiian understanding of the contact situation was not able to contain the reality which it encompassed, and so it was transformed. The chiefs, practicing the above analogy, early took on European names, clothing, and life styles in a heated competition. But there is another logic involved, not discussed by Sahlins. The identification with Europe was equivalent to the absorption of foreign *mana*, the *mana* of the more highly ranked, associated with the source of power and wealth, and patently a reality made concrete in the British presence. This all seems clearly similar to West African royals and chiefs who claim descent from Mecca and take on Arab names, to situations in Central Africa where aristocrats took on Portuguese names and titles, to the general illusion often found throughout the ethnographic world that dominant groups claim separate ethnic origin from the indigenous people. If power is defined as coming from an external source, those in power have every advantage in iden-tifying with it. Is this the application of a specific cultural model or the working of a social logic? But there is more involved than models here, for the example of King Kamehameha who 'never tired of asking passing European visitors if he did not live "just like King George"' (140), gave up much of the European paraphernalia as he approached the end of his life, making it clear that his position was not in any way dependent on a foreign extravagance.

204 • JONATHAN FRIEDMAN

The conclusions that Sahlins draws from his discussions entail not only 'a theory of history' but a 'criticism of basic Western distinctions . . . history and structure . . . stability and change' (143). He argues that history is always structural, just as structure is historical, and that 'culture functions as a *synthesis* of stability and change, past and present, diachrony and synchrony' (144). This is the core of the dialectical model where the practice of received categories alters their content because the world does not conform to our cultural presuppositions. To claim that this is somehow against the grain of Western thought is clearly somewhat of an overstatement. After all, such dichotomies have been criticized from classical Greek philosophy to Spinoza and nineteenth-century dialectics. Sahlins's own dialectic of culture and praxis is itself unmistakably reminiscent of a whole tradition of European thought that he has not seen fit to acknowledge. Most recent, and close to his own approach, are certain of the variants of structural and structuralist Marxism represented by Godelier, Rey, and even myself.[42] Sahlins takes the dialectic further in addressing himself specifically to cultural form, something which has also been part of the critique of materialist reductionism in Marxism.[43]

But Sahlins's culturalism, much more than a recognition of cultural form, gives his dialectic a very particular content. This becomes clear as he closes in on the 'relation of cultural concepts to human experience, or the problem of symbolic reference' a 'phenomenology of symbolic action' (145). The absolutely core question is whether the relation of 'cultural concepts to human experience' is one of 'symbolic reference'? Sahlins's very Boasian answer is that

> [h]uman social experience is the appropriation of specific percepts by general concepts : an ordering of men and the objects of their existence according to a scheme of cultural categories which is never the only one possible, but in that sense is arbitrary and historical. (145)

Is this to say, then, that the relations between people take their structure from a cultural model? It would appear so. Then social life in general is the same as a game or a ritual or perhaps a movement, insofar as it is an implementation of a program. The other half of the dialectic is that in practising these symbolic plans we enter a context that has 'its own reasons' that subject the symbols to new referents and alter their meaning. In the crunch, Sahlins falls back on the same dichotomy that he hoped to have superseded, between structure (cultural) and event, which as Sahlins defines them, are quite *irreducible* to one another. And yet he denies precisely this when he insists that 'all structure or system is phenomenally evenementiel' so that 'event is the empirical form of system' (153). Now if this were really the case, there could be no dialectic of structure and event since the two are related as essence and appearance. There is absolutely no way of knowing what Sahlins has in mind here. Perhaps it is the old structuralist notion that the appearance of structure in observable social forms depends on the way it interacts with its environment, so that a given structure always appears as a set of variants or transformations generated by a dialectical interaction.[44] If so, then the 'event as empirical form' is no more than another more mystifying way of expressing the dialectical dichotomy between structure and practice. If we read this text without resorting to such strained interpretations, however, it is a tricky way of having one's cake and eating it, since it quite frankly eliminates the opposition between structure and event which is the explicit basis of Sahlins's model.

Is it best, then, simply to forget this little aside as a mere disguise of the real issue? I think not, for in the final analysis, while events can and do have properties and 'reasons stemming from other worlds (systems)' (153), their significance is a projection of the cultural structure. Thus 'the event is a happening interpreted' (153), and we are back at the start of our discussion (9). If events are interpretations, and still have a life of their own in some other realm of reality, what then is the nature of such realms and why are they so manifestly irrelevant as structures in their own right? What kind of totality, after all, have we got here? Culture appears to be a sign system that in its practice and transformation assumes the form of events whose only significance is the result of their interpretations within the culture that generates them. Here is the answer to the seeming contradiction between Sahlins's presentation of structure and event as opposed, on the one hand, and event as a mere manifestation of structure, on the other. If events are only such by virtue of being interpreted within a cultural scheme, then the opposition between structure and event is merely an aspect of a total process which subsumes all practice within culture. All the 'other worlds' and 'reasons of their own' are only significant as 'happenings interpreted.' They have no autonomous existence in Sahlins's understanding. In spite of all efforts to provide a dialectic of culture and practice, we are left in the end with only culture. In spite of all attempts to place culture in history, he always and everywhere reduces history to culture. Is this, then, the *Marshall Touch*, like the poor, old Lydian king; everything he gets his hands on turns to culture?

A. Madame la Culture

Do clothes make the man? If Sahlins's model is, in its outlines, reminiscent of a structuralist-Marxist dialectic, its cultural guise does much to transform its basic nature. In certain respects, perhaps crucial, we witness a rapprochement with a kind of Hegelian-Fichtean world view. Sahlins overcomes the dichotomy of structure and event by reducing, in spite of all efforts to the contrary, the latter to the former. There is no World-Culture equivalent to the World-Spirit, so we are still safely within the bounds of a realist history *inclusive* of different cultural forms. But within any cultural realm, and cultural realms are all there is in history, the world proceeds according to Hegelian principles whereby *every aspect* of social process is encapsulated within culture. We might all agree on avoiding the 'twin anthropological (or historical) errors of materialism and idealism' (154). But cultural subsumption, even if it is in the last instance, remains the complementary equivalent of another famous last instance. The question is whether the 'burden of "reality"' has its 'real effects' always 'in the *terms* of some cultural scheme' (154), or whether social reality is *constituted of* structures of meaning, but not *constituted by* such structures. The difference is by no means trivial, since it implies that structure is embedded in lived experience in a variety of significant ways, not merely as plans or grammars, but as the actual form of experience and the constitutive identities of subjects; that cultural schemes are not for the most part programs of action, but properties of reality that observers abstract and often reify; finally that the so-called burden of reality is not something which is at once external and at the same time subsumed by cultural categories, but is an immediate aspect of the totality of praxis as well as the structure of the conditions of praxis. Generalized exchange circles to business cycles, Kondratieff curves to *gumsa-gumlao* oscillations[45]—all are just as real and as structured as any culturally planned behaviour, even if they are not expressions of any culture's intentions.

My argument is felicitously illustrated by Sahlins's final onslaught on the practically medieval scholasticism of Hindess and Hirst[46] which they themselves totally devastated in a subsequent publication.[47] They 'eliminate' the value of history by the simple claim that 'historical events do not exist [in] and can have no material effectivity in the present' and that the conditions of existence of social relations in the present 'necessarily exist and are reproduced in the present' as well.[48] Sahlins's answer to this is that 'culture is precisely the organization of the current situation in the terms of a past' (155). Now as I understand Hindess and Hirst, they are making a mere existential point: that the only way that past existences can have any present existence is by their *reproduction* in the present, in other words by a practice that is *situated* in the present. To counter that the present is organized by the past is to miss the point, since it begs the question of why, how, and who. The unproblematical use of culture as that which imprints the past in the current situation eliminates the conditions of practice. Why should anyone organize the present in terms of the past? What is it that makes for the fact of empirical, temporal continuity of cultural form even where it is transformed? Is it because we walk around with theories for our practice, recipe books for our social existence? Or is it, as I would suggest, because the conditions of our existence, our social relations, and even the constitution of ourselves as subjects, are structured and transformed in the very flow of events that is our praxis and even more, the process of social reproduction in which our praxis participates. The continuity in history is not that of events, but of relations, and it is a continuity that is not easily susceptible to a past/ present dichotomy. Events are, by definition, discontinuities, as opposed to processes of social reproduction which are, by definition, continuous. In the cultural determinist framework, there would not appear to be any such relations and processes. If there is only culture and its practice, its generated events, then it is perfectly understandable that history must be conceived as the repetition of the script, the imposition of the past on the present.

The dialectic of which I have spoken is one that is located between a total social praxis and its conditions of existence. This praxis includes, like *habitus*, strategies and intentions that in their specificity are by definition cultural. Sahlins's dialectics is located between *culture* and *its conditions of existence*, that is between cultural form, abstracted from practice, and its implementation. It is, as such, a mere aspect of social praxis! And the division of praxis into code and event, sense and interest, is truly arbitrary, as if every 'sense' did not have an 'interest' and every 'interest' a 'sense.' The only segment of a larger world that impinges itself upon the cultural subject is the immediate environment of action. All the other, non-intentional properties of reality that are essential to our dialectic are only interesting to Sahlins insofar as they effect changes in the code itself. They never achieve the status of structure, for example, social structure, structures of identity, structures of reproduction.[49]

There is a clear unity in all of these dialectically unified oppositions; culture/practice, structure/event, 'pre-existing concept and unintended consequence' (152). They are all based on the relation of the individual subject to intended actions. Instead of a universal principle of practice, such as maximization, there are particular paradigms of significance that are the source of intentions. Thus, events are produced via the individual practice of the code. And if things don't turn out looking like the code itself, because of the burden of reality, the only thing left in the end is the code, since reality is always subsumed by culture. Sahlins would no doubt protest that I have not understood him. He would refer to his explicit statements to the effect that 'objective properties' and significance are 'two sides of the same thing' (150). I have not argued against his intentions, with which I am in complete agreement, but with what I see as the impossibility of carrying them out within a cultural determinist framework. For instead of envisaging material and symbolic properties as part of a single process, *containing more than either culture or practice*, he sees materiality as an appendage to culture in action, only relevant as a perturbation of the cultural scheme.

As I understand it, culture is applied in Sahlins's fashion where we can speak of a project, the acting out of a scheme. This occurs in a very limited way in ritual where a certain bracketing makes it possible to mold a situation, perform a play. It occurs in its fully dialectical form in social movements, whose cultural projects seek to reorganize either a segment or all of social reality according to an 'a priori' scheme. It is not unusual that social practices can assume the form of ritual, that presidents can act out old movies, that whole societies can act out origin myths, in the right circumstances. But not all the time! Unless he argues that social systems are either rituals or movements, which surely have some of the qualities of the relation between individual intention and action, I don't see how Sahlins can maintain such a model of the nature of society and history.

Is not the dialectic of culture and practice an artifact of the anthropologist's relation to his object? If our cherished otherness is no more than cultural difference,[50] and we abstract what it is that is different from its concrete events, and translate it into a way of producing those events, we arrive, naturally, at some notion of culture as code, grammar, program. They do what they do because they are what they are. Different cultures-different histories, different cultures-different social forms, different rules-different games. Behind it all, the empty subject of capitalist civilization, different islands-different worlds whose relation to reality is understood in terms of the game; role playing, rule using, and, by implication, cultural practice, where society is the spinoff of individual intentionality, and where the only tangible being is *Madame la Culture*, subject of history.

* The essay by Jonathan Friedman with which this exchange begins was first published in *History and Theory* 26 (1987), pp. 72–99 (© Wesleyan University), and is reprinted here by kind permission of the journal's editors and its publishers, Wesleyan University. It is followed by a reply from Marshall Sahlins which is being published for the first time in *Critique of Anthropology*.

NOTES

1. Claude Lévi-Strauss, *The Savage Mind* (London, 1966), 130–131.
2. Marshall Sahlins, *Culture and Practical Reason* (Chicago, 1976), 56.
3. Jonathan Friedman, 'Civilization Cycles and the History of Primitivism,' *Social Analysis* 14 (1983), 31–52.
4. Marshall Sahlins, 'Raw Women, Cooked Men, and Other "Great Things" of the Fiji Islands,' in *The Ethnography of Cannibalism*. Special Publication, Society for Psychological Anthropology, ed. P. Brown and D. Tuzin (Berkeley, 1983), 72–93.

5. Marshall Sahlins, *Historical Metaphors and Mythical Realities: Structure in Early History of the Sandwich Islands Kingdom.* Association for the Study of Anthropology in Oceania, Special Publication No.1 (Ann Arbor, 1981), 72.

6. K. Ekholm and J. Friedman, 'Towards a Global Anthropology,' in *History and Underdevelopment*, ed. L. Blussé, H.L.Wesseling, and G.Winius (Leiden, 1980); K. Ekholm, 'External Exchange and the Transformation of Central African Social Systems,' in *The Evolution of Social Systems*, ed. J. Friedman and M. Rowlands (London 1977); K. Ekholm, '. . . Sad Stories of the Death of Kings: The Involution of Divine Kingship,' *Ethnos* 50 (1985), 248–272; J. Friedman, 'Catastrophe and Continuity in Social Evolution' in *Theory and Explanation in Archaeology*, eds. C. Renfrew, M. Rowlands, and B. Segraves (New York, 1982), 175–196; J. Friedman, 'Captain Cook, Culture and the World System,' *Journal of Pacific History* 20 (1985), 191–201; J. Friedman, 'Post-structuralism and the New Moon,' *Ethos* 50 (1985), 123–133; J. Friedman, 'Our Time, Their Time, World Time: The Transformation of Temporal Modes,' *Ethos* 50 (1985), 168–183; E. Wolf, *Europe and the People without History* (Berkeley, 1982).

7. Sahlins, *Historical Metaphors and Mythical Realities*, (Ann Arbor, 1981).

8. Sahlins envisages his dialectic as an absolutely general model of the relation between culture and context: 'As a description of the social deployment—and functional revaluation—of meanings in action, it need not be restricted to circumstances of intercultural contact' (xiv).

9. In a recent, and as yet unpublished, manuscript ('Fiji: A Tale of Three Kingdoms.' Paper for symposium, 'Symbolism Through Time.' Wenner-Gren Foundation for Anthropological Research. Fez, Morocco, 12–21 January 1986), Sahlins has indeed attempted to reveal an indigenous historical dialectic in Fiji, where the context of warfare among three kingdoms is responsible for cultural variations on a common 'deep structure.' The manuscript is not clear, however, in its present state, on how structure and practice relate to one another in this analysis.

10. I borrow this term from Clifford Geertz.

11. W. Ellis, *An Authentic Narrative of a Voyage Performed by Captain Cook* (London, 1782), II, 153.

12. Clifford Geertz, 'Anti-Anti Relativism,' *American Anthropologist* (1984), 275.

13. Sahlins, *Historical Metaphors and Mythical Realities*, (Ann Arbor, 1981).

14. P. Bourdieu, *Outline of a Theory of Practice* (Cambridge, Eng., 1977); *Le sens pratique* (Paris, 1981).

15. Bourdieu, *Le sens pratique* (Paris, 1979).

16. Bourdieu, *Ce que parler veut dire* (Paris, 1983).

17. F. Alberoni, *Movement and Institution* (New York, 1984).

18. Luc de Heusch, *Essais sur le symbolism de l'inceste royal en Afrique* (Brussels, 1958); *Le pouvoir et le sacré.* Annales du Centre D'Etudes des Religions 1 (Brussels, 1962); *Le roi ivre ou l'origine de l'état* (Paris, 1972); *Rois nés d'un coeur de vache* (Paris, 1982).

19. Luc de Heusch, *Why Marry Her?* (Cambridge, Eng., 1981), 19–24.

20. A word about Clastres is in order before proceeding. A common interpretation and critique of his work is based in a serious misrepresentation of his concept of power. *Society against the State* (1977) is not about primitive society's premonitions concerning the eventualities of state power and an attempt to prevent social evolution. His approach is very much more structural than that. Primitive societies, at least those of South America, upon which he bases the entirety of

his discussion, are said to practice a kind of anti-power that takes the form of socially castrated chiefs who, while occupying the locus of social power, are in their practical relation to society a negation of that which he represents. The power negated in such societies is not something belonging to an imagined future, but a continuous presence, an immanent danger that requires a never ending struggle. Marcel Gauchet has developed Clastres's idea even further in an important essay where he suggests that the very self-representation of society as society implies a symbolic structure of power as external force, a Nature upon which society is dependent, that is the basis for both the practice of anti-power and the potential form of the state (Gauchet, 'La dette du sens et les racines de l'état,' *Libre* 2 [1977], 5–43).

21. L. de Heusch, *Le roi ivre*, and *Rois nés d' un coeur de vache* (Paris, 1982); A. Adler, 'Le Pouvoir et l'interdit,' in *Systèmes de signes* (Paris, 1978), 25–40; A. Adler, *La mort est le masque du roi* (Paris, 1982), 25–40.

22. Georges Dumézil, *Mitra-Varuna* (Paris, 1948).

23. *Ibid.*, 77.

24. Sahlins does, in fact, argue that there is a third term in the Fijian structure, generated by 'the conjunction of chief and people, sea and land' (99) which parallels the Indo-European scheme detailed by Dumézil. But, as we shall argue, this 'tripartite pyramidal scheme' (99) is an extension of dualism and is everywhere resolved into a dual structure.

25. A.M. Hocart, 'Chieftainship and the Sister's Son in the Pacific,' *American Anthropologist* 17 (1915), 631–646; *Lau Islands, Fiji*. Bishop Museum Bulletin 62 (Honolulu, 1929); *The Northern States of Fiji*. Royal Anthropological Institute of Great Britain and Ireland, Occasional Publication 11 (London, 1952).

26. Hocart, 'Chieftainship and the Sister's Son.'

27. I am not, of course, suggesting that protein value is of any significance. But a more existential understanding of the constitution of cultural (of course) experience is clearly in order here. Work on the structure of the person (M.C. Ortigues and E. Ortigues, *Oedipe Africain* [Paris, 1984]; M. Augé; *Génie du paganisme* [Paris, 1982]; 'Ordre biologique, ordre social: la maladie, forme élémentaire de l'événement,' in *Le Sens du mal: Anthropologie, histoire, sociologie et la maladie*, eds. M.Augé and C.Herzlich [Paris, 1984]; F. Héritier, 'L'identité Samo,' *in L'identité: Séminaire dirigé e par Claude Lévi-Strauss* [Paris, 1977]; 'Stérilité, aridité, sécheresse: Quelques invariants de la pensée symbolique,' in *Le Sens du mal*) will certainly prove crucial in understanding the internal necessity of cannibalism in given conditions, a necessity that organizes desire and not just the intellect.

28. Sahlins, 'Fiji: A Tale of Three Kingdoms.'

29. *Ibid.*, 22.

30. Compare this to Dumézil's trichotomy which in its Indian version is closest to the Fijian Structure. Here we have the priestly function, combining the opposed *celeritas* and *gravitas* of *Mitra/Varuna* itself ranking above the warrior function represented by the lesser god *Aryaman*, opposed, finally to the people: *Brahman/Kshatria/Vaishya* order + violence/war/agriculture: sacred rule/secular rule/people. The dualism here, between sacred and secular, order and violence, rulers and people are contained within a larger scheme of encompassment that is not reducible to a process of dichotomization. Whether the sacred Fijian chief represents the land in relation to his sea warriors, or the sea in relation to his subject commoners, the same dualist oppositions organize the representations.

31. R. Needham, *Primordial Characters* (Charlottesville, 1978).

32. J. Friedman, 'Notes on Structure and History in Oceania,' *Folk* 23, 1981, 275–295; 'Catastrophe and Continuity in Social Evolution.'

33. Friedman, 'Notes on Structure and History in Oceania,' 281–287.

34. K. Ekholm, *Power and Prestige: The Rise and Fall of the Kongo Kingdom* (Uppsala, 1972) in Historical Transformations: The Anthropology of Global Systems, eds. K. Ekholm and J. Friedman (Lanham, 2008); 'External Exchange and the Transformation of Central African Social Systems,' '. . . Sad Stories of the Death of Kings.' (Ethnos, 1985), 248–272.

35. Ekholm, 'Sad Stories,' Ethnos, 266–267.

36. Hocart, *The Northern States of Fiji* 7–8; Sahlins, 'Fiji, A Tale of Three Kingdoms,' 62.

37. D. Tuzin, 'Cannibalism and Arapesh Cosmology: A Wartime Incident with the Japanese,' in *The Ethnography of Cannibalism*, in P. Brown and D. Tuzon, eds. (Washington DC, 1983), 67.

38. Sahlins himself notes how at least one kingdom, Verata, looked with abhorrence upon the practice of cannibalism and possessed none of the ceremonial parapher-nalia usually associated with it. (Sahlins, 'Fiji: A Tale of Three Kingdoms,' 64; W.T. Pritchard, *Polynesian Reminiscences* (1866) [London, 1968]).

39. Sahlins, 'Fiji: A Tale of Three Kingdoms,' 101.

40. Lévi-Strauss, *The Savage Mind* (Chicago, 1966).

41. C. Lévi-Strauss, 'Structuralism and Ecology.' Gildersleeve Lecture delivered 28 March 1972. Barnard College, New York.

42. Many one-time structural and structuralist Marxists have developed beyond their original concepts, criticizing the implicit 'logic of the productive forces' of all varieties of Marxist models, the failure to take into consideration the dom-inance of the imaginary structures of social life and recognizing the nonlocal character of social reproduction (Friedman, 'Marxism, Structuralism, and Vulgar Materialism,' *Man* 9 [1974], 444–469; Friedman, 'Marxist Theory and Systems of Total Reproduction,' *Critique of Anthropology* 7 [1976], 3–16).

43. Friedman, 'The Place of Fetishism and the Problem of Materialist Interpretations,' in *Critique of Anthropology* 1 (1974), 26–62; L. Colletti, 'Marxism and the Dialectic,' *New Left Review* 93 (1975), 3–29. 'Relations of production come to be fetishes because fetishes come to be relations of production, because a social structure . . . comes to dominate the process of reproduction, an element whose internal properties do not correspond to its material functions' ('The Place of Fetishism,' 57). 'Social reproduction *only* takes place through social forms and society lives its reproduction *in* these forms' (59).

44. Sahlins seems here to be playing with the distinction between the abstract and the concrete: 'As a set of meaningful relations between categories, the cultural order is only virtual. It exists in potentia merely. So the meaning of any specific cultural form is all its possible uses in the community as a whole' (153). This, of course, is merely a restatement of the relation between *langue* and *parole*, deep structure and final string. The unanswered question is the nature and locus of the 'virtual.' If it is grammar, then we presumably carry it around in our heads. If it is structure in the Lévi-Straussian sense, it is, I would argue, embedded in social process as properties of both intended and nonintended forms. The circular space of generalized exchange is not part of a cultural plan, but a deducible aspect of social practice. It may be the case that it is we who make the deduction, but the

social space in question is certainly just as much a part of the cultural life of the society in question as are marriage rules.

45. E.R. Leach, *Political Systems of Highland Burma* (London, 1954).
46. B. Hindess and P. Hirst, *Pre-Capitalist Modes of Production* (London, 1975).
47. B. Hindess and P. Hirst, *Mode of Production and Social Formation* (London, 1977).
48. Hindess and Hirst, *Pre-Capitalist Modes*, 312.
49. There is an interesting parallel here with the work of Giddens. Just as Sahlins tends to reduce culture to codes, Giddens reduces structure to rules. In both cases, we are left with a universal subject and a set of paradigms of action which are applied to an external reality that in turn generates unintended results (A. Giddens, *Central Problems in Social Theory* [London, 1979]). The dialectic of structure and practice is encompassed by Giddens's 'duality of structure.' Lurking behind both paradigms is a more elaborate methodological individualism.
50. J. Boon, *Other Tribes, Other Scribes: Symbolic Anthropology in the Comparative Study of Cultures, History, Religion and Texts* (Cambridge, Eng., 1982).

Chapter 11

Deserted Islands of History: A Reply to Jonathan Friedman

Marshall Sahlins

I do not wish to appear churlish or insensitive to the generous compliment Mr. Jonathan Friedman pays me by reviewing *Islands of History* and other writings of mine at such length.[1] Friedman clearly cannot say enough good things about these works. So I would never accuse him of misunderstanding the text—even though he thinks that I will (p. 35). Where could he have gotten that idea? Anyhow, it cannot be some simple misunderstanding, as that presumes a certain innocence on the reviewer's part; whereas, what Friedman produces is a sustained misrepresentation of my work, from start to finish.

Again and again he tries to force what I am saying into the procrustean bed of 'cultural determinism.' A curiously antique and positivist discourse—or does Friedman really think I am Leslie White reincarnated as Lévi-Strauss? But the worst part is not this systematic corruption of ideas I use and interpretations I offer. Something more complexly perverse comes out of Friedman's prodigious efforts to misconstrue the central argument of these essays: especially the argument—in opposition to all received 'culturalism'—about how cultural forms are changed in the course of their reproduction, by virtue of their submission to real-pragmatic conditions of human action (*praxis*). Friedman wants to make out that I completely dissolve the *realia* of practice into pre-existing cultural schemes, or that for me 'everything is generated by a cultural code' (p. 13). Never mind that the phrase 'cultural code' does not even appear in *Islands of History*, not once; nonetheless, having thus reduced my argument, he reproaches it as a species of 'reductionism.' Still this is not the worst part. The worst part is when positions explicitly developed in *Islands of History* reappear in Friedman's review as criticisms of the book. This happens too often. And it means that I cannot really say that Friedman misunderstands the text, since I can as often agree with him. But neither is his piece accurately described as a review, since it reads more like another chapter in the life of Yossarian.

I will illustrate my objections on grounds Friedman has chosen, by unpacking the issues in the passage (p. 35) where he says, 'Sahlins would no doubt protest that I have not understood him. He would refer to his explicit statements to the effect that "objective properties" and significance are "two sides of the same thing"(150).'[2] These sentences are fairly taken as a kind of condensed symbol of Friedman's method, beginning with the bizarre fact that on the page of *Islands* to which he refers (Sahlins, p. 150) there is no discussion whatever of a relation between 'objective properties' and 'significance,' nor is it said anywhere else that these are two sides of the same thing. Whatever Friedman might mean by 'explicit statements to the effect,' such a proposition from the perspective of this book would be at best trivial and otherwise basically misleading. The discussion that Friedman thus characterizes actually concerns the relations between 'sense' and 'interest,' and it issues in statements explicitly opposed to the idea that 'everything is generated by a cultural code.'

In this discussion, 'sense' designates the Saussurean value of the sign, its concept as fixed by contrasts to other signs, while 'interest' is the pragmatic value or the difference the sign makes to the people using it. So the text indeed says that 'sense' and 'interest' are two sides of the same thing, the sign: the first in relation to other signs, the second in relation to acting subjects. If 'sense' is the life of signs in the community, 'interest' is the sign in people's lives—whence certain powers of the second to affect the first. Note that in the page prior to his own allusion to this discussion, Friedman observes that I do not appreciate that every sense has an interest and vice versa: rather, I make a 'truly arbitrary' division of praxis 'into code and event, sense and interest . . . as if every "sense" did not have an "interest" and every "interest" a "sense"' (his p. 34). To complete the air of *Catch 22* it would only be necessary for Friedman to criticize me for collapsing the event into the 'code,' as if these two were the same thing—which of course he does (pp. 32–33). Alternatively the same effect can be achieved by comparing what *Islands* does say about sense and interest with this idea that everything comes down to the cultural code. What the text does say is that in the capacity of interests, cultural categories are referred by people to the world, thus putting the categories at pragmatic risk and in the event changing their conventional sense.

Briefly, the argument is that while sense and interest are two sides of the same thing, my interest in something is not the same as its sense—in the way for example, that my necessity for milk, or perhaps allergy to it, is not the same as its exchange value. The interest engages the signified thing in my practical situation, the difference it makes to me, whereas the sense is its differential or positional value in a social universe of such values. Yet as practically engaged in interested ways, the conventional senses of signs are submitted to multiple risks. They are risked by reference to objects, which may well have properties and consequences not foreseen in the received sense; they are risked in the projects of intelligent subjects who remain capable of improvising relations and permutations of sense likewise previously unknown; they are risked in social relations between persons of different interests and unequal powers of objectifying their own interpretations; etc. But if the values of signs are thus affected in action, so then are the relationships between signs affected; and if the relationships are thus changed, so then have the senses of signs been altered by their uses, by their existence as human life.[3] In the historical analyses of *Islands*, several dimensions of the argument on practical risks are synthesized in the notion awkwardly called 'the structure of the conjuncture'. The phrase is meant to describe the organization of the historical event as a practico-symbolic process, developing its own proper dynamic (p. 125) out of the tactical interplay of different values and interests in specific pragmatic circumstances. Or, in one summary definition: 'the practical realization of the cultural categories in a specific historic context, as expressed in the interested action of the historic agents, including the microsociology of their interaction.'[4] This idea of a conjunctural structure is deployed at some length and by name in several of the historical studies in *Islands*, especially with regard to the death of Cook (pp. 125,127; *cf. xvii*, 67,152–154). It was also fairly critical in a previous work, of which Friedman takes note, *Historical Metaphors and Mythical Realities*. Nevertheless, he pretends I have found such structures of the conjuncture 'apparently not worthy of investigation or perhaps . . . simply impossible to approach' (his p. 13).

On the other hand, inasmuch as in the most generous of all his compliments Friedman says that the clarity of my prose is not at issue, it is worth trying to figure out why he makes such surrealist translations of it.[5] Consider, for instance, this metamorphosis of 'sense' and 'interest' into 'significance' and 'objective properties.' On the evidence, Friedman does perceive these items as a kind of proportion, that sense is to interest as significance is to objective properties. By the same evidence one can deduce that for him the common contrast in the proportion is between symbolic and material properties; even as he is sure that my project is to eliminate the material by subsuming it in a symbolic order which alone is systematic. So the quaint characterization of *Islands* as 'cultural determinism' or 'culturalism' appears now in a different light: it is a gesture of becoming delicacy on Friedman's part, as these are clearly euphemisms for 'idealism.' And this helps explain why Friedman goes on to the effect that '"objective properties" and significance are two sides of the same thing.'[6] He imagines it was some kind of pathetic attempt on my part to recognize the existence of the real world: good intentions alas deceived by a theoretical commitment to privileging the cultural code.

To understand Friedman's bowdlerized textual readings, then, it is necessary to reverse the logic just described, that is, to see them as *sequitur* to a just war on the 'totalitarian' principle of 'cultural determinism.' Beginning with the settled opinion that I disregard the structures of the real-material world, and that I conflate them instead with people's *post factum* symbolic interpretations, Friedman is disposed to misrepresent in a parallel manner all propositions in which he is able to construe an analogous contrast of 'objective properties' and 'significance.' So far as he is concerned they are so many equivalent expressions of the same cultural idealism. He thus manages to put into practice what he accuses me of doing in theory, viz., dissolving the realities—in this case, of the text—within *a priori* cultural schemes. But Friedman should know that the real theory of *Islands* is that material realities, such as authors, are often ornery relative to the ways people are pleased to think them.

It gets richer yet. In the best tradition of the academic *pensée sauvage*, Friedman is able to detect a 'common structure' in my writings from the binary classifications—significance/objective properties—of his own intellectual code:

> There is a common structure in these oppositions: structure versus practice, prescription versus performance, mythopractice versus *habitus*. It is the structure outlined in *Culture and Practical Reason* that opposes culture and practice and that insists that culture is everywhere the determinant. These essays represent an application of cultural determinism to historical process, an attempt to translate all forms of historical movement into an expression of culture as a 'model for' the production of reality. There is, in other words, nothing that is not culturally generated! (p. 12, *exclamation in original*).[7]

Since in fact there are no 'explicit statements to the effect' of this cultural idealism in the texts at issue, the presumption must be that I have been speaking such culturalist prose all along without knowing it. But this cannot be. I have learned my 'cultural determinism' from masters. If I really believed such a cockamamie theory, I would know how to defend it.

Yet to defend it would require such brilliant notions as that the cultural categories organize experience prescriptively, univocally, and otherwise independently of the *realia* of the experience. On the other hand, the converse proposition (as Friedman knows) is equally inane, that reality is a 'model for' the production of culture: as if the symbolic life were the self-consciousness of the world, rehearsing as names the given differences between things. The world does not thus refer to itself in people's words or the constructions they put upon it. If it did, then everyone would construe the same objects or situations in the same way—which is untrue even among people of the same society, let alone those of different societies. People refer variously to the same kinds of things: in their own ways, according to their respective schemes of intelligibility. And there must be something in the nature of a scheme, if there is intelligibility.

Empirical realities, then, are appropriated as social meanings, as worldly instances of cultural classes. The meanings may or may not have been known before; moreover, as selective valuations of experience they can only imperfectly notice the 'objective properties'—descriptions of which are inexhaustible. Nonetheless, worldly experiences are socialized as referential tokens of cultural types, of concepts that can be conceivably motivated in the existing scheme. Notice that just because there is a culture this does not mean there is no invention or novel response to material realities—albeit *by the same token*, the realities will then have effects of a distinct cultural type. We come thus to the anthropology I have tried to advance in *Islands* and other studies going back to *Culture and Practical Reason*—another book concerning which Friedman's appreciation is limited.

The main idea is that real-material forces function in culture as meaningful values, values that are not *a priori* stipulated by the 'objective properties,' nor therefore are they the only ones possible, but in terms of which these objective properties have determinate historical effects. As for example gold, in the physical composition of which no metallurgist ever discovered 'wealth,' although it is in this capacity of wealth that the natural distribution of the ore becomes a reality of world-historical significance (see note 3). Even things whose 'utility' seems to lie in their physical composition, as rain is good for growing crops, have to wait the cultural order that gives them such effect. And if there is drought and famine, shall we have infanticide, senilicide, migration (of whom?) or irrigation?—or perhaps first kill the king? Precisely by the relations that constitute a material-something as a positional value in a scheme of persons and the objects of their existence, the materiality of this something unfolds as a certain force.

Such material realities of course have reasons, movements, and structures of their own—as do cyclones and earthquakes, or for that matter Captain Cook and imperial capitalism. And equally evident, they have compelling effects on people's lives. Still their efficacies differ in the lives of different peoples. According to their specific capacities as culture, their general compulsions as force are variously realized. By these cultural mediations, the material realities become *historical* realities, the natural forces *historical* forces. Otherwise, human history is a branch of physics.[8]

'In other words'—here is Friedman's translation of the prose I have been speaking thusly all this time—'there is nothing that is not culturally generated!'

Obviously we have a gap of ontological proportions. In the perspective I just described, 'cultural' is anything that is ordered or configured by the human symbolic faculty, anything whose mode of existence is thus symbolically constituted. The opposition is to whatever is 'natural': *not* to what is 'real' or 'material'—otherwise there is no such thing as a domestic horse. But for Friedman there is a fundamental incommensurability between the material and the symbolic, between reality and the 'cultural code.' So when I say that in human affairs perception is at the same time an historic conception, or experience an interpretation, he gets panicky and, while accusing me of obliterating the real in the cultural, he is compelled to recuperate the distinction in anthropologically reckless ways, as by contrasting social structure (or social relations) to cultural codes in the way that the substantial is different from the symbolic (e.g. pp. 9, 34). This is reckless and obscurantist because human social structures are symbolic orders, meaningful constitutions of human relations in the terms of which the material realities find their historic effects.[9]

And should the ethnologist forget that when an elephant tramples an Azande's garden, the owner is likely to accuse some kinsman in the vicinity of witchcraft? Or that the Azande will do so even though he knows it is a natural property of elephants to trample gardens? But it is not a property of elephants to trample *property* (let alone *your* garden).

Appropriated in the human realm, the material realities acquire historical motions that cannot be predicated directly from their 'objective properties.' There is no adequate relation between the destruction of one's garden by an elephant and accusing a kinsman of witchcraft, except by the way of Azande cultural order. Yet this is a true effect of material reality, of trampling elephants, on the course of Azande society.

On the other hand, some other people, for instance George Orwell, would just shoot the bloody elephant. That happenings such as elephants, or Captain Cook sailing into some Pacific island, although *sui generis* from the perspective of the people to whom they happen, will nonetheless engender historic reactions of different kinds and proportions according to the diverse ways they are assimilated in local cultural orders, which is to say according to the significances variously attributed to them—this is also the idea in *Islands* about 'structure and event' that Friedman makes such a mess of. Beginning (as we have seen) by faulting me for opposing structure and event in a 'truly arbitrary' fashion (p. 32), Friedman ends by complaining again that I abusively confuse them, collapsing the event into the structure as 'an aspect of a total process which subsumes all practice within culture' (p. 32). In between, Friedman's argument wanders perplexedly between these alternatives. For just so, he is hung up on an obsessive dualism of the real and the symbolic; whereas, the text of *Islands* he thus strains to subsume is an argument in three terms—happenings, structures, and events—in which, moreover, the event is the *relation* between the other two. 'Or in other words, an event is not just happening in the world; it is a *relation* between a certain happening and a given symbolic system' (*Islands*, p. 153, emphasis in the original).[10] Once more, the reasoning is that historical outcomes cannot be predicated from the phenomenon-in-itself, the 'objective properties' of the happening. The consequences of an earthquake on wandering Chichimec hunters and gatherers cannot be compared, as an event, with the effect of tremors of the same magnitude in the same place when it had become Mexico City.[11]

And all this is no less true of happenings of exotic cultural origins, such as the advent of Captain Cook in Kealakekua Bay, Hawaii. They are variously comprehended, absorbed, amplified, impeded, diverted and otherwise orchestrated and transmitted along the lines of local cultural schemes. In *Islands*, I deliberately chose to exemplify by an historic case of amplification, where the disproportion between the apparent innocence of the circumstances (from a Western viewpoint) and the seriousness of the consequences (from the vantage of the local people) would highlight the historical work of the cultural order.[12] The story was about how, by an Hawaiian logic, the original divinity of the British was eroded when Cook's sailors carried their intimacies with Hawaiian women to the extent of eating with them. By Vancouver's visit fourteen years later the British were prohibited from even entering the temple where Cook had been ritually greeted as the god Lono, on grounds that the Whites had polluted themselves by co-dining with women. 'Events thus cannot be understood,' this discussion concludes, 'apart from the values attributed to them: the significance that transforms a mere happening into a fateful conjuncture. What is to some people a radical event may appear to others as a date for lunch' (*Islands*, 153).

This indifference on Friedman's part to the ways people culturally organize what happens to them, and thereby achieve their own histories, this indifference, I say, is not a matter of principle only. Or perhaps it is not at all a matter of principle, since he seems to make more or less explicit statements to something like the opposite effect (e.g. pp. 10–11). Be that as it may, it is at least a settled practice, as when he hastens to disregard the several historical studies in *Islands* by stuffing the societies involved into their appropriate cases in his private museum of speculative developmental types—or in a really gross caricature of Fiji, degenerative types. Again, when considering certain remarkable episodes of the World System in the Pacific, such as the Hawaiians' sacrifice of Cook, or the serious battles waged by the New Zealand Maori to down the flagpole erected by the British above the Bay of Islands, Friedman finds these perfectly transparent reactions to the gestures of Western imperialism. They are adequately accounted for by what the British were doing, so that to his satisfaction what the British were doing was historically responsible for what the Polynesians were doing. It is not just that Friedman ignores that Cook (as numerous other Western captains) had emerged with impunity from many similar scrapes with Polynesian chiefs—although, precisely, these affairs lacked the cosmic tensions developing over the weeks of antecedent rituals in Hawaii.[13] Nor is the problem simply that in explaining the Maori flagpole wars in terms of the ambiguities of the British colonial presence—economically attractive but politically sinister—Friedman forgets that the British did the like all over the world without evoking the spectacular tactics of the Maori hero Hone Heke. 'Let us fight,' he said, 'with the flagpole alone!' What then are we to make of Friedman's consistent mistaking of the famous Maori's name (as 'Hono Heke')? (This must sound to New Zealanders like analyzing John DiMaggio's 56-game hitting streak would to New York baseball fans.) Could it be a question of *method*: for instance, a method in which 'specific determinations evoke in theory the same suspicions that persons do in reality?'[14] Friedman's explanations of Pacific events are reminiscent of the historiographic principle discovered in earlier Western writings by Dorothy Shineberg: 'there must be a white man behind every brown.'[15] It is as if the indigenous peoples could not have their own reasons for acting as they did. And by thus ignoring the historical work of the indigenous peoples, the method inadvertently becomes the superstructural expression of the very imperialism its practitioners despise. It appears as the self-consciousness of the World System itself: as though the academic anthropologist or historian would intellectually complete the project of an imperialism that has already materially invaded the lives of others by now denying them any cultural autonomy, coherence or authenticity.

For the remainder of what Friedman says about *Islands* and the other works, one must at some point leave it to the interested reader to judge the reviewer's respect of the texts.[16] Of the specific analyses of Hawaiian and Fijian history, Friedman's representations are just as good as they are for performative structures, mythopraxis, sense and reference, structures of the conjuncture, and other concepts adopted in these works. In a brilliant witticism, Friedman asks in this connection if it is 'then, the *Marshall Touch*, like the poor, old Lydian King; everything he gets his hands on turns to culture?' (p. 33) But Friedman could be as mistaken about the identity of the academic magical king as he is of the Phrygian Midas. For it is Friedman himself, with a wave of the wand of 'cultural determinism' who is able to make all these understandings of *Islands* just disappear, transforming them into 'generative schemes' and so many other guises of the same idealism. And then with a triumphant flourish, he restores the original from behind his own ear. 'Mythopraxis' he writes, 'is best conceived not as a generative scheme, but as an interpretative or definition space within which practice finds its meaning' (p. 21).[17]

Clearly then, that citation from Sartre was not apt. Sartre was criticising a certain vulgar Marxism as 'a project of elimination. The method is identical with [the] Terror in its inflexible refusal to differentiate.' But Friedman is well known for his own strictures on an analogous materialism. Besides, here everything happens as if the Committee of Public Safety were made up of the Marx *Brothers*.

NOTES

1. Jonathan Friedman, 'Review Essay: Islands of History,' *History and Theory* 26 (1987), pp. 72–99. I refer to Friedman's review by page numbers for the *Critique of Anthropology* reprint in parentheses.
2. I cite in full the paragraph from which these sentences are taken (as I will later discuss the entire line of reasoning):

> There is a clear unity in all of these dialectically unified oppositions; culture/practice, structure/event, 'pre-existing concept and unintended consequence' (152). They are all based in the relation of the individual subject to intended actions. [What could this mean?] Instead of a universal principal of practice, such as maximization, there are particular paradigms of significance that are the source of intentions. Thus, events are produced via the individual practice of the code. And if things don't turn out looking like the code itself, because of the burden of reality, the only thing left in the end is the code, since reality is always subsumed by culture. Sahlins would no doubt protest that I have not understood him. He would refer to his explicit statements to the effect that 'objective properties' and significance are 'two sides of the same thing' (150). I have not argued against his intentions, with which I am in complete agreement, but with what I see as the impossibility of carrying them out within a cultural determinist framework. For instead of envisaging material and symbolic properties as part of a single process, *containing more than either culture or practice*, he sees materiality as an appendage to culture in action, only relevant as a perturbation of the cultural scheme (p. 35).

3. See the Introduction and Chapter 5 of *Islands*; or see M. Sahlins, 'Catégories culturelles et pratiques historiques,' *Critique* 456 (1985), pp. 537–558. I should explain that I have here adopted Saussure's well known analogy between exchange-value and semiotic value because Marx says something of very similar implication about the fetishism of commodities. 'So far,' he wrote in *Capital*, 'no chemist has ever discovered exchange value in either a pearl or a diamond' (New York: International Publishers, 1967, v.1, 83, *cf*. pp. 72–74). And I invoke the materialist master not to put myself in the right (or left), but to set up an understanding of the 'symbolic' in human affairs as a meaning which cannot be determined in the 'objective

properties,' yet through which these properties (such as the natural distribution of diamonds) have practical and historical effects. This basic understanding is another which Friedman cannot accord me, as shall be seen momentarily.

4. *Islands, xiv.* I believe Friedman has the like in mind when he offers, as antidotes to my reductionist ideas of 'mythopraxis,' the observation that social practice 'is organized around currently meaningful situations and strategies, all of which are defined in the context of contemporary social relations' (his p. 21). On remaining defects of this assertion, and of Friedman's treatment of mythopraxis, see note 16, below.

5. Indeed Friedman writes, 'If it is possible to differ on points of theory and analysis, this is thanks to the splendid clarity achieved in these texts' (p. 14). That's nice. I cannot recall that any reviewer has ever said the like of my work; even the most favourably inclined complain about the opaqueness of the style. Alas, judging from the present case they are probably right, and Friedman is once again being wrong-headed about the text.

6. See note 2, above.

7. Friedman here refers to M. Sahlins, *Culture and Practical Reason*, Chicago: University of Chicago Press, 1976. At least the recklessness of his argument gives some insight into the weird syllogism by which Friedman repeatedly taxes mine: Sahlins radically opposes culture and practice; Sahlins assimilates practice to culture; therefore Sahlins radically confuses culture and practice—thus ignoring reality.

8. So, we are 'not forced to adopt the idealist alternative, conceiving culture as walking about in the thin air of symbols. It is not that the material forces and constraints are left out of account, or that they have no real effects on cultural order. It is that the nature of the effects cannot be read from the nature of the forces, for the material effects depend on their cultural encompassment' (*Culture and Practical Reason*, p. 206).

9. Hence I agree altogether that there are real social structures greater than practice, as of generalized exchange, by which history is orchestrated. This criticism of Friedman's was my point all along.

10. Or again: 'An event is not simply a phenomenal happening, even though as a phenomenon it has reasons and forces of its own, apart from any given symbolic scheme. An event becomes such as it is interpreted . . . The event is a *relation* between a happening and a structure (or structures): an encompassment of the phenomenon-in-itself as a meaningful value, from which follows its specific historical efficacy' (*Islands xiv*, emphasis in original).

11. 'Washington, Sept. 26 [1987] (AP)—Building design contributed to much of the damage in the 1985 Mexico City earthquake that killed more than 4,000 people, according to a new United States government study'.

> 'The report noted that a high percentage of damage occurred in buildings from 6–17 stories high. It is said the natural period of motion—the time to complete a vibration—of such buildings was amplified by the ground motion of the drained lake bed on which Mexico City lies. These buildings and the earth movement had periods of motion that were roughly equal, about two seconds, resulting in serious damage. Taller and shorter buildings were less likely to be affected, the study found . . .'

> 'The lack of symmetrical design in buildings was found to be the second most common problem. Asymmetrical designs allowed buildings to twist, placing excessive stress on the structures.' *New York Times*, 27 September 1987.

12. Talk of unintended consequences: what a poor choice this turned out to be when subsumed in the dualistic code of a review bent on privileging the real and criticizing the ideal.

13. It should be noted that Cook was specifically identified with the Hawaiian god Lono, by name and ritual procedures, before his death and not just *ex post facto* as Friedman would prefer to believe. This is testified to by contemporary documents of Cook's voyage, even the published ones (*cf.* Sahlins, *Historical Metaphors*). On other, analogous scrapes of Cook in Tonga and Tahiti, see, e.g., E.C. Beaglehole, *The Journals of Captain Cook*, v.1. (1955), pp. 114–116; v.2 (1969), pp. 217–220; v.3 (1967), pp. 133–134, pp. 229–232).

14. J.-P. Sartre, *Search for a Method*. New York: Vintage Books, 1968, p. 48.

15. D. Shineberg, *They Came for the Sandalwood*. Melbourne: Melbourne University Press, 1967, p. 214.

16. Unfortunately with regard to Fiji this will be nigh impossible because Friedman cites a considerable manuscript of 80-odd typed pages called 'Feejee: A Tale of Three Kingdoms' which I had not intended to publish in that form. Prepared for a Wenner-Gren conference, this paper was passed to Friedman by a third party unknown to me and cited by him without my authorization, though on the cover it says 'Not for publication' and on the first page 'Do not cite.' For the rest, Mr. Friedman's representation of the contents is framed with his habitual scrupulousness.

17. Compare *Islands*, 55. *et passim*. This unexceptional characterization of mythopraxis by Friedman would leave in doubt only his next sentence, cited earlier: 'Social practice is organized around currently meaningful situations and strategies, all of which are defined in a context of contemporary social relations' (p. 15). Nor is the obscurity too much relieved by the succeeding sentence, indicating that currently meaningful situations are such metaphors as usurping the throne (p. 15).

PART VII
Fighting over Commodities and History

There is venom in this discussion that should not be allowed to distract from or disguise the seriousness or scale of the underlying disagreements. Seemingly, at the core is a difference in emphasis on commodities (and the definition of commodities) on one hand and commodity-fetishism on the other; but also at issue are fundamental disagreements about the purpose of anthropological explanation.

Taussig, who is best known for his writing on fetishism and colonialism in South America, attacks books by Wolf (*Europe and the People without History*, 1982) and Mintz (*Sweetness and Power*, 1985) that represent an historical anthropology that relates local scale and global landscape to movements of capital in global networks of the production, distribution and consumption of commodities. The arguments in the books in question have cultural settings with specific referents (e.g., sugar produced in the Caribbean through the labour of African slaves and consumed in hot drinks in Europe), and display a variety of temporal and spatial features, but the super ordinate setting is global-capitalism-as-culture, and the fundamental disagreement turns on the adequacy of the theoretical tools employed, not on the accuracy of the material invoked or even the conclusions reached. Taussig's disdainful regard for the historical anthropology rendered by Wolf and Mintz displays a zeal to break with the past that is symptomatic of several key shifts in the attention of the discipline, most notably the shift represented in the literary turn.

In retrospect, one of the striking features of the attack on Wolf and Mintz (which is paralleled, although in briefer form, in Tyler's response to Scholte in this volume) is the fact that the proposed shift into a more open, interpretive mode of anthropology—theoretically open and resistant to the discipline of explanatory purpose—should seem to require such strident denunciation of other, competing approaches.

The fundamental disagreement over explanatory versus hermeneutic goals has been a mainstay of anthropological theorizing over the past century and this encounter between Wolf/Mintz and Taussig shows it with particular clarity.

Chapter 12

History as a Commodity in Some Recent American (Anthropological) Literature

Michael Taussig

There are no facts *as such*. We must always begin by introducing a meaning in order for there to be a fact.

—Nietzsche, quoted in R. Barthes, 'The Discourse of History'

Sundering truth from falsehood is the goal of the materialist method, not its point of departure. In other words, its point of departure is the object riddled with error, with conjecture. The distinctions with which the materialist method, discriminative from the outset, starts are distinctions within this highly mixed object, and it cannot present this object as mixed or uncritical enough.

—Walter Benjamin, 'Addendum to "The Paris of the Second Empire in Baudelaire"'

Guide Books

Two highly polished books about commodities have recently been launched onto the U.S. market. The results of lifetimes of thought, both seize on the commodity in the belief or the hope that the firmer they grasp it, the more likely they are to shake us free of the illusions we have about explaining society. Preeminently they are guide books for American Anthropology, which they wish to save from various fates—a descent into triviality, losing sense of purpose. It's as if Anthropology, once an item in a dull university catalog, had like the commodity itself risen from mere thinghood to acquire life and soul, albeit sickly and deformed and in need of saving.

Studies of the everyday in modern life, of the changing character of mundane matters like food, viewed from the joined perspective of production and consumption, use and function, and concerned with the differential emergence and variation of meaning, may be one way to inspirit a discipline now dangerously close to losing its sense of purpose (Sidney Mintz, *Sweetness and Power*, p. 213).

In 1968 I wrote that anthropology needed to discover history, a history that could account for the ways in which the social system of the modern world came into being, and that would strive to make analytic sense of all societies, including our own [because] our methods were becoming more sophisticated but their yield seemed increasingly commonplace. To stem a descent into triviality, I thought we needed to search out the causes of the present in the past. Only in this way could we come to comprehend the forces that impel societies and cultures here and now. This book grew out of these convictions (Eric Wolf, *Europe and the People without History*, p. ix).

LIFESAVERS

I have been thrown two life jackets, one to inspire, the other to stem descent, yet I fear the sea is too cold and choppy to use them, much as I might want to. Like Kafka I'm sure there's hope, but I'm not sure if it's for us. This is the sea of commodities, vast and treacherous. Most of the time the best one can do is tread water. Kafka said he suffered from seasickness on dry land, but the builders of these life jackets don't have much time for that sort of talk, and I suppose that befits the grim purpose of saving lives. Not for them the resort to play or trickery, the slow digesting of experience(s), the place of dream in the commodity as utopian wishing, emotions, interpretation, and all that goes along with observing oneself observing. Yet sometimes I think the designers of these jackets do not realize quite how serious our situation is, how the sea surrounds us on all sides, commodities determining the very way we try to size up things, objectify and subjectify the world and in doing so create colliding realities, how the horizon wavers, advances and recedes, making us giddy as the currents from the deep pull and tear us in all directions. More mysterious than table-turning, Marx said in his famous chapter on the fetishism of commodities and its secret—therewith bringing to a close that massive first step of an introduction to *Capital* concerned not merely with the vexing question of value but with *problematizing the commodity-form* itself. Marx was not happy with the solid, open-faced appearance that commodities acquired as things, complete unto themselves. And with what fiendish delight did he point to the dazzling epistemological somersaults undertaken by commodities and upon ourselves, first as things, then as spirits. Fetishism was the term he used and we, in a post-Frankfurt/Adorno/Benjamin age, are now somewhat accustomed not only to attempts to work through the effects of the coupling and decoupling of reification with fetishization but also to the shocking conclusions that Adorno, for one, drew; namely, that this somersaulting, this coupling and decoupling, constituted the basis of capitalist culture as well as the insuperable block to the Kantian antinomies. There could be no solution inside philosophy to the epistemological problems posed by our type of economy. Ours was the age of contradiction par excellence, an age of fragmentation and incoherence in which (according to the *Communist Manifesto* and Marshall Berman) 'all that is sold melts into air.' Georg Lukàcs, in a classic paper on reification, opined in the mid-1920s that at this stage of capitalism there was no problem that did not lead back to the question of the commodity-form, the central structural problem of capitalist society in *all* its aspects. The basis of this commodity-form, he wrote, 'is that a relation between people takes on the character of a thing and thus acquires "phantom objectivity," an autonomy that seems so strictly rational and all-embracing as to conceal every trace of its fundamental nature; the relation between people.' Exceedingly strange, therefore, that our two commodity authors should be attempting to save us without so much as a nod to Marx for his warnings about the commodity's two-facedness and double-dealing—especially when we consider the dependence on him they manifest throughout their work. On looking over their books one is tempted to conclude that works which cannot trade blow for blow with the commodity as thing and the commodity as fetish are destined to reproduce the very phantom objectivity Lukàcs pointed to. And they do this not only in the name of critique, but to save us.

TITLES

There is Sidney Mintz's book *Sweetness and Power: The Place of Sugar in Modern History*, and Eric Wolf's *Europe and the People without History*. Both titles have something to tell us. Professor Mintz's is congenial in assuring me that there is an entity, Modern History, with *places* in it for commodities like shelving in the supermarket. Our task is to find where the sugar is kept, and in search of it, we learn much about the whole. As a guide, Mintz is charming and modest. His text depends much on the subjunctive mood, a lot of perhaps and maybe, a nudge here and there, every now and then a grand slam where bits are smooshed together to the benefit of capital and power. In short it is a text, a poetics, of sweetness *and* power. As such it is to be sharply distinguished from the poetics of Wolf's commodity-book, which proceeds in a straight line through History seen as progressive stages in the unfolding of a Totality. Wolf knows the supermarket so well that all he has to do is pull a few items off the shelves to illustrate the interlocking connections that constitute aforesaid Totality, and his tone is authoritative. The poetics of sweetness and power takes on added significance when Mintz speaks eloquently of a sense of mystery he found in sugar from the beginning of his Caribbean awakening, a mystery that is largely but not completely put to rest by finding out about and being able to envision as so many internal rela- tions of sugar the trading relations between Europe, Africa, and the sugar islands and land south of Florida; the stupendous importance of sugar in the development of capitalism; the complex puzzle of Demand (as in Supply and Demand); aristocratic luxury taste and lower-class imitating; the possible role of sugar in sweetening and fueling the bitter life of the English laborer; and so forth. But the mystery lingers. No matter how many connections of (what one might choose to call) the historical sort Mintz brings to light, it is we, with our specific conventions, convictions, and curiosity, who provide that light (of intelligibility)—and thereby continue to puzzle about the connections between meaning (sweetness) and power.

Wolf's entitling is, to put it mildly, a study in irony, for the implica- tion is that many or all Third World people have been *falsely* portrayed (particularly by anthropologists, he will say) as not having History (First Irony). Then there is the Marxist or Marxist-Populist convention by which it is a sign of revolutionary solidarity to affirm the existence of those passive objects of others' History-making, 'people (truly) without history' (Second Irony). Both formulations effortlessly reify History as some-thing to be possessed, and both are subject in his book to a Third or meta-irony by the surprising absence of the Histories of the people without history. It is Wolf's way of looking at History as the History of the Commodity that causes this dehistoricization of History. He takes the materialist or bourgeois meaning of the commodity, not the one that bedevils Marx in the long first section of *Capital*, with the result that History itself becomes a fetish, a live being with a spirit of its own. This fetish-power Wolf renders as Capital Accumulation. People then become things, truly without History.

MEN MAKE STORIES

'Men make history,' states Wolf in his Afterword, following Marx, 'but not under conditions of their own choosing.' Men (and women) make stories too, and since the Enlightenment they have often called them Histories. The wonder is how such stories, removed from the authority of the lived experience of the story-teller, are constructed so as to seem (in the words of Roland Barthes) *to tell themselves*. Like the commodity, (hi)story has two modes; in its thing-form it is something that the (hi)sto- rian can rise above and manipulate; in its fetish-form it is self-empowered and irresistibly real. As commodity, therefore, History is the story that men make and makes men. In this way the Historian humbly finds that privileged position, that Archimedean point, outside of History whereby History in its telling can be evaded. This point outside and above history is the phantom to which the historian striving for objectivity, the phantom objectivity of Lukàcs, aspires. Both of these books about the commodity and history are phantomized in this way.

Irresistibly Real

In this type of History 'everything happens,' writes Barthes, 'as if the discourse or the linguistic existence was merely a pure and simple "copy" of another existence, situated in an extra-structural field, the "real."'

Not so much 'arguments' and 'points' but first the creation and sustenance of a feeling of the real, out there—this is the major ideological task of the discourse of history, and it involves a mode of representation which denies the act of representing. Raymond Williams writes that language is not merely an instrument but also a source of experience. Yet to the sustenance of the 'reality-effect' of historical discourse it is essential that writing be understood as only instrumental—our instrument with which we copy reality out there, reality serene in its independence from its representation. (The reality with which we are not so much concerned as involved, of course, is the one that asks us not about the existence of this table or that tree but about social relationships, social knowledge in both its implicit and its explicit dimensions, labor and labor-power.)

The Reality of Modernity

Might not commodity fetishism create modes of representation which undo as well as sustain this 'effect of the real'?

Barthes writes that historical discourse is the only one in which the referent is addressed as external to the discourse, though without its ever being possible to reach it outside this discourse.

This superb and supreme insolubility of the referent, smug in its own thinghood, is of course a phantom, a contrivance that masquerades as self-made in its occupying Lukàcs's space of phantom objectivity. Its very phantasmic character, however, beckons us toward modes of representation in which representation itself is represented. These modes are Modernism. And it is their task to link arms with phantoms so as to problematize reference. They do not openly contest the fetishism of commodities so much as trip them up in their own epistemological murk.

Professor Mintz calls not only for an 'anthropology of modern life' and 'of the changing character of mundane matters like food', but for an anthropology that retains 'a full appreciation of humanity's historical nature as a species' (p. 213). He invokes the modern against the primitive. He sees Primitivism as an essential part of anthropologists' undoing and castigates Romanticism, that whipping boy of Realists.

Yet is not his very insistence here testimony to the dependence of the modern on Primitivism? What could be more archaic, if not primitive, than the impassioning appeal to humanity's historical nature as species? And might not the commodity itself, which is what his book is about, be testimony to this precise dependence and conflation of Primitivism and Modernism? Think here of Walter Benjamin's *Passagenwerk*, the Paris Arcades Project of the 1930s, with his pointed concern to show us the ways by which the commodity, in its very modernity and mundaneness, conjured up the archaic and the exotic, the primitive and the mythic. It was as if, in our secular and scientific age, fancy found its home no longer in the stories and gods of times gone by but in commodities, as fetishes and as things.[1] A dreamworld lay before us in the mythic meanings of commodities, the promise they held. The primitive was made anew by the new, and it was the child's fresh eye that brought the always-the-same in the commodity to the adult's sense of change and 'progress' in this age of the modern—this age for which Mintz wants an anthropology. But little of this implosion of the made-up past in the present meets Mintz's adult eye, despite his poignant call for an anthropology of the modern in the mundane. Like the way both he and Professor Wolf eye the commodity, so modernity is here deproblematized; it is the latest slice in the homogenous flow of time.

Marlboro Man

In leather and denim he sits, high on his galloping horse, way above the freeway, swinging his lariat yet perfectly relaxed as the cars hum and the semis scream past underneath, their drivers half in and half out of consciousness in that funny semi-awake/semi-dream state of near hypnosis that characterizes not only highway driving but much of modernity as well. And what could be more rationalistic than the freeway, the shortest distance between two points in a straight line, cruise control, every exit numbered. Progress too. He's high already. Must be fifty feet up there dwarfing us, going too fast to do more than glimpse him galloping in another century through the grey midwestern summer sky as we approach Detroit or cross the Bay Bridge to Oakland.

Visceral Meaning

Tobacco: a capital substance, and a mystical one too; a killer and a necessity. It enters not only the freeway of our imagination, as it does for shamans in the Orinoco Delta, but the blood that is our biological life-stream. Its meanings overwhelm us. Up there in the sky with his lariat and with the gods, more alive than you or me, the Marlboro Man. But sugar, where rides its champion? This is a question not so much of 'advertising' (a term that instantly makes one switch off one's politico-aesthetic scanner) but of the mythification of substances in a non-mythifying age of marketing rationality. Why tobacco one way and sugar another? Why should Mintz's book on the meaning-and-power of sugar in modern history contain next to nothing that can help us? And what happens to 'meaning' when it becomes 'taste'? Might not we call on Mintz, by the material facts of the matter, to create a new field not of power and meaning but of power and . . . visceral meaning? And what might that be? (With some surprise I note that what people mean by meaning, when they regard it as secondary to something 'more basic' like 'power' or one or another of *les grandes recits*, is so terribly staid, so framed, cognitive, and uptight. No place for emotions or visceral meanings here.)

RITUAL

The study of 'consumption' is essential to Mintz's mystery of sugar. The commodity passes in its life-circuit from exchange-value to use-value where, anthropologist as he is, Mintz scents the strategic importance of ritual in creating and maintaining sugar's demand. In doing so he subtly reminds us of some of anthropology's claim to distinction, what makes it different from other human sciences. He is using anthropology, showing us its power. Yet his doing so weakens its power, for what we get are textbookish clichés about ritual as a crude functionalizer: rituals into which sugar was 'wedged' (*sic*) reproduce social status and social divisions; sugar drifts down the social ladder as it becomes cheaper and more plentiful and drifts down further to be used as a sign of . . . one is not sure exactly, but it is used in rituals of separation and departure and, of course, the ritual of tea and the tea break in work. But we seem to be sliding, for what a ritual banquet of the ruling class or the ritual of a funeral means is not quite the same as what we mean when we speak of the ritual of a cup of tea in modern times, one of the many 'rituals' of everyday life. In fact, we do not say ritual (that's more a professionalized anthropological smirk). What people say are things like (recalling my childhood) 'a cuppa tea, a Bex, and a good lie down'—a sigh of pleasure/a cry of pain and muted protest, associated particularly with or attributed to working-class women in Sydney (Bex is an across-the-counter analgesic). It is a pity that Mintz never takes us into one of these rituals of the modern everyday so often named and hence claimed in the explanation of consumption. But perhaps modernity would stretch anthropology out of shape.

—We can drink it black, Stephen said. There's a lemon in the locker.
—O, damn you and your Paris fads, Buck Mulligan said. I want Sandycove milk.

Haines came in from the doorway and said quietly:

—That woman is coming up with the milk.
—The blessings of God on you, Buck Mulligan cried, jumping up from his chair. Sit down. Pour out the tea there. The sugar is in the bag. Here I can't go fumbling at the damned eggs. He hacked through the fry on the dish and slapped it out on three plates saying:
—*In nomine Patris et Filii et Spiritus Sancti*. Haines sat down to pour out the tea.
—I'm giving you two lumps each, he said. But, I say, Mulligan, you do make strong tea, don't you?

   Buck Mulligan hewing thick slices from the loaf said in an old woman's wheedling voice:

—When I makes tea, I makes tea, as old Mother Grogan said. And when I makes water, I makes water.
—By Jove, it's tea, Haines said.

Buck Mulligan went on hewing and wheedling:

—So I do, Mrs Cahill, says she. *Begob, ma'am*, says Mrs Cahill, *God send you don't make them in the one pot*. He lunged towards his messmates in turn a thick slice of bread, impaled on his knife.
—That's folk, he said very earnestly, for your book Haines.

An unusual group in some ways only, students in James Joyce's Dublin, July 16, 1904. Yet this is clearly life surging around the sugary rite, and how its sense differs from the naming and claiming and functionalizing of the rites of that what we might call a premodern Anthropology, enmeshed in the fiction of the real, wishes to recruit for the explanation of demand! How its sudden swerves of pace and direction, its gathering of angles, imprecisions, and layers, suggest conflicting realities at work in any instant of Modernity! But where would that leave an anthropology of the modern everyday.

PRACTICES

Mintz talks of practices of consumption (p. 154) as well as of rituals, and in much the same way. Practices of consumption 'mark the distribution of power' within the organization of society, for example. Comforting words are 'mark' and 'organization,' reassuringly solid for the necessary task of bestowing a sense of coherence on the world. But of 'power,' the wished-for bedrock, there are other views. Michel de Certeau, for example, writes on what he calls the logic of everyday practices and, more pointedly, on the complication posed for the study of such practices by the constant disruption of such logic. In his words, 'these practices themselves alternately exacerbate and disrupt our logics' (note, exacerbate *and* disrupt). Research into these practices, as much as the practices themselves, contains what he calls 'regrets'—the havoc played on the logic of explanation and of analysis by the play of chance in everyday life-practice, the ineffability of certain experiences constituting those practices, the grayness of the epistemic murk habituating our life-forms. The study of practices in everyday modern life leads, he concludes, to a *'polemological* analysis of culture. Like law (one of its models), culture articulates conflicts and alternately legitimizes, displaces, or controls the superior force. It develops in an atmosphere of tensions, and often of violence [and] the tactics of consumption, the ingenious ways in which the weak make use of the strong, thus lend a political dimension to everyday practices.'[2]

De Certeau thus sees power as not only entailed in practices of consumption but destabilized as well. This is quite distinct—as writing practice—from what a text like Mintz's achieves. *Sweetness and Power*, in the very earnestness with which it continuously strives to reduce such things as 'practices of consumption' to 'power' as the bedrock, constantly affirms and sustains that power. Just as the commodity is deproblematized, and the Modern too (seen as the latest slice in the flow of homogenous time), so power itself is reified, and critique cast in conventional terms sustains convention.

SLIPPERINESS AND POWER

One of the things that amazes me reading a book like this, with its wealth of materials and enormity of scope and drama, is how little it amazes me. There is no estrangement. Not only is this anthropology of the everyday textualized so that the everyday remains everyday, but the sense of slipperiness of power, what de Certeau conveys, is anathema to it. Instead the text itself is slippery, to grease the huge determinisms of capital's narrative. This is a text that creates its effects with the subjunctive, the perhaps, the subtle, the sugary understatement—yet it is implacable as the closing of a coffin-lid in sealing fate. One example:

> The history of sugar in the United Kingdom has been marked by many 'accidental' events, such as the introduction of bitter stimulant beverages in the mid-seventeenth century. But sugar consumption's rise there-after was not accidental; it was the direct consequence of underlying forces in British society and of the exercise of power (p. 150).

SYMBOLING

Mintz writes (pp. 153–54) that 'birth and death are universal in the sense that they happen to all human beings; our capacity to symbolize, to endow anything with meaning and then act in terms of that meaning, is similarly universal and intrinsic to our nature—like learning to walk or to speak (or being born or dying). But which materials we link to events and endow with meaning are unpredictably subject to cultural and historical forces.'

Meaning is thus subject (unpredictably) to forces. But what is the meaning of those forces? How did they escape symbolization? Where is the privileged point outside meaning whereby judgement on meaning can be rendered?

In Mintz's book this point is social relations and the distribution of power in society. Unlike birth and death such relations are not subject to our capacity to symbolize. There lies our hope. They escape fate.

HISTORY AND DIFFERENCE

'If there is any explanation it is historical.' With these words Professor Mintz banishes hermeneutics to intellectual purgatory. Meaning becomes History. 'When we pass onto our children the meanings of what we do, our explanation consists largely of instructions to what we learned to do before them' (p. 158). It is left to the historian's historian to ask about the learner's learning, and history is thus what exists—truly 'the past in the present,' to quote Professor Wolf. But one has questions about a view that chains the present to the past in this way. Do not the children pass something onto their elders?

What most anthropologists think about meaning can be summed up, Mintz says, by paraphrasing Clifford Geertz: human beings are caught in webs of signification they themselves have spun. Mintz strongly objects. Not only is meaning historical, it is also determined by differences between groups in society (in an older earthier discourse, by class struggle). 'The assumption of a homogenous web,' he writes, 'may mask, instead of reveal, how meanings are generated and transmitted. This is perhaps the point where meaning and power touch most clearly' (p. 158).

TOUCHING

'The profound changes in dietary and consumption patterns in eighteenth and nineteenth century Europe were not random or fortuitous, but the direct consequence of the same momentum that created a world economy, shaping the asymmetrical relationship between metropolitan centers and their colonies [and] the tremendous productive apparatuses, both technical and human, of modern capitalism. But this is not to say that these changes were intended' (pp. 158–59).

Touching is the trope which Professor Mintz uses to displace the 'web of meaning.' Touching is what sweetness-and-power is all about. Touching consists in:

(a) listing dates and prices and volumes of sugar production and consumption; and
(b) giving some (to my mind extraordinarily limited) sense of the symbolism of sugar; and
(c) touching (a) with (b), implying some meaningful connection exists between the two

when in fact what makes the connection meaningful in Mintz's text is a quality brought from outside—from Reality, from History, from the great narrative of Capitalism ('the same momentum that created a world economy').

SWEETNESS AND POWER

Touching involves the artful confounding of 'cause' with metonymy. Although historical discourse of the type Mintz employs strains to give the appearance of manifesting, if not establishing, 'causal' connections, what it really gives us is the continuous parading and constellating of bits and pieces to an imagined whole—bits and pieces of the world and world history in sugar.

When, at the very close of his book, and with his perennial charm and modesty, Professor Mintz suggests that his 'connecting so minor a matter as sugar to the state of the world in general may seem like yet another chorus of the bone song—the hip bone's connected to the leg bone, etc.' (p. 214)—we see quite clearly how the artful confounding of metonymic with causal analysis works. It succeeds (throughout the text, not just here at the strategic moment of closure) through Mintz's very sweetness, the sense of the author that the text tirelessly creates, with his wonderfully developed poetics of understatement, modesty, and subtlety.

Thus can the very next sentence after the bone song-disclaimer read, in a slashingly different key, 'But we have already seen how sucrose, this "favored child of capitalism"—in Fernando Ortiz' lapidary phrase—epitomized the transition from one kind of society to another.'

Thus does the bone song become, through its own sweetness, power—the power of the story that seems to tell itself.

Undoing History

Because of its furtive yet complete dependence on a narrative, that of Capitalism, to make its metonymic connections appear causal ones that can make 'meaning' seem like something secondary to 'History,' Mintz's contribution to an Anthropology of the Modern Everyday does little more than reproduce a premodern anthropology chained ever more firmly to its past. To adopt the jargon: the task is not to do history but to undo it.

One way of doing this is precisely that of the bone song. We consciously dismiss the commodified storytelling of causal analysis and instead make the juxtaposition of metonyms our way of 'doing history' through its undoing—not for us the rosary beads and chains of causes and effects. Then would we be confronted not by the power of Historical Discourse but by a quite different collation of meaning and power as generated by a modernist text of the modern and the mundane, striking with the left hand (the hand of accident and fortuity so abhorred by Mintz), irregularly challenging the inviolablity of the referent, constantly problematizing reality instead of sustaining it by resort to the awesome power of Capital.

Stemming Descent

I am sitting in a hot and waterless sugar plantation town in western Colombia, reading Professor Wolf's book about commodities and colonies, *Europe and the People without History*. I have been coming back to this town every year since 1969. Everything Wolf writes in his book about plantation development strikes me as curiously over-general and, when applied to what I know about the history of the people of this town and of the surrounding plantations, wrong. What am I to make of the sort of knowledge this book creates, this book aimed at stemming a descent into triviality?

Wolf's book is built on the impassioned appeal to make broader connections. Part One is titled 'Connections,' in bold type above a double-page reproduction of one of the de Brys's engravings made in the year 1599, depicting a moving caravan of armed traders together with their laden camels and mules. Why with this demand to broaden the context is there a terrible narrowing of interest? Why with the demand to look for connection is there blindness to the unexpected?

There are no surprises in this history of history-less peoples, and no escaping it either. It is more remorseless than fate. Making connections here means referring the part to the whole. The whole is already known. It is the world of trade and production. It is the whole world as a metaphysical entity. Its driving force is Capital Accumulation. Its destination is History.

Incidentally, the de Brys' engravings, several of them dramatically featured in this book, are now emblematic of the European conquest of the New World, a graphic cliché like the use of Mayan glyphs to serve as signs of Latin America. But the de Brys, commissioned by Protestant Dutch and English merchants, rivals of the Spanish, never traveled far from Paris and certainly never saw the New World. Their task was to create images with which others—such as us, today—would see that world's newness. And they peopled it with humans taken from Classical ideals, from (the idea of) ancient Greece.

What sort of connections does the use of such imagery suggest we make? Perpetuated conventions raise the question of how we can ever see the newness of the New World. Could that be the true aim of History?

How strange that this book, so enthusiastically rooted in the deep soil of historical determinism, should itself be able to escape the ways by which history transmutes connections into conventions.

The plentiful use of maps of the world and its parts is interesting in this regard, because maps function to authorize, even more than photographs, the idea of the real. If the de Brys images authorize the 'once upon a time' of History, then the maps complement that realization with the notion that reality is not so much represented as copied.

This book is like a map, a copy, of the world. It looks down onto the world. But where does it look from, and how did it get there?

Curious, how one reads and says, So what? Is this not all terribly obvious, or an academicization of the obvious? It produces a strange effect. I, the reader, must be missing something—and the book is no longer obvious but mysterious. It's all very well to talk so much about Historical Political Economy and of The Three Modes of Production that constitute World History. But aren't there other modes of production to consider? What about the mode of textual production, alongside if not prior to the kinship, the tributary, and the capitalist modes of production? What about modes of production of the real? And anyway, didn't Marx subtitle his *Capital* a *critique* of political economy?

Overarching, thrusting, penetrating, choking, consolidating, expanding, shifting of gears, more thrusting—these are the terms this book pours forth. We seem to be caught between a machine and certain sorts of sexual acts, the colony a woman's thighs, capitalism a penis, capitalism as juggernaut. The text evinces a strange pleasure in recounting this activity. It seems to be more than the pleasure of always being right. (In Kafka's penal colony the official in charge of the torture machine puts himself into it and then sets it going, inscribing the death sentence in words on his very body. He enjoys it.)

—'External warfare, trade, and internal consolidation created new states in Europe [and] agriculture ceased to grow, perhaps because the available technology reached the limits of its productivity. The climate worsened' (p. 108).
—'Trade and warfare necessarily fed upon each other.'
—'The State needed the merchants.'

Thus does this writing animate things and abstractions of things; war becomes a person, a spirit, or a god. It creates States. So does trade. They feed on each other. Internal consolidation also creates (States). Agriculture stops growing. Technology reaches. And all this spiritualization of things is on a par with natural process; 'the climate worsened.' This mode of production of reality parallels Marx's ironic, teasing observations about commodity fetishism whereby people become like things and things become like people. Only Wolf's fetishism is not ironic. He is serious. He animates things in the same way as Capital. But as we know, the life thereby endowed is spectral.

A text that so closely reproduces the life-force of capital as its own innermost mode of production is a bullying text. In its attempt at critique through relentless repetition of the terrific power of capital, such a text joins forces with that power. Grim determinism and grim determination to 'face reality' combine. How could we undo this combination in a way that would never let itself be assimilated to capital's fetish power?

Authoritarian realism: in siding with the power of capital through this mode of reality production, everything loose is nailed down, as the expression goes. Nailed down to what? To an integrated (imaginary) whole.

This totality is made in part through the continuous use of violent verbs in the passive voice. The usage not only makes the violence of the text strategically ambivalent—both violent and controlled (by whom? by what?)—but also creates the sense of past-perfect action completed, action finalized. It makes it difficult to see history as a living force in the present. Instead history comes across as judgment, and the Final one at that.

I keep coming back to the question: What is history? What is historical explanation? What is historical understanding? The answer seems to be taken for granted in the text. I must be the only one who doesn't follow. Surely, 'history,' like religion, is here endowed with the moral authority of the past?

One gets only a negative idea of what historical understanding is: it is not what anthropologists did or still do in studying so-called primitives as pristine survivals from a timeless past. But one cannot define history and historical understanding from their (supposed) absence, like filling an empty bucket. Everything is securely established in this text, and the first thing securely established is the inviolability of the text's own procedures and modes of explaining. History is never given the chance to marshal a counterattack and devour the means by which it is invoked.

'There were several reasons for Huron success in this role' is typical of the text's attempts to recreate a world in which everything has its reasonable reason. In this instance of the Hurons' relationship with the French, the Hurons 'occupied a strategic location for [trade] exchanges.' In fact it boils down not to several but to one Reason capable of infinite multiplication.

Explanation is thus a matter of 'unravelling the chains of causes and effects at work in the lives of particular populations' as 'the totality [which is the world] developed over time' (p. 385). What more could one say? As against 'the totality' not people, but 'populations.'

What about people, the 'people without history'? Wolf distinguishes his way of creating historical understanding from that of the (now largely defunct) Modernization School (with its concept of 'traditional society'), and from that of André Gunder Frank and of Immanuel Wallerstein, by the fact that they all omit considerations of the pre-capitalist modes of existence of the 'micropopulations habitually studied by anthropologists,' and 'of the manner in which these modes were penetrated, subordinated, destroyed, or absorbed, first by the growing market and subsequently by industrial capitalism' (p. 23). Wolf distinguishes his own position by its undertaking an examination of just such penetration, subordination, destruction, and absorption—of how (for example) 'Mundurucú or Meo were drawn into the larger system to suffer its impact and to become its agents' (p. 23). The totality rests its immense weight on this examination.

I read statistics and see maps bordered with anthropological jargon of authenticity and titles of classes (the planter class, peasants, wage labor, serfdom). Categories unfold like the Stations of the Cross: the scenes are static, but with faith the believer is moved toward the great ascent. In the section 'The Movement of Commodities' the first example of how Wolf's Historical Political Economy will shatter anthropological understanding of the dreadful ahistorical variety concerns rice and the concept of the 'loosely structured social system' advanced by John Embree in 1950 to characterize, so Wolf writes, Thai society. There is a growling and huffing in the text at this crucial point, but one gathers that anthropological discourse concerning Thai society is both single-voiced and intent on claiming non-historical 'reasons' for such looseness of structure. 'Yet,' continues and concludes Wolf, 'the features of [the Thai village] Bang Chan that led to its characterization as "loosely structured"—like the features of other Thai villages caught up in the rice economy in other ways—must [*sic*] be understood not merely as social structure of a certain kind but as the outcome of the expansion of commodity production' (p. 321).

That's Rice. That's the examination and illustration of how the people without history in Thailand got theirs—enormously inconclusive; a mouse's squeak. And remember, this is the book that begins with the plea to make connections. Next comes Meat. The Aborigines of Australia are fitted into Meat, where we find one paragraph of eleven lines about the people without history, a paragraph that tells us (a) pastoralists and natives clashed over land and water, and the natives were largely overrun, some like 'the Walbiri' (people without history are rarely differentiated) becoming wage hands, and (b) the anthropologist Mervyn Megitt 'noted that in the mid-1950s the Walbiri made use of their increased leisure, freed from the stringent demands of food collecting by the transition to wage work, to intensify their social and ceremonial activities' (p. 321). Next, Bananas.

Not a word inviting us to wonder what those 'ceremonial activities' might be saying to us about commodification as seen from the central desert—about the meat that enters into labor-power and the labor-power that enters into meat—let alone what it means to have time bourgeoisified into 'work' and 'leisure time.' Instead, this supposed critique of commodities sustains their very cultural categories.

Bananas. Here the 'examination' of the effect on 'populations' of the movement of commodities, the examination designed to manifest the unraveling of chains of causes and effects as they intertwine in the totality, concludes in the same spirit as Meat, with a similarly curiously out-of-place 'set-piece' apparently aimed at showing the causative role of the commodity economy on 'culture' as 'effect'—that mechanization was probably the main cause of a 'native millenarian movement' (note the jargon) among banana plantation workers in western Panama.

There cannot be even a whisper in a totalizing project such as Professor Wolf's that this native millenarian movement may have something to teach us about the equally millenarian movement of commodities. Its function in history is to be his example. But might there not be in this 'reaction' in western Panama a theory of history and the commodity from which we could all 'react' in *our* turn, so as to gain not that sublime point outside history to which Professor Wolf strives, but the see-sawing inside-and-outside mobility of positions required to match and mismatch the fetishized view of commodified reality to which Wolf's text grants such eloquent, indeed overwhelming, testimony.

Notes

1. See Susan Buck-Morss's article on the *Passagenwerk* in *New German Critique*, no. 29 (1983), which is especially helpful on this argument.
2. Michel de Certeau, *The Practice of Everyday Life* (Berkeley: University of California Press, 1984), pp. xvi–xvii.

Chapter 13

WHITHER COMMODITIES? REPLY TO MICHAEL TAUSSIG

SIDNEY W. MINTZ AND ERIC R. WOLF

We have had ample opportunity to study Michael Taussig's objections to our work, which he originally intended to publish in two versions in two places, although, in the event, only one has appeared. At the risk of making Taussig's commentary more intelligible than he may have intended it to be, we will begin by outlining what we understand to be our critic's difficulties with *Sweetness and Power* (which he was once asked to review; hereafter *S&P*), and *Europe and the People Without History* (which he was not asked to review, but reviewed anyway; hereafter *EPWH*).

Taussig does not like either book. *He* does not like what we say, and *he* does not like the way we say it. Taussig seems unwilling to imagine that others might have projects different from his own. This makes him readier than he ought to be to rely upon a rhetoric of denunciation. Venting his own 'visceral' reactions, he has turned an ancient argument among many different figures in the sociocultural disciplines into a discursus that struck us as more than slightly self-referential. According to him, we are historical when we should be hermeneutical; we study the history of commodities, rather than studying commodity fetishism; we treat commodities as things, rather than as fetish objects *and* things; we talk of causes instead of talking of 'visceral meanings', and by our naturalizing we appear to make inevitable in capitalism what is really only contingent. This listing gives Taussig's critique more coherence than it possesses, but we see no need to replicate either his longwindedness or his vagueness.

We are not the positivist, naturalizing devils Taussig makes us out to be. We have even had our share of encounters with the problems of subjectivity and reflexivity. Mintz once authored a book entitled *Worker in the Cane: A Puerto Rican Life History* (1960); and Wolf (with Edward Hansen) wrote a multi-perspectival, 'Brechtian' presentation of *The Human Condition in Latin America* (1972). But it is indeed the case that, in *S&P* and *EPWH*, we take the position that human arrangements

244 • SIDNEY W. MINTZ AND ERIC R. WOLF

are best understood by a grasp of the bases and workings of material life, through what Marx, in *A Contribution to the Critique of Political Economy*, called 'production and productive consumption' and 'consumption and consumptive production'. We have tried to apply this approach in historically specific ways, and not only abstractly. Our insistence on a historical orientation is not new for either of us. It is exemplified, for instance, in the first paper we published together (Mintz and Wolf 1950), and in much of our subsequent work. We employ historical perspectives because both of us feel that material conditions and their consequences for social life are best weighed and best understood when seen in their development over time.

Contrary to what Taussig says of our work, we have no interest in teleological history. We do not see history as a series of stepping-stones toward the achievement of some transcendental goal. We are also unconcerned with history as a discourse that installs the effects of the real. Our concern with history is primarily methodological. Studying phenomena in their temporal dimension is not an end in itself, but a way of getting at causal forces and their incremental or diminishing consequences. Taussig concluded that we are antiquated fuddy-duddies because we look for chains of cause and effect. But our aim is to explain human arrangements as well as to interpret them. We believe that explanation requires conceptions of causality; we want to clarify causation because we aspire to understand why human beings make their own history, but under determinant and constraining conditions. We do not believe that history is just what people feel it is; we think we have a commitment to try to understand the 'facts' that undergird their lives. From where we stand, both action *and* choice obey a causal structure of possibilities. We want to know what determines the shape of these structures of possibilities, in both time and space. In our books, we devoted our efforts to the history of the processes by which particular goods became commodities within world capitalism. *S&P* deals with one such commodity, *EPWH* with a number of different commodities. But Taussig says we don't study commodity fetishism, which is what he would have studied had he been us. Worse, we cavalierly fail to acknowledge our debt to the man who gave the world the concept of commodity fetishism, Karl Marx. Taussig thinks that by our not dealing with the fetishistic nature of commodities, we fall into the trap of falsely hypostatizing things; we treat things as if they were things. Dopes (he says) . . . can't you see that they're *not* things? Don't you recognize that they can *only* be understood if their fetishistic nature is given as much importance as their thing-nature? That's what Marx was talking about . . . he tells us. By treating things as things, by favoring history over visceral reactions (thus banishing 'hermeneutics to intellectual purgatory'), we make everything inevitable, and we take the magic away from the relationship between persons and things. Not for us, he chides us, 'the resort to play or trickery, the slow digesting of experience(s), the place of dream in the commodity as utopian wishing, emotions, interpretation, and all that goes along with observing oneself observing.'

We would answer that, no, we don't resort intentionally to play or trickery. We *have* done some digesting of experience, and both *S&P* and *EPWH* embody portions of our experience (though they might not be recognizable as such by everybody). As for the place of dream in the commodity as . . . etc, etc, it is after all simply that we were trying to do something else. Most readers and reviewers seemed to notice as much without prodding. Now, 'All that goes along with observing oneself observing' sounds like . . . well, you know, I mean like *great*, man. But do we all have to do it?

We suggest that there is a difference between tracing the history of particular commodities in the western world, and employing Marx's concept of commodity fetishism to interpret the relationships among persons as mediated through commodities. The world of commodities, as Marx sought to describe it, was an emerging capitalist world of producers and consumers, a world remade by their changing relations to the means of production, and by the changing significance of exchange in that world. Through these changes producers and consumers of commodities came to stand in qualitatively different relationships to each other. But this new world of commodities as defined by Marx did not arise with a thunderclap; it did not appear overnight; it did not happen everywhere at the same time, or at the same rate, or in exactly the same way. We remain in doubt about the total variety of ways in which such transitions may occur; we are not yet confident that we can abstract from a large number of well-understood cases in order to frame universal rules about how the world became capitalistic. We believe that studies of single cases can help us understand what happened, but without always clarifying the general processes they exemplify. Hence we recognize that to speak of 'capitalist' and 'precapitalist', while highly convenient to swift and tidy exposition, is also risky . . . a shortcut and an abstraction. The uneven process by which things became commodities was gradual and many-sided and took centuries; it has not ended and there persist serious arguments about when it began. All this admitted, it is nonetheless possible to study, as part of the rise of capitalism, how particular commodities came to be produced for sale in distant markets, within organizations created by capitalist entrepreneurs, uniting labor, land, capital goods and variable amounts of capital in new settings. Such commodities reached consumers whose relationships to the new world market differed widely, and in many different ways, from those of their

246 • SIDNEY W. MINTZ AND ERIC R. WOLF

specific producers. If one studies how palm oil or sugar or cocoa or oil or diamonds become commodities within an expanding world market, one notes that the relationships between their specific producers and consumers were similarly specific. The fetishism characteristic of the perception of those commodities is not a property of the commodities themselves but of their phenomenological status in systems of production, exchange and consumption of a capitalist kind. But all parts of those systems are not necessarily evolved to the same degree or in the same fashion. The parts of the world taken up into the system started out much differentiated among themselves, culturally, economically and otherwise. Those outsiders who came to engineer them into the system shared with each other their eventual intentions, perhaps, but not much else. Oil here, woven cloth there; sharecropping here, contract labor there; alienated land here, rented land there. Different systems of kinship, of religious belief, were invoked within newly organized ways of doing familiar things differently, or of doing different things in familiar ways.

To address the challenge of adequate analysis of this variety, it should not be enough to say that the victims have been put on the capitalist road; nor to explore, however imaginatively, their subjective reactions to their plight. That they are victims is likely; that the outcomes vary is certain; that there is much more to the story is even more certain. Both of us in different ways tried in the books reviewed to grapple with the worrisome questions which a study of the cultural history of commodities brings in its wake. If the commodities whose history we study as a means of explaining the progress of capitalism outside Europe are to be interpreted in terms of their fetishistic character, then this is a *different* task from analyzing the growth of a world in which the relationships between producers and consumers come to be analyzable through commodities. Neither such kind of study can be labelled 'wrong' because it exists. They are different kinds of study.

The study of the fetishism of commodities has become interesting to many scholars now, inside and outside of anthropology. That interest rests heavily upon analyses of the ways that contemporary consumers in the West integrate their consumption into the regnant framework of 'buyers' culture'. But this, too, is different from the study of the history of commodities; from the study of how these *particular* things became commodities; and from the study of the variety of processes involved in the emergence of uneven and widely distributed capitalist forms, inside the West as well as outside it. To learn about the concept of commodity fetishism (and to teach about it), to make its study part of anthropology, is a useful activity. We pointed to the importance of the concept ourselves, in a joint paper first published slightly more than thirty years ago (Wolf and Mintz 1957). But neither of the books causing Taussig's distress was aimed at analyzing this concept. We wonder what useful purpose it serves . . . though we have no doubt that it serves some . . . to attack us for not having written books different from the ones we wrote.

Taussig favors over our methods a methodology of 'collation of meanings and power as generated by a modernist text of the modern and the mundane.' This is not what we do, and we are not convinced that it is a procedure superior to our own.

Extrapolating and juxtaposing tell-tale meanings ripped—doubtless with lots of gut feeling—from tattered books of life provides one way of apprehending something called reality; but there's the rub. Such *brico-lage*, even when inspired, leads not to explanation but to revelation. No wonder Taussig festoons his discussion with quotations from Fredrich Nietzsche and Walter Benjamin, the latter a seeker after deliverance for whom the goal of knowledge was Messianic redemption, the former a prophet of nihilism for whom the value of an idea lay in its power to enhance 'life'.

Life, yes; but for whom and against whom? Taussig prefers such inspirational soundings to what he calls 'the rosary beads and chains of causes and effects'. No materialist rosary in his musings, we concede in our role as fuddy-duddies; but not much responsibility to reality, either. Instead, Prometheus-Taussig invites us to transcend 'the inviolability of the referent', presumably through 'collation'. But 'collation' sounds dangerously like a methodology that emphasizes style of presentation more than it does 'the referent'. The referent sometimes gets lost in the text altogether, because of what turn out to be irresistible temptations to show off, to sound off, and to take it off . . . on the determinate causes of which we do not comment.

Taussig says we want to install a 'fetishized view of commodified reality'. He is exercised by what he understands as our invocation of a 'fetish-power' (his words) called Capitalist Accumulation. In our tracings of commodities and their implications for people's lives, he finds us 'trivializing' anthropology. What appeals to *him* in Marx is the Old Man's 'unhappiness' about commodity fetishism. It is clear that Taussig has read Part I of *Das Kapital*. But his reading is heavily social-psychological, cosmological, and culturalist, with rather less attention to Marx's demonstration of how this form of fetishism informs the division of labor under capitalism. Perhaps he failed to read Part VII of that same work by Marx, called *The Accumulation of Capital*. Wolf, in his book, tried to show how people's lives became intertwined in the production and movement of particular commodities (including, yes, meat), and how their lives were changed as a consequence of these intertwined connections. Mintz wrote his book about how sucrose . . . sugar . . . penetrated and altered the lives of its users: the ways its meanings changed, and the way they changed its meanings. Neither of us sought to write a history or sociology or social psychology of commodities as such; we used the trajectories of commodities as 'tracers' through the veins and arteries of a developing political and economic system. If people do not live the way they did in 1400, how does one account for how they live now? Looking for causes we found them in the ways by which people were drawn into the circuits of capital and became increasingly subject to the processes that Marx labelled 'the accumulation of capital'. Taussig dislikes this 'fetishized view of a commodified reality'. Does he think this is something we imposed upon that reality?

We assure Taussig that we don't much care for capitalism, either. Nonetheless, we were greatly intrigued, as we read his interpretation, by his apparent success in staying entirely outside the system of commodity production and consumption in the course of his own social reproduction. How, indeed, does Dr. Taussig do it? Does he shave with obsidian chips of his own manufacture? Does he live in a tent of buffalo hide? Are his feet sheathed in the skins of alligators that he has himself harpooned? Can we learn to do it, too? And if not, why not? And if this impression, which we gather from his criticisms of our work, is incorrect; if he has not managed, Houdini-like, to stay entirely independent of this system we all apparently dislike, perhaps he can explain to us why the same question we put to him should not be put to Iroquois fur hunters, to Mundurucú, to Meo, or to Caribbean plantation laborers. What are the ways in which they were drawn into the capitalist world? May we not ask them what we ask Dr. Taussig?

That people can react differentially and in contradictory fashion to these involvements is hardly news. Even Taussig's own project of opposing our 'fetishized view of a commodified reality' with one that is presumably non-fetishized and non-commodified is clearly predicated upon some sort of involvement with a commodified world. In the end, then, perhaps we can comprehend Taussig's motivations for such an attempt. But we would question both the reasoning that underlies it, and the fashion in which it has been put forward.

ABOUT THE EDITOR

Stephen Nugent teaches anthropology at Goldsmiths, University of London, and is director of the Centre for Visual Anthropology there. His long-term interest in Brazilian Amazonia is represented in his books, *Big Mouth* (1990), *Amazonian Caboclo Society* (1993), *Some Other Amazonians* (2004) and *Scoping the Amazon* (2007). He is an editor of the journal *Critique of Anthropology*.